How Designers Think

To Rosie

How Designers Think

The Design Process Demystified

Fourth edition

Bryan Lawson

AMSTERDAM • BOSTON • HEIDELBERG • LONDON • NEW YORK • OXFORD
PARIS • SAN DIEGO • SAN FRANCISCO • SINGAPORE • SYDNEY • TOKYO
Architectural Press is an imprint of Elsevier

Architectural Press

Architectural Press is an imprint of Elsevier
Linacre House, Jordan Hill, Oxford OX2 8DP
30 Corporate Drive, Suite 400, Burlington, MA 01803

First published 1980
Paperback edition 1983
Reprinted 1986, 1988
Second edition 1990
Reprinted 1991, 1994
Third edition 1997
Reprinted 1999, 2000, 2001, 2002, 2003, 2005
Fourth edition 2006

British Library Cataloguing in Publication Data
A catalogue record for this book is available from the British Library

Library of Congress Cataloguing in Publication Data
A catalogue record for this book is available from the Library of Congress

ISBN–13: 978-0-7506-6077-8
ISBN–10: 0-7506-6077-5

For more information on all Architectural Press publications
please visit our website at www.architecturalpress.com

Printed and bound in Great Britain by Biddles Ltd, King's Lynn, Norfolk
06 07 08 09 10   10 9 8 7 6 5 4 3 2 1

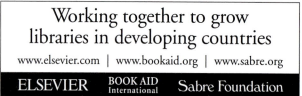

Working together to grow
libraries in developing countries

www.elsevier.com | www.bookaid.org | www.sabre.org

ELSEVIER   BOOK AID International   Sabre Foundation

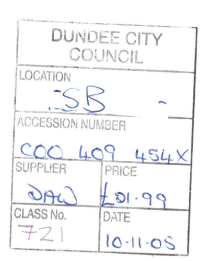

Contents

Preface

This book now has far too long a history for my liking. It is frightening to think that it was first published now nearly a quarter of a century ago. It has been in continuous print ever since and many people have been kind enough to say how it has helped them with their studies, research or just developing their design process. Needless to say there are many others who have been rather more critical of some of the ideas and most of their arguments have been taken into account as the book has progressed through previous editions to this fourth one.

The book was not originally intended to be prescriptive and that continues to be the case. It is an attempt to draw together much of what I know about designing. That understanding has, of course, come from many years' research. But this understanding also comes from teaching designers from a wide range of backgrounds. I have taught students of architecture, interior design, product and industrial design, urban design and town planning, landscape, graphics as well as those who develop virtual worlds such as websites and animated films. I have also taught in the areas of ergonomics, systems design and computer programming. These students have repeatedly amused, surprised and entertained me. They have always taught me new things and occasionally astonished me. That they do not realise some things are thought to be difficult is often the charm and advantage of such novice students and every now and then they show that it is possible to make the complex simple and to resolve the intractable. This is why design is such a drug, so fascinating and yet of course so frequently frustrating and infuriating. I have been privileged to meet many wonderful designers, some of them very well known and others less so. We have discussed the ideas in this book. Often highly successful designers warn me at the start of these discussions that they can more easily describe their designs than their processes. Actually, it usually turns out that they can say a great deal more about their processes than they had previously realised they could. It may seem odd to some readers that I say relatively little about the finished work of some of these successful designers. The fact is that much more has been written about their designs than their processes so I make no apology for saying very little about product here and concentrating on process.

If I were to start writing this book from scratch now I would probably do it differently. Since I first published this book I have written two others on related matters, *Design in Mind* and *What Designers Know*. The latter is actually a companion book to this one. I have revised this fourth edition in the light of more recent research but also in the knowledge that *What Designers Know* is now also published. Effectively both books taken together represent my latest thinking. This fourth edition has two totally new chapters at the end. The chapters in the third edition on designing with drawings and designing with computers have been removed. Both of those essentially looked at the way design knowledge is transferred between the human mind and some external representation. The main ideas that grow out of that study can now be found in a much more developed form in *What Designers Know*. The first new chapter here discusses the idea of design as conversation. Not only has this view of design grown in popularity over the time this book has been in print, but it now offers a way of thinking about many of the important issues concerning the ways the designers work in teams, with drawings and with computers. The second new chapter rather rashly tries to summarise the range of activities that I believe make up the design process. It also incorporates and summarises some of the lessons only recently available to us about how really expert designers work and how this might be different from the way novice designers work.

There are therefore now three points of summary in the book. The model of design problems which is developed in Chapter 6, the intermediate conclusions of Chapter 7 and the final summary of design activities in Chapter 16. I very much doubt that this is the end of the story. I am sure that many people will tell me that it is not and that we shall continue to have the same interesting and fascinating debates that I have been lucky to be part of for so many years.

I have researched the design process for over four decades now and met with most of those who contribute significantly and repeatedly to the field and I have greatly benefited from discussion with all the people involved. The Design Thinking Research Symposia and the Creativity and Cognition Conferences have offered particular inspirations. I have supervised many research students and benefited from collaborating with them. I am greatly indebted to all those who have helped me to form these fumbling ideas as we grope towards an understanding of that most magical of all human cognitive endeavours, designing.

Bryan Lawson

Acknowledgements

I am greatly indebted to the many design students I have taught over the years who frequently challenge their tutor's own ideas through their creative imagination. In particular I am grateful for the many discussions and debates we have had over many years in my research group and with other colleagues. There are too many who have contributed in this way to name but if they remain interested enough to read this, then I hope they will know who they are!

I must thank the designers who have allowed themselves to be subjected to my investigation. Many of them have substantial reputations and have been brave enough to open up their minds to me. I hope they will feel I have done their talents justice here.

I am also indebted to the following for supplying illustrations:

Richard Seymour of Seymour/Powell, London, UK for Figures 10.4, and 15.2;

Ken Yeang of T. R. Hamzah and Yeang Sdn Bhd, Kuala Lumpur, Malaysia for Figure 10.5;

Richard MacCormac of MacCormac, Jamieson, Prichard, London, UK for Figures 11.5, 11.6 and 14.3;

Professor Peter Blundell Jones of The University of Sheffield, UK for Figure 11.7;

Kit Allsopp of Kit Allsopp Architects, London, UK for Figures 12.1 and 12.2;

Michael Wilford of Michael Wilford and Partners, London, UK for Figure 12.3;

Eva Jiricna of Eva Jiricna Architects, London, UK for Figure 12.4;

Robert Venturi of Venturi, Scott Brown and Associates, Philadelphia, USA for Figures 12.5 and 12.6;

Geoff Jones of Building and Urban Design Associates, Birmingham, UK for Figure 13.9;

Steven Groak of the Ove Arup Partnership, London, UK for the idea behind Figure 15.3;

Richard Burton of Ahrends, Koralek and Burton, London, UK for Figures 14.1 and 14.2;

Peter Durand London, UK for Figure 14.4;

Ian Ritchie of Ian Ritchie Associates, London, UK for Figure 15.1.

PART ONE

WHAT IS DESIGN?

1

Introduction

Put a group of architects, urban designers and planners in a sight-seeing bus and their actions will define the limits of their concerns. The architects will take photographs of buildings, or highways or bridges. The urban designers will wait for that moment when all three are juxtaposed. The planners will be too busy talking to look out of the window.

Denise Scott Brown, *AD Urban Concepts*

To regard thinking as a skill rather than a gift is the first step towards doing something to improve that skill.

Edward de Bono, *Practical Thinking*

Design

The very word 'design' is the first problem we must confront in this book since it is in everyday use and yet given quite specific and different meanings by particular groups of people. We might begin by noting that 'design' is both a noun and a verb and can refer either to the end product or to the process. Relatively recently the word 'designer' has even become an adjective rather than a noun. Although on the one hand this can be seen to trivialise design to the status of mere fashion, this adjectival use implies something that will be important to us in this book. It implies that not all design is equally valuable and that perhaps the work of some designers is regarded as more important. In this book we shall not be studying how design can offer us the fashion accessory. In fact we shall not be much concerned directly with the end products of design. This book is primarily about design as a process. We shall be concerned with how that process works, what we understand about it and do not, and how it is learned and performed by professionals and experts. We shall be interested in how the process can be supported with computers and by working in groups. We shall be interested in how all the various stakeholders can make their voice heard.

To some extent we can see design as a generic activity, and yet there appear to be real differences between the end products created by designers in various domains. One of the questions running throughout the book then will be the extent to which designers have common processes and the extent to which these might vary both between domains and between individuals. A structural engineer may describe the process of calculating the dimensions of a beam in a building as design. In truth such a process is almost entirely mechanical. You apply several mathematical formulae and insert the appropriate values for various loads known to act on the beam and the required size results. It is quite understandable that an engineer might use the word 'design' here since this process is quite different from the task of 'analysis', by which the loads are properly determined. However, a fashion designer creating a new collection might be slightly puzzled by the engineer's use of the word 'design'. The engineer's process seems to us to be relatively precise, systematic and even mechanical, whereas fashion design seems more imaginative, unpredictable and spontaneous. The engineer knows more or less what is required from the outset. In this case a beam that has the properties of being able to span the required distance and hold up the known loads. The fashion designer's knowledge of what is required is likely to be much vaguer. The collection should attract attention and sell well and probably enhance the reputation of the design company. However, this information tells us much less about the nature of the end product of the design process than that available to the engineer designing a beam.

Actually both these descriptions are to some extent caricatures since good engineering requires considerable imagination and can often be unpredictable in its outcome, and good fashion is unlikely to be achieved without considerable technical knowledge. Many forms of design then, deal with both precise and vague ideas, call for systematic and chaotic thinking, need both imaginative thought and mechanical calculation. However, a group of design fields seem to lie near the middle of this spectrum of design activity. The three-dimensional and environmental design fields of architecture, interior design, product and industrial design, urban and landscape design, all require the designer to produce beautiful and also practically useful and well functioning end products. In most cases realising designs in these fields is likely to require very considerable technical knowledge and expertise, as well as being visually imaginative and ability to design. Designers in these fields generate objects or places which may have a major impact on the quality of life of many people. Mistakes can seriously inconvenience, may well be expensive and can even be dangerous. On the other hand, very good design can approach the power of art and music to lift the spirit and enrich our lives.

Architecture is one of the most centrally placed fields in this spectrum of design, and is probably the most frequently written about. Since the author is an architect, there will be many architectural examples in this book. However, this is not a book about architecture, or indeed about any of the products of design. It is a book about design problems, what makes them so special and how to understand them, and it is about the processes of design and how to learn, develop and practise them.

Already here we have begun to concentrate on professional designers such as architects, fashion designers and engineers. But there is a paradox here about design. Design is now clearly a highly professional activity for some people, and the very best designers are greatly valued and we admire what they do enormously. And yet design is also an everyday activity that we all do. We design our own rooms, we decide how to arrange things on shelves or in storage systems, we design our own appearance every morning, we plant, cultivate and maintain our gardens, we select food and prepare our meals, we plan our holidays. All these everyday domestic jobs can be seen as design tasks or at least design-like tasks. When we are at work we are still designing by planning our time, arranging the desktops of our computers, arranging rooms for meetings, and so we could go on. We may not aggrandise these humble tasks with the word 'design', but they share many of the characteristics of professional design tasks.

We can see, however, that these tasks vary in a number of ways that begin to give us some clues about the nature of designing. Some of these tasks are really a matter of selection and combination of predetermined items. In some cases we might also create these items. Occasionally we might create something so new and special that others may wish to copy what we have done. Professional designers are generally much more likely to do this. But professional designers also design for other people rather than just themselves. They have to learn to understand problems that other people may find it hard to describe and create good solutions for them. Such work requires more than just a 'feeling' for materials, forms, shapes or colours; it requires a wide range of skills. Today then professional designers are highly educated and trained.

Design education

Design education in the form we know it today is a relatively recent phenomenon. That a designer needs formal instruction and periods of academic study and that this should be conducted in an educational institution are now commonly accepted ideas. The history of design education shows a progressive move from the workplace into the college and university studio. In a recent attempt to interpret the history of architectural education linked to establishment of the Prince of Wales Institute of Architecture, this change is interpreted as a series of political conspiracies (Crinson and Lubbock 1994). Certainly it is possible to argue that academically based design education lacks contact with the makers of things, but then as we shall see in the next chapter this reflects practice. The designers of today can no longer be trained to follow a set of procedures since the rate of change of the world in which they must work would soon leave them behind. We can no longer afford to immerse the student of architecture or product design in a few traditional crafts. Rather they must learn to appreciate and exploit new technology as it develops.

We are also seeing quite new design domains springing up as a result of technology. I have been lucky enough to spend some time working in the design faculty of a university entirely devoted to multi-media. Designers there learn to animate, to create web-sites, to design virtual worlds and to create new ways for people to relate to, and use, highly complex technology. Such design domains were unimaginable when the first edition of this book was published and yet today they are extremely popular with students. Even further along the spectrum of design fields we find the system designers and software designers who create the applications that we all use to write books, manipulate images and give lectures. Many contemporary products have in them hardware and software that are combined and integrated in a manner that makes the distinction increasingly irrelevant. Mobile phones, MP3 players and handheld personal computers are not only appearing, but converging and transforming into new kinds of devices. Such areas of design are changing our lives not only physically but socially. Until recently we would have thought of software and system designers as lying outside the scope of a book like this. However increasingly I am finding that people who work in those fields are seeing relevance in the ideas here and as a consequence are beginning to question the traditional ways in which such designers have been educated.

In the twentieth century technology began to develop so quickly that, for the first time in our history, the change was palpable within a single lifetime. Design has always been connected with our contemporary intellectual endeavour including art, science and philosophy. During that period we saw a change in design that was at the time thought to be more profound and fundamental than any of the stylistic periods that had preceded it. It was even known by its direct connection to the contemporary, 'modernism'. This name implied that it provided a full stop at the end of design history and I was taught by tutors who genuinely believed that. This set of ideas has so profoundly influenced the way that we think about design that sometimes it is hard to disentangle. Only now are we beginning to see that it is possible for design to move on from modernism. We shall not here be primarily concerned with design as style, but nor can we think about process in isolation.

Design education has recently emerged from a period of treating history as deserving academic study but making little connection with the present. Thankfully those notions of modernism as the last word in design have been largely rejected and the design student of today is expected not only to appreciate historical work in its own right but to use it to inform contemporary design.

Design education has some very common features that transcend countries and design domains. Design schools characteristically use both the physical and conceptual studio as their central educational device. Conceptually the studio is a process of learning by doing, in which students are set a series of design problems to solve. They thus learn how to design largely by doing it, rather than by studying it or analysing it. It seems almost impossible to learn design without actually doing it. However the ideas in this book may offer a complementary resource. One of the weaknesses of the traditional studio is that students, in paying so much attention to the end product of their labours, fail to reflect sufficiently on their process. Physically the studio is a place where students gather and work under the supervision of their tutors. The studio is often assumed to replicate the offices of professional designers in the domain. However, one of the perennial problems here is that so much of the real professional world is very difficult to replicate in the college or university. In particular there is usually an absence of clients with real problems, doubts, budgets and time constraints.

It is often difficult therefore for design students to develop a process which enables them to relate appropriately to the other stakeholders in design. Rather it is easier for them to develop very personally self-reflective processes aimed chiefly at satisfying themselves and possibly their tutors. Thus, the educational studio can easily become a place of fantasy removed from the needs of the real world in which the students will work when they graduate. Not only does this tend to distort the skill balance in the process, but also the sets of values which the students acquire. Hubbard showed for example that town planners tend to acquire a different set of values about architecture to the public they represent and serve (Hubbard 1996). Similarly Wilson showed that architects use different evaluative systems to others about buildings (Wilson 1996). She also showed that this tendency is acquired during education. More disturbingly this work also revealed a strong correlation between preferences within each school of architecture and that these preferences are linked to style. Almost certainly design schools do not intend these effects so perhaps this indicates some significant problems with the studio concept of design education.

Throughout this book we shall see how many influences a designer must be open to and how many arguments there are about their relative importance in practice. Design education, like design itself, will probably always be controversial. Traditions have grown up which show structural variations not only between countries but also between the various design fields.

The extent to which the various design fields share a common process is a matter for considerable debate. That designers educated in each of these fields tend to take a different view of problems is less contentious. Furniture designers will tell you that they can spot furniture designed by an architect as opposed to someone trained in furniture design. Some say that architects design furniture to sit in space and not obstruct it; others will tell you that architects simply do not understand the nature of the materials used in furniture and consequently assemble it as they would a building. It is now commonly accepted that the United Kingdom construction industry is too divided and confrontational and that the various consultants and contractors involved tend to be combative when the client would like them to be co-operative. A recent report suggested a solution to all this would be to educate them all through some kind of common university degree only allowing specialisation later (Bill 1990). Such an idea, while well meaning, is fundamentally flawed. It assumes that there is a pool of 18-year-old students with more or less blank minds and personalities who might be attracted to take such a degree. In fact we know the truth to be very different. Very few students applying to university apply for courses in more than one area of the construction industry. Similarly, very few students apply to study more than one design field. Thus, although architecture and product design seem very closely related there is little contact between the fields. The internationally acclaimed British product designer Richard Seymour is not surprised by this.

> Although some architecture and some product designs look very close it is really the extreme end of the bow of the architecture tree rubbing up against a leaf at the extremity of the product design tree. We tend to think that they are very similar, but they are not. Fundamentally their roots are completely different.
>
> Lawson (1994)

For Richard Seymour, the separation between these professions begins very early and crucially before the period of tertiary education which might be held responsible for the divide. His view is that these 'roots' are put down much earlier in life and that by the time we come to select our profession, the choice is effectively already made. Richard Seymour observes that most product designers come from a background of achievement in practical crafts like metalwork and woodwork.

> The product designer is used to working with physical entities and the nature of materials and experiences them through seeing and feeling.

The English system of upper school education may aggravate these difficulties since pupils must choose to study only about four subjects. The universities then demand particular subjects before granting admission to each degree. Thus you might well be offered a place to study for a degree in architecture even if you had not studied mathematics, but almost certainly the same university would not grant you a place to study civil engineering. So the specialisation of students has already begun at school.

Whether it is the education system or the very nature of the students who select themselves, the atmosphere and social norms in the lecture theatres, studios and laboratories in the university departments of architecture, civil engineering and product design are different from the very beginning. The students speak differently, dress differently and have different images of themselves and the lives ahead of them. We must be cautious therefore in assuming that all design fields can be considered to share common ground. What is certain is that design is a distinctive mental activity, and we shall progressively explore its characteristics through this book.

However, we shall also discover that design can be extremely varied and we shall see that successful designers can employ quite different processes whatever their educational background.

Design technologies

This chapter began with a brief look at some of the differences between the way fashion designers and civil engineers might design. Another very important difference between them is the technology they must understand and use to achieve their ends. Designers must not only decide what effects they wish to achieve, they must also know how to achieve them. So our civil engineer must understand the structural properties of concrete and steel, whereas our fashion designer must appreciate the characteristics of different fabrics. Again this a simple caricature since both must know far more than this, but the point is made to demonstrate that their grasp of technology has to be relevant to their design field. Traditionally we tend to use the end products of design to differentiate between designers. Thus a client may go to one kind of designer for a bridge, another for a building, yet another for a chair and so on.

Many designers dabble in fields other than those in which they were trained, such as the famous architect Mies van der Rohe who designed a chair for his German Pavilion at the Barcelona International Exhibition of 1929, which to this day appears in the lobbies of banks and hotels all over the world. Very few designers are actually trained in more than one field such as the highly acclaimed architect/engineer Santiago Calatrava. Some designers are even difficult to classify such as Philippe Starck who designs buildings, interiors, furniture and household items. It is interesting that some of the most famous inventions of modern times were made by people who had not been specifically trained to work in the field in which they made their contribution (Clegg 1969):

Invention	Inventor
Safety razor	Traveller in corks
Kodachrome films	Musician
Ball-point pen	Sculptor
Automatic telephone	Undertaker
Parking meter	Journalist
Pneumatic tyre	Veterinary surgeon
Long-playing record	Television engineer

Classifying design by its end product seems to be rather putting the cart before the horse, for the solution is something which is formed by the design process and has not existed in advance of it. The real reason for classifying design in this way has less to do with the design process but is instead a reflection of our increasingly specialised technologies. Engineers are different from architects not just because they may use a different design process but more importantly because they understand about different materials and requirements. Unfortunately this sort of specialisation can easily become a strait-jacket for designers, directing their mental processes towards a predefined goal. It is thus too easy for the architect to assume that the solution to a client's problem is a new building. Often it is not! If we are not careful then design education might restrict rather than enhance the ability of the students to think creatively.

The cautionary tale of the scientist, the engineer, the architect and the church tower illustrates this phenomenon. These three were standing outside the church arguing about the height of the tower when a local shopkeeper who was passing by suggested a competition. He was very proud of a new barometer which he now stocked in his shop and in order to advertise it he offered a prize to the one who could most accurately discover the height of the tower using one of his barometers. The scientist carefully measured the barometric pressure at the foot of the tower and again at the top, and from the difference he calculated the height. The engineer, scorning this technique, climbed to the top, dropped the barometer and timed the period of its fall. However, it was the architect who, to the surprise of all, was the most accurate. He simply went inside the church and offered the barometer to the verger in exchange for allowing him to examine the original drawings of the church!

Many design problems are equally amenable to such varied treatment but seldom do clients have the foresight of our shopkeeper. Let us briefly examine such a situation. Imagine that a railway company has for many years been offering catering facilities on selected trains and has now discovered that this part of the business is making a financial loss. What should be done? An advertising agency might suggest that they should design a completely new image with the food repackaged and differently advertised. An industrial designer might well suggest that the real problem is with the design of the buffet car. Perhaps if passengers were able to obtain and consume food in every coach they would buy more than if they had to walk down the train. An operations research consultant would probably concentrate on whether the buffet cars were on the right trains and so on.

It is quite possible that none of our professional experts was right. Perhaps the food was just not very appetising and too expensive? In fact, probably all the experts have something to contribute in designing a solution. The danger is that each may be conditioned by their education and the design technology they understand. Design situations vary not just because the problems are dissimilar but also because designers habitually adopt different approaches. In this book we shall spend some time discussing both design problems and design approaches.

What does design involve?

Barnes Wallis is perhaps most famous for his wartime invention of the bouncing bomb immortalised in the film of the 'dam-busters'. However his career achievements went much further with a whole succession of innovative pieces of aviation design including aircraft, airships and many smaller items. However, at the age of sixteen, Barnes Wallis failed his London matriculation examination (Whitfield 1975). It seems likely that this was a result of undergoing a form of Armstrong's heuristic education at Christ's Hospital, which did little to prepare its pupils for such examinations but rather concentrated on teaching them to think. Barnes Wallis recalls 'I knew nothing, except how to think, how to grapple with a problem and then go on grappling with it until you had solved it'. Later Barnes Wallis was to complete his London University first degree in astonishingly quick time, taking only five months!

Later in life Barnes Wallis was quite prepared to take technical advice, but never accepted help with design itself: 'If I wanted the answer to a question for which I could not do the mathematics I would go to someone who could . . . to that extent I would ask for advice and help . . . never a contribution to a solution'. Even at an early age it was the quality of Barnes Wallis' thinking and his approach to problems as much as his technical expertise which enabled him to produce so many original aeronautical designs.

For many of the kinds of design we are considering, it is important not just to be technically competent but also to have a well developed aesthetic appreciation. Space, form and line, as well as colour and texture, are the very tools of the trade for the environmental, product or graphic designer. The end product of such design will always be visible to the user who may also move inside or pick up the designer's artefact. The designer must understand our aesthetic experience, particularly of the visual world, and in this sense designers share territory with artists. For these reasons alone, and there are some others we shall come to later, designers also tend to work in a very visual way. Designers almost always draw, often paint and frequently construct models and prototypes. The archetypal image of the designer is of someone sitting at a drawing board. But what is clear is that designers express their ideas and work in a very visual and graphical kind of way. It would be very hard indeed to become a good designer without developing the ability to draw well. Indeed designers' drawings can often be very beautiful.

Sometimes the drawings of designers become art objects in their own right and get exhibited. We must leave until later a discussion of why the practice of designing should not be considered as psychologically equivalent to the creation of art. Suffice it now to say that design demands more than just aesthetic appreciation. How many critics of design, even those with the most penetrating perception, find it easier to design than to criticise?

Perhaps there can be no exhaustive list of the areas of expertise needed by designers, although we shall attempt to get close to this by the end of the book. However, there is one more set of skills that designers need which we should at least introduce here. The vast majority of the artefacts we design are created for particular groups of users. Designers must understand something of the nature of these users and their needs whether it is in terms of the ergonomics of chairs or the semiotics of graphics. Along with a recognition that the design process itself should be studied, design education has more recently included material from the behavioural and social sciences. Yet designers are no more social scientists than they are artists or technologists.

This book is not about science, art or technology, but the designer cannot escape the influences of these three very broad categories of intellectual endeavour. One of the essential difficulties and fascinations of designing is the need to embrace so many different kinds of thought and knowledge. Scientists may be able to do their job perfectly well without even the faintest notion of how artists think, and artists for their part certainly do not depend upon scientific method. For designers life is not so simple, they must appreciate the nature of both art and science and in addition they must be able to design! What then exactly is this activity of design? That we must leave until the next chapter but we can already see that it involves a sophisticated mental process capable of manipulating many kinds of information, blending them all into a coherent set of ideas and finally generating some realisation of those ideas. Usually this realisation takes the form of a drawing but, as we have seen it could equally well be a new timetable. It is the process rather than the end product of design which chiefly interests us in this book.

Design as a skill

Design is a highly complex and sophisticated skill. It is not a mystical ability given only to those with recondite powers but a skill which, for many, must be learnt and practised rather like the playing of a sport or a musical instrument. Consider then the following two passages:

> Flex the knees slightly and, while your upper body inclines towards the ball, keep from bending over too much at the waist. The arms are extended fully but naturally towards the ball without any great feeling of reaching out for the ball . . . start the club back with that left arm straight letting the right elbow fold itself against the body . . . the head should be held over the ball . . . the head is the fixed pivot about which the body and swing must function.
>
> Lee Trevino (1972) *I Can Help Your Game*

> Keeping the lips gently closed, extend them a little towards the corners as when half smiling, care being taken not to turn them inwards at all during the process. The 'smile', rather a sardonic one perhaps, should draw in the cheeks against the teeth at the sides and the muscular action will produce a firmness of the lips towards the corners. Now, on blowing across the embouchure towards its outer edge, the breadth will make a small opening in the middle of the lips and, when the jet of air thus formed strikes the outer edge the flute head will sound.
>
> F. B. Chapman (1973) *Flute Technique*

These two passages come from books about skills. Both are skills which I have spent a lifetime miserably failing to perfect; playing golf and playing the flute. My well-thumbed copies of these books offer me a series of suggestions as to where I should direct my attention. Both authors concentrate on telling their readers how it feels to be doing it right. A few people may pick up a golf club and swing it naturally or make a beautiful sound on a flute. For them these books may be of little help, but for the vast majority, the skills must be acquired initially by attention to detail. It is in the very nature of highly developed skills that we can perform them unconsciously. The expert golfer is not thinking about the golf swing but about the golf course, the weather and the opponents. To perform well the flautist must forget the techniques of embouchure and breath control and fingering systems, and concentrate on interpreting the music as the composer intended. You could not possibly give expression to music with your head full of Chapman's advice about the lips. So it is with design. We probably work best when we think least about our technique. Beginners however must first analyse and practise all the elements of their skill and we should remember that even the most talented of professional golfers or musicians still benefit from lessons all the way through their careers.

While we are used to the idea that physical skills like riding a bicycle, swimming and playing a musical instrument must be learned and practised, we are less ready to recognise that thinking might need similar attention as was suggested by the famous British philosopher Ryle (1949):

> Thought is very much a matter of drills and skills.

Later the psychologist Bartlett (1958) echoed this sentiment:

> Thinking should be treated as a complex and high level kind of skill.

More recently there have been many writers who have exhorted their readers to practise this skill of thinking. One of the most notable, Edward de Bono (1968) summarises the message of such writers:

> On the whole, it must be more important to be skilful in thinking than to be stuffed with facts.

Before we can properly study how designers think, we need to develop a better understanding of the nature of design and the characteristics of design problems and their solutions. The first two sections of this book will explore this territory before the third main section on design thinking. The book as a whole is devoted to developing the idea that design thinking is a skill. Indeed it is a very complex and sophisticated skill, but still one which can be analysed, taken apart, developed and practised. In the end though, to get the best results, designers must perform like golfers and flautists. They should forget all the stuff they have been taught about technique and just go out and do it!

References

Bartlett, F. C. (1958). *Thinking*. London, George Allen and Unwin.

Bill, P. Ed. (1990). *Building towards 2001*. London, National Contractors Group.

Clegg, G. L. (1969). *The Design of Design*. Cambridge, Cambridge University Press.

Crinson, M. and Lubbock, J. (1994). *Architecture: Art or Profession*? Manchester, Manchester University Press.

de Bono, E. (1968). *The Five Day Course in Thinking*. Harmondsworth, Allen Lane.

Hubbard, P. (1996). Conflicting interpretations of architecture: an empirical investigation. *Journal of Environmental Psychology* **16**: 75–92.

Lawson, B. R. (1994). Architects are losing out in the professional divide. *The Architects' Journal* **199**(16): 13–14.

Ryle, G. (1949). *The Concept of Mind*. London, Hutchinson.

Whitfield, P. R. (1975). *Creativity in Industry*. Harmondsworth, Penguin.

Wilson, M. A. (1996). The socialization of architectural preference. *Journal of Environmental Psychology* **16**: 33–44.

2

The changing role of the designer

A bee puts to shame many an architect in the construction of her cells but what distinguishes the worst of architects from the best of bees is this, that the architect raises his structure in imagination before he erects it in reality. At the end of every labour process we get a result that already existed in the imagination of the labourer at its beginning.

Karl Marx, *Das Capital*

Architecture offers quite extraordinary opportunities to serve the community, to enhance the landscape, refresh the environment and to advance mankind – the successful architect needs training to overcome these pitfalls however and start earning some serious money.

Stephen Fry, *Paperweight*

Vernacular or craft design

In the industrialised world design has become a professional activity. There is now a whole range of designers each educated and trained to design objects for quite specific purposes. There are graphics designers who arrange the myriad of images we look at, product designers who create the items we use in our everyday lives and architects who design the buildings we live and work in. At university now it is also possible to take courses on interior design, theatre design, urban design, landscape design, fashion and textile design, and of course there are degrees in civil and structural engineering, electrical and electronic engineering, mechanical engineering and chemical and process engineering. So it seems there is a designer with a university degree who has been trained to design every article we buy, consume or inhabit. However, it has not always been so, nor is it so now in many other societies. Design as we know it in the industrialised world is a relatively recent idea.

Some years ago a group of my first year architecture students at Sheffield University were working on a project devised to get them to think about the design process. This project was specifically set up to get the students to concentrate on process rather than product, and for this reason did not involve buildings. Instead the students had to work in groups to design a machine to process marbles (Fig. 2.1). Nine marbles had to be poured into the machine at one end from a plastic cup and the machine was required to deliver two, three and four marbles respectively into three other plastic cups after a certain period of time. The students were also expected to record and later analyse how they had made decisions and interacted with each other during the design process. During the project, the studio was full of noise, not only from the clacking of marbles as machines were tested and found in need of improvement but also from the arguments which raged as to how the improvements could, or should be made. Inevitably most designs began by being complicated and unreliable,

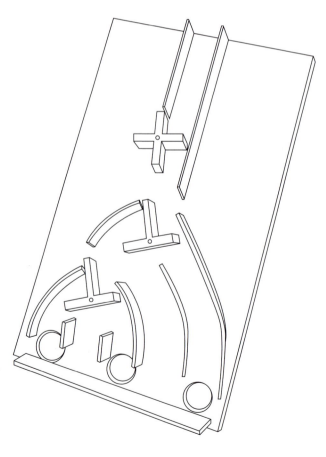

Figure 2.1
Part of a marble machine designed by a group of architecture students using a highly self-conscious process

and the groups gradually moved towards simpler and more reliable machines. The most reliable solutions were generally those which had few moving parts, not many different materials and were easy to construct. As is often the case with design, such solutions also tend to look pleasing and visually explain how they work.

One night it snowed very heavily, and the next morning the students quite spontaneously decided to abandon their work and turned their attention to building an igloo in a nearby park (Fig. 2.2). The igloo was very successful. It stood up strongly and could accommodate about ten people with the internal temperature rising well above that of the ambient air. Indeed the igloo was so well made that it attracted the attention of the local radio station who came along and conducted an interview with us inside!

What was even more remarkable however was the change of process. Out in the park the students left behind not only their marble machines but also their arguments on design. The students immediately, and without any deliberation switched from the highly self-conscious and introspective mode of thinking encouraged by their project work to a natural unselfconscious action-based approach.

There were no protracted discussions or disagreements about the form of the igloo, its siting, size or even construction and there were certainly no drawings produced. They simply got on and built it. In fact these students shared a roughly common image of an igloo in

Figure 2.2
The same architecture students designed and built an igloo but used an unselfconscious approach

what we might fancifully describe as their collective consciousness. In this respect their behaviour bears a much greater resemblance to the Eskimo way of providing shelter than to the role of architect for which they were all being trained. Actually the common image of an igloo which these students shared and successfully realised was not entirely accurate in detail, for with their western preconceptions they built up the walls in horizontal courses whereas the Eskimo form of construction is usually a continuous rising spiral ramp (Fig. 2.3).

As the igloo was completed the students' theoretical education began to take over again. There was much discussion about the compressive and tensile strength of compacted snow. The difficulties of building arches and vaulting with a material weak in tension were recognised. It was also realised that snow, even though it may be cold to touch, can be a very effective thermal insulator. You would be very unlikely indeed to overhear such a discussion amongst Eskimos. Under normal conditions igloos are built in a vernacular manner. For the Eskimo there is no design problem but rather a traditional form of solution with variations to suit different circumstances which are selected and constructed without a thought of the principles involved.

In the past many objects have been consistently made to very sophisticated designs with a similar lack of understanding of the theoretical background. This procedure is often referred to as

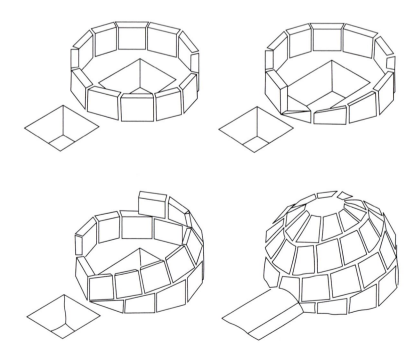

Figure 2.3
The traditional method of igloo construction

'blacksmith design' after the craftsman who traditionally designed objects as he made them, working to undrawn traditional patterns handed down from generation to generation. There is a fascinating account of this kind of design to be found in George Sturt's book *The Wheelwright's Shop* (Sturt 1923). Sturt suddenly found himself in charge of a wheelwright's shop in 1884 on the death of his father. In his book he recalls his struggle to understand what he describes as 'a folk industry carried on in a folk method'.

Of particular interest here is the difficulty which Sturt found with the dishing of cartwheels. He quickly realised that wheels for horse-drawn vehicles were always constructed in a rather elaborate dished shape like that of a saucer, but the reason for this eluded Sturt. (Fig. 2.4) From his description we can see how Sturt's wheelwrights worked all their lives with the curious combination of constructional skill and theoretical ignorance that is so characteristic of such crafts-men. So Sturt continued the tradition of building such wheels for many years without really understanding why. He realised that the dished wheel itself must be much more complex to make than a flat one. However the design necessitated even further complexities resulting in the wheel being tilted outwards and angled in towards the front (Fig. 2.5). Not surprisingly then, he was not content to remain in ignorance of the reasons behind the design.

Sturt first suspected that the dish was to give the wheel a direction in which to distort when the hot iron tyre was tightened on by cooling, but Jenkins (1972) has shown that dishing preceded the introduction of iron tyres. One other reason that occurred to Sturt

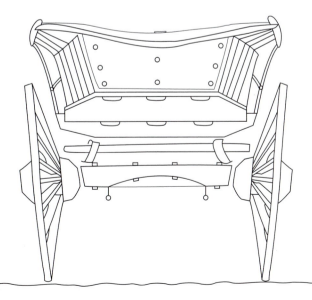

Figure 2.4
The cartwheel for horse-drawn vehicles was constructed in a complex dished shape

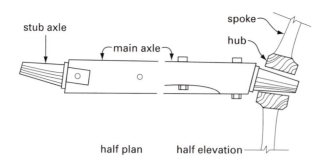

spoke

hub

stub axle

main axle

half plan

half elevation

Figure 2.5
The axle had to be tilted down (pitch) to enable the cartwheel to transfer load nearly vertically to the ground, and then angled forward (foreway) to prevent the cartwheel falling off

was the advantage gained from the widening of the cart towards the top thus allowing overhanging loads to be carried. This could be achieved since that part of the dished wheel which transfers the load from axle to road must be vertical, and thus the upper half of the wheel leans outwards. This may have more validity than Sturt realised since legislation in 1773 restricted the track of broad wheeled vehicles to a maximum of 68 inches. Although dished cartwheels were narrow enough to be exempt from this legislation, the roads would have probably got so rutted by the broad wheeled vehicles that a cart with a wider track would have had to ride on rough ground.

Eventually Sturt discovered what he thought to be the 'true' reason for dishing. The convex form of the wheel was capable not just of bearing the downward load but also the lateral thrust caused by the horse's natural gait which tends to throw the cart from side to side with each stride, but this is still by no means the total picture. Several writers have since commented on Sturt's analysis and in particular Cross (1975) has pointed out that the dished wheel also needed foreway. To keep the bottom half of the wheel vertical the axle must slope down towards the wheel. In turn this produces a tendency for the wheel to slide off the axle which has to be countered by also pointing the axle forward slightly thus turning the wheel in at the front. The resultant 'foreway' forces the wheel back down the axle as the cart moves forwards. Cross appears to argue that this is a forerunner of the toe-in used on modern cars to give them better cornering characteristics. This is probably not accurate since, as Clegg (1969) has argued, this modern toe-in is really needed to counter a lateral thrust caused by pneumatic rubber tyres not present in the solid cartwheel.

There probably is no one 'true' reason for the dishing of cartwheels but rather a great number of interrelated advantages. This is very characteristic of the craft-based design process. After many generations of evolution the end product becomes a totally integrated response to the problem. Thus if any part is altered the complete system may fail in several ways. Such a process served extremely well when the problem remained stable over many years as with the igloo and the cartwheel. Should the problem suddenly change, however, the vernacular or craft process is unlikely to yield suitable results. If Sturt could not understand the principles involved in cartwheel dishing how would he have responded to the challenge of designing a wheel for a steam-driven or even a modern petrol-driven vehicle with pneumatic tyres?

The professionalisation of design

In the vernacular process designing is very closely associated with making. The Eskimos do not require an architect to design the igloo in which they live and George Sturt offered a complete design-and-build service to customers requiring wheels. In the modern western world things are often rather different. An average British house and its contents represent the end products of a whole galaxy of professionalised design processes. The house itself was probably designed by an architect and sited in an area designated as residential by a town planner. Inside, the furnishings and fabrics, the furniture, the machinery and gadgets have all been created by designers who have probably never even once dirtied their hands with the manufacturing of these artefacts. The architect may have got muddy boots on the site when talking to the builder once in a while, but that is about as far as it goes. Why should this be? Does this separation of designing from making promote better design? We shall return to this question soon, but first we must examine the social context of this changed role for designers.

Approximately one in ten of the population of Great Britain may now be described as engaged upon a professional occupation. Most of the professions as we now know them are relatively recent phenomena and only really began to grow to the current proportions during the nineteenth century (Elliot 1972). The Royal Institute of British Architects (RIBA) was founded during this period. As early as 1791 there was an 'Architects' Club' and later a number of Architectural Societies. The inevitable process of professionalisation had begun, and by 1834 the Institute of British Architects was founded. This body was no longer just a club or society but an organisation of like-minded men with aspirations to raise, control and unify standards of practice. The Royal Charter of 1837 began the process of acquiring social status for architects, and eventually the introduction of examinations and registration gave legal status. Indeed, in the United Kingdom, the very title architect is legally protected to this day. The whole process of professionalisation led inevitably to the body of architects becoming a legally protected and socially respected exclusive élite. The present remoteness of architects from builders and users alike was thus assured. For this reason many architects were unhappy about the formation of the RIBA, and there are still those today who argue that the legal barriers erected between designer and builder are not conducive to good architecture. In recent years the RIBA has relaxed many of its earlier rules and now allows members to be directors of building firms, to advertise and generally behave in a more commercial manner than was originally required by the code of conduct. Professionalism, however, was in reality not concerned with design or the design process but rather with the search for status and control, and this can be seen amongst the design-based and non-design-based professions alike. Undoubtedly this control has led to increasingly higher standards of education and examination, but whether it has led to better practice is a more open question.

The division of labour between those who design and those who make has now become a keystone of our technological society. To some it may seem ironic that our very dependence on professional designers is largely based on the need to solve the problems created by the use of advanced technology. The design of a highland croft is a totally different proposition to the provision of housing in the noisy, congested city. The city centre site may bring with it social problems of privacy and community, risks to safety such as the spread of fire or disease, to say nothing of the problems of providing access or preventing pollution. The list of difficulties unknown to the builders of igloos or highland crofts is almost endless. Moreover each city centre site will present a different combination of these problems. Such variable and complex situations seem to demand the attention of experienced professional designers who are not just technically capable, but also trained in the act of design decision-making itself.

Christopher Alexander (1964) has presented one of the most concise and lucid discussions of this shift in the designer's role. Alexander argues that the unselfconscious craft-based approach to design must inevitably give way to the self-conscious professionalised process when a society is subjected to a sudden and rapid change which is culturally irreversible. Such changes may be the result of contact with more advanced societies either in the form of invasion and colonisation or, as seen more recently, in the more insidious infiltration caused by overseas aid to the underdeveloped countries. In this country the Industrial Revolution provided such a change. The newly found mechanised means of production were to be the cultural pivot upon which society turned. The seeds of the nineteenth century respect for professions and the twentieth century faith in technology were sown. Changes in both the materials and technologies available became too rapid for the craftsman's evolutionary process to cope. Thus the design process as we have known it in recent times has come about not as the result of careful and wilful planing but rather as a response to changes in the wider social and cultural context in which design is practised. The professional specialised designer producing drawings from which others build has come to be such a stable and familiar image that we now regard this process as the traditional form of design.

The traditional design process

The questions we must ask ourselves are how well has this new traditional design process served us and will it change? It has, indeed, always been undergoing a certain amount of change, and there are signs that many designers are now searching for a new, as yet ill-defined, role in society. Why should this be?

Initially the separating of designing from making had the effect not only of isolating designers but also of making them the centre of attention. Alexander (1964) himself commented perceptively on this development:

> The artist's self-conscious recognition of his individuality has a deep effect on the process of form-making. Each form is now seen as the work of a single man, and its success is his achievement only.

This recognition of individual achievement can easily give rise to the cult of the individual. In educational terms it led to the articled pupillage system of teaching design. A young architect would be put under the care of a recognised master of the art and the hope was that as the result of an extended period of this service, the skills peculiar to this individual master would rub off. Even in the schools of architecture students would be asked to design in the manner of a particular individual. To be successful designers had to acquire a clearly identifiable image, still seen in the flamboyant portrayal of designers in books and films. The great architects of the modern movement such as Le Corbusier or Frank Lloyd Wright not only designed buildings with an identifiable style, but also behaved and wrote eccentrically about their work. In this country those architects who were unhappy about the growing influence of the Royal Institute of British Architects in the late nineteenth century argued that architecture was an individual art and should not be regularised and controlled. Kaye (1960) argued that this period of professional-isation did actually coincide with a period of rigidity of architectural style.

Design by drawing

The separation of the designer from making also results in a central role for the drawing. If the designer is no longer a craftsman actu-ally making the object, then he or she must instead communicate instructions to those who will make it. Primarily and traditionally the drawing has been the most popular way of giving such instructions. In such a process the client no longer buys the finished article but rather is delivered of a design, again usually primarily described through drawings. Such drawings are generally known as 'presenta-tion drawings' as opposed to the 'production drawings' done for the purposes of construction.

However, in the context of this book, an even more important drawing is the 'design drawing'. Such a drawing is done by the designer not to communicate with others but rather as part of the very thinking process itself which we call design. In a most felicitous phrase Donald Schön (1983) has described the designer as 'having a conversation with the drawing'. So central is the role of the draw-ing in this design process that Jones (1970) describes the whole process as 'design by drawing'. Jones goes on to discuss both the strengths and weakness of a design process so reliant on the draw-ing. Compared with the vernacular process, the designer working in this way has great manipulative freedom. Parts of the proposed solution can be adjusted and the implications immediately investi-gated without incurring the time and cost of constructing the final product. The process of drawing and redrawing could continue until all the problems the designer could see were resolved. This vastly greater 'perceptual span', as Jones called it, enables designers to make much more fundamental changes and innovations within one design than would have ever been possible in the vernacular process, and solves the problems posed by the increasing rate of change in technology and society. Such a design process then encourages experimentation and liberates the designer's creative imagination in a quite revolutionary way, making the process almost unrecognisable to the vernacular craftsman.

Whilst design by drawing clearly has many advantages over the vernacular process, it is not without some disadvantages. The drawing is in some ways a very limited model of the final end product of design, and yet in a world increasingly dependent on visual communication it seems authoritative. The designer can see from a drawing how the final design will look but, unfortunately, not necessarily how it will work. The drawing offers a reasonably accurate and reliable model of appearance but not necessarily of performance. Architects could thus design quite new forms of housing never previously constructed once new technology enabled the high-rise block. What they could not necessarily see from their drawings were the social problems which were to appear so obvious years later when these buildings were in use.

Even the appearance of designs can be misleadingly presented by design drawings. The drawings which a designer chooses to make whilst designing tend to be highly codified and rarely connect with our direct experience of the final design. Architects, for example, probably design most frequently with the plan, which is a very poor representation of the experience of moving around in a building. For all these reasons we devote a whole chapter to the role of drawing in the design process later in this book.

Design by science

As designs became more revolutionary and progressive, so the failures of the design by drawing process became more obvious, particularly in the field of architecture. It became apparent that if we were to continue separating designing from making, and also to continue the rapid rate of change and innovation, then new forms of modelling the final design were urgently required.

It was precisely this concern that led Alexander to write his famous work *Notes on the Synthesis of Form* in 1964. He argued that we were far too optimistic in expecting anything like satisfactory results from a drawing-board based design process. How could a few hours or days of effort on the part of a designer replace the result of centuries of adaptation and evolution embodied in the vernacular product? Alexander proposed a method of structuring design problems that would allow designers to see a graphical representation of the structure of non-visual problems.

This piece of work had an extraordinarily lasting effect on thinking about design method. It is all the more remarkable since there is only one reported attempt to use the method and that did not result in any obvious success (Hanson 1969). The reason for the failure of Alexander's method results from his erroneous assumptions about the true nature of design problems, and we discuss this in the next chapter. However, that generation of design methodology for which Alexander's work now stands as a symbol was motivated by the common unease shared by designers about the inadequacy of their models of reality. Unfortunately the new models, which were frequently borrowed from operations research or behaviourist psychology, were to prove just as inadequate and inaccurate as designing by drawing (Daley 1969). Perhaps the real reason for the influence of Alexander's work was that it signalled yet another change in the designer's role. The issue no longer seemed to be one of protecting the individuality and identity of designers but, rather, had become the problem of exercising what Jones called 'collective control' over designers' activities. Somehow the whole process had to become more open to inspection and critical evaluation. The model of scientific method proved irresistible. Scientists made explicit not just their results but also their procedures. Their work could be replicated and criticised and their methods were above suspicion. How nice it would be if designers followed such a clear, open and public process! This idea caused many writers to develop models of the design process itself and we shall examine some of these in the next section. But where does all this leave the designer's role in society today?

Future roles of the designer

In our current state of uncertainty it is hardly valid to give a definitive view of the future, or even present, role of the designer. Cross (1975) asks us to consider whether we are now entering a post-industrial society and consequently in need of a post-industrial design process. The difficulty with this question is really how one views the prospect of life in such a post-industrial society. This issue is essentially a political debate about the extent to which we wish to decentralise the centres of power in our society. Some writers hail the looming energy crisis as providing the critical push towards a return to self-sufficiency. Others claim that the inertia of our technological development is too great to be stopped and that we shall find other means of providing centralised forms of energy. Thus our views about the future role of designers are inevitably linked to the kind of direction in which we wish society to go. Markus (1972) suggests three broad views which designers today may hold about their role in society.

The first role is essentially conservative, centred around the continued dominance of the professional institutions. In such a role designers remain unconnected with either clients or makers. They passively await the client's commission, produce a design and withdraw from the scene. There are already real problems with this approach. In the case of architecture the client may often be some branch of government or a large commercial organisation, and in such cases architects frequently become employees rather than consultants. We might expect that an architect seeking out this conservative role would be supported by the RIBA, but professional bodies tend to respond to threats against their roles by gradually redefining their role (Elliot 1972). Thus, when the traditional role of building designer is threatened by obsolescence, changing technology or the changing nature of the client, architects may either seek to redefine themselves as the leaders of a multi-professional team or withdraw to the earlier territory of aesthetic and functional designer. It seems doubtful that a professional body such as the RIBA can continue for long to support both the general private practitioner and salaried government employee. In many ways this role has come under a considerable double threat recently. Governments in many countries seem to be following the lead given by Margaret Thatcher in dismantling public sector service professional departments and by portraying the professional bodies and institutes as protectionist rather than concerned with the public good.

The opposite to this conservative approach is actively to seek different structural changes in society but which also would result in the end of professionalism as we know it. Such a revolutionary approach would lead the designer to associate directly with user groups. Since this kind of designer is also likely to believe in a decentralised society he or she would be happiest when dealing with the disadvantaged, such as the tenants of slum clearance areas, or the revolutionary such as self-sufficiency communes. In this role the designer deliberately forsakes positions of independence and power. Such designers no longer see themselves as leaders but as campaigners and spokespeople. A significant difficulty with this role is that since these kinds of client/user groups are unlikely to control any resources valued outside their limited societies, the designer loses all influence over other designers except by the power of example.

The third, middle, path lies between these two extremes, and is much more difficult to identify except in vague terms. In this role, designers remain professionally qualified specialists but try to involve the users of their designs in the process. These more participatory approaches to design may include a whole range of relatively new techniques, ranging from the public inquiry through gaming and simulation through to the recent computer-aided design procedures. All these techniques embody an attempt on the designer's part to identify the crucial aspects of the problem, make them explicit, and suggest alternative courses of action for comment by the non-designer participants. Designers following this approach are likely to have abandoned the traditional idea that the individual designer is dominant in the process, but they may still believe they have some specialised decision-making skills to offer. We return to the problems created by this approach in two special chapters on designing with others and designing with computers at the end of the book.

References

Alexander, C. (1964). *Notes on the synthesis of form*. New York, McGraw Hill.

Clegg, G. L. (1969). *The Design of Design*. Cambridge, Cambridge University Press.

Cross, N. (1975). *Design and Technology*. Milton Keynes, Open University Press.

Daley, J. (1969). A philosophical critique of behaviourism in architectural design. *Design Method in Architecture*. London, Lund Humphries.

Elliot, P. (1972). *The Sociology of the Professions*. London, Macmillan.

Hanson, K. (1969). Design from linked requirements in a housing problem. *Design Methods in Architecture*. London, Lund Humphries.

Jenkins, J. G. (1972). *The English Farm Wagon*. Newton Abbot, David and Charles.

Jones, J. C. (1970). *Design Methods: seeds of human futures*. New York, John Wiley.

Kaye, B. (1960). *The Development of the Architectural Profession in Britain: a sociological study*. London, Allen and Unwin.

Markus, T. A. (1972). A doughnut model of the environment and its design. *Design Participation*. London, Academy Editions.

Schön, D. A. (1983). *The Reflective Practitioner: How professionals think in action*. London, Temple Smith.

Sturt, G. (1923). *The Wheelwright's Shop*. Cambridge, Cambridge University Press.

3

Route maps of
the design process

The six phases of a design project:

1. Enthusiasm
2. Disillusionment
3. Panic
4. Search for the guilty
5. Punishment of the innocent
6. Praise for the non-participants

Notice on the wall of the Greater London Council Architects
Department
(According to Astragal AJ, 22 March 1978)

'Now for the evidence,' said the King, 'and then the sentence.' 'No!'
said the Queen, 'first the sentence, and then the evidence!'
'Nonsense!' cried Alice, so loudly that everybody jumped, 'the idea
of having the sentence first!'

Lewis Carroll, *Alice Through the Looking Glass*

Definitions of design

So far in this book we have not actually attempted a definition of
what is and is not design. We have explored the variety and
complexity of the designer's role and seen something of the way
this has developed over time. We have also seen a little of the
enormous variety of types of design and discussed the dimensions
along which they vary. To attempt a definition of design too
soon might easily lead to a narrow and restricted view. To understand fully the nature of design it is necessary not only to seek
out the similarities between different design situations, but also
to recognise the very real differences. Inevitably, each of us will
approach this general understanding of design from our own particular background.

This is all too apparent when writers attempt a comprehensive definition of design. What sort of designer might have offered the following definition?

> The optimum solution to the sum of the true needs of a particular set of circumstances.

Is it more likely that such a definition is the idea of an engineer or an interior designer? Is it meaningful to talk of 'optimum solutions' or 'true needs' in connection with interior design? In fact Matchett who defined design this way, comes from an engineering background (Matchett 1968). This definition suggests at least two ways in which design situations can vary. Matchett's use of 'optimum' indicates that the results of design as he knows it can be measured against established criteria of success. This may well be the case for the design of a machine where output can be quantified on one or more scales of measurement, but it hardly applies to the design of a stage set or a building interior. Matchett's definition also assumes that all the 'true needs' of a circumstance can be listed. More often than not, however, designers are by no means sure of all the needs of a situation. This is because not all design problems relate to equally purposeful activities. For example, it is much easier to define the needs to be satisfied in a lecture theatre than in a domestic living-room.

Some pronouncements about design would have us believe that these differences are not really very important. This is taken to an extreme by Sydney Gregory (1966) in his early book on design methodology:

> The process of design is the same whether it deals with the design of a new oil refinery, the construction of a cathedral or the writing of Dante's Divine Comedy.

Perhaps what Gregory was really telling us, was that when he designed or wrote he personally used a similar process. Whilst this might have worked for Sydney Gregory it seems unlikely that it would have worked for Dante, who showed no interest as far as we know in chemical engineering! It is more likely that design involves some skills which are so generic that we could reasonably say they apply to all forms of design practice, but it also seems likely that some skills are quite specific to certain types of design. It would also seem reasonable to suggest that the balance of skills required by each type of designer is different.

Certainly all designers need to be creative and we will deal with creative thinking in a later chapter. Some designers, such as architects, interior and product designers need a highly developed visual sense and usually need to be able to draw well. We deal with designing by drawing in another chapter. Other designers at the more engineering end of the spectrum are likely to need higher numeracy skills and so on.

Of course it is possible to arrive at a definition of design which allows for both the disparate and the common features. Chris Jones (1970) gives what he regarded as the 'ultimate definition' of design:

> To initiate change in man-made things.

All designers could probably agree that this applies to what they do, but does it really help? Such a definition is probably too general and abstract to be useful in helping us to understand design. Do we really need a simple definition of design or should we accept that design is too complex a matter to be summarised in less than a book? The answer is probably that we shall never really find a single satisfactory definition but that the searching is probably much more important than the finding. Chris Jones (1966) had already recognised just how difficult this search is in his earlier description of design: 'The performing of a very complicated act of faith.'

Some maps of the design process

Many writers have tried to chart a route through the process from beginning to end. The common idea behind all these 'maps' of the design process is that it consists of a sequence of distinct and identifiable activities which occur in some predictable and identifiably logical order. This seems at first sight to be quite a sensible way of analysing design. Logically it seems that the designer must do a number of things in order to progress from the first stages of getting a problem to the final stages of defining a solution. Unfortunately, as we shall see, these assumptions turn out to be rather rash. Indeed Lewis Carroll's Queen may well have made rather a good designer with her apparently ridiculous suggestion that the sentence should precede the evidence!

However, let us proceed to examine some of these maps in order to see how useful they are. The first map we might examine is that laid out for use by architects in the RIBA *Architectural Practice and Management Handbook* (1965). The handbook tells us that the design process may be divided into four phases:

Phase 1 assimilation
The accumulation and ordering of general information and information specifically related to the problem in hand.

Phase 2 general study
The investigation of the nature of the problem.
The investigation of possible solutions or means of solution.

Phase 3 development
The development and refinement of one or more of the tentative
   solutions isolated during phase 2.

Phase 4 communication
The communication of one or more solutions to people inside or
   outside the design team.

However, a more detailed reading of the RIBA handbook reveals that these four phases are not necessarily sequential although it may seem logical that the overall development of a design will progress from phase 1 to phase 4. To see how this might actually work, however, we shall examine the transitions between the phases.

   Actually, it is quite difficult for the designer to know what infor-mation to gather in phase 1 until there has been some investiga-tion of the problem in phase 2. With the introduction of systematic design methods into design education it became fashionable to require students to prepare reports accompanying their designs. Frequently such reports contain a great deal of information, slav-ishly gathered at the beginning of the project. As a regular reader of such reports, I have become used to testing this information to see how it has had an impact on the design. In fact, students are often unable to point to any material effect on their solutions for quite large sections of their gathered data. One of the dangers here is that since gathering information is rather less mentally demanding than solving problems there is always a temptation to put off the transition from phase 1 to phase 2. Professional designers are unlikely to succumb to this temptation since they need to earn their living, but students often do, and such a map often serves only to encourage unproductive procrastination!

   The detailed development of solutions (phase 3) rarely goes smoothly to one inevitable conclusion. In fact such work often reveals the weaknesses in the designer's understanding of the problem and grasp of all the relevant information. In other words there is a need to return to phase 2 activities!

Even more sobering is the experience common to all designers, that when they show possible solutions to their clients (phase 4) only then will the clients see that they have described the problem badly (phase 1).

We could go on analysing the map in this way, but the general lesson would remain the same. Although it may seem logical that the activities listed here should be performed in the order shown by the map, the reality is much more confused. What the map does is to tell us that designers have to gather information about a problem, study it, devise a solution and draw it, though not necessarily in that order. The RIBA handbook is very honest here in declaring that there are likely to be unpredictable jumps between the four phases. What it does not tell us is how often or in what way these jumps are made (Fig. 3.1).

If we turn on through the pages of the RIBA handbook there is yet another, much larger scale map to be found. Because of its immense detail this 'Plan of Work', as it is called, looks much more promising at first sight. The plan of work consists of twelve stages described as a logical course of action:

A Inception
B Feasibility
C Outline proposals
D Scheme design
E Detail design
F Production information
G Bills of quantities
H Tender action
J Project planning
K Operations on site
L Completion
M Feed-back

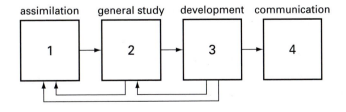

Figure 3.1
A map of the design process according to the RIBA plan of work

35

The handbook rather revealingly also shows a simplified version in what it describes as 'usual terminology':

A–B Briefing
C–D Sketch plans
E–H Working drawings
J–M Site operations

From this we can see the plan of work for what it really is; a description not of the process but of the products of that process. It tells us not how the architect works but, what must be produced in terms of feasibility reports, sketch plans and production drawings. Further, it also details the services provided by the architect in terms of obtaining planning approval and supervising the construction of the building.

Architects used to be paid their fees according to a standard level and pattern which formed part of the Conditions of Engagement for Architects. Today fees are a matter of negotiation between architects and their clients and both the level of their remuneration and the pattern of payments is very variable. However, it remains the case that an architectural project may last for a long time, often many years, and thus architects, if they are to be solvent, need payments before the end of their work. Historically, then, the RIBA plan of work was used to determine agreed stages of work which could attract staged payments. So the plan of work may also be seen as part of a business transaction; it tells clients what they will get, and describes what architects must do. It does not necessarily tell us how it is done.

The plan of work also describes what the other members of the design team (quantity surveyor, engineers etc.) will do, and how they will relate to the architect; with the architect clearly portrayed as the manager and leader of this team. This further reveals the plan of work to be part of the architectural profession's propaganda exercise to stake a claim as leader of the multi-disciplinary building design team. Again this is now by no means a commonly shared view of the architect's role! None of this should be taken as criticism of the RIBA plan of work, which probably performs its functions quite adequately, but in the end we probably learn from it more about the history of the role of the RIBA than about the nature of architectural design processes.

Two academics, Tom Markus (1969b) and Tom Maver (1970) produced rather more elaborate maps of the architectural design process (Fig. 3.2). They argued that a complete picture of design

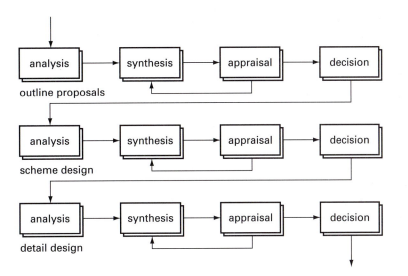

outline proposals

scheme design

detail design

Figure 3.2
The Markus/Maver map
of the design process

method requires both a 'decision sequence' and a 'design process' or 'morphology'. They suggest that we need to go through the decision sequence of analysis, synthesis, appraisal and decision at increasingly detailed levels of the design process (stages 2, 3, 4 and 5 in the RIBA handbook). Since the concepts of analysis, synthesis, and evaluation or appraisal occur frequently in the literature on design methodology it is worth attempting some rough definitions before examining these maps in more detail.

Analysis involves the exploration of relationships, looking for patterns in the information available, and the classification of objectives. Analysis is the ordering and structuring of the problem. Synthesis on the other hand is characterised by an attempt to move forward and create a response to the problem – the generation of solutions. Appraisal involves the critical evaluation of suggested solutions against the objectives identified in the analysis phase. To see how these three functions of analysis, synthesis and evaluation are related in practice we might examine the thoughts of a chess player deciding on the next move. The procedure suggests that first our player might analyse the current position on the board by studying all the relations between the pieces; the pieces that are being threatened and how, and which of the unoccupied squares remain unguarded. The next task would be to clarify objectives. Obviously the ultimate long-term object of the game is to win, but at this particular stage the priorities between attack or defence and between immediate or eventual gain have to be decided. The synthesis stage would be to suggest a move, which might emerge either as a complete idea or in parts, such as moving a particular piece, occupying a particular square or threatening a particular piece, and so on. This idea then needs evaluating against the objectives before finally deciding whether or not to make the particular move.

To return to the Markus/Maver map, we have already seen how maps of the design process may need to allow for return loops from an activity to that preceding it. The first move thought of by our chess player may on examination prove unwise, or even dangerous, and so it is with design. This accounts for the return loop in the Markus/Maver decision sequence from appraisal to synthesis, which in simple terms calls for the designer to have another idea since the previous one turned out to be inadequate.

The presence of this return loop in the diagram, however, raises another question. Why is it the only return loop? Might not the development of a solution suggest more analysis is needed? Even in the game of chess a proposed move may reveal a new problem and suggest that the original perception of the state of the game was incomplete and that further analysis is necessary. This is even more frequently the case in design where the problem is not totally described, as on a chess board. This was long ago recognised by John Page (1963) who warned the 1962 Conference on Design Methods at Manchester:

> In the majority of practical design situations, by the time you have produced this and found out that and made a synthesis, you realise you have forgotten to analyse something else here, and you have to go round the cycle and produce a modified synthesis, and so on.

So we are inevitably led to the conclusion that our map should actually show a return loop from each function to all preceding functions. However, there is yet another problem with this map (Fig. 3.3). It suggests, again apparently logically, that the designer proceeds from the general to the specific, from 'outline proposals' to 'detail design'. Actual study of the way designers work reveals this to be rather less clear than it may seem. Conventionally the Markus/Maver map of the design process for architects suggests that the early

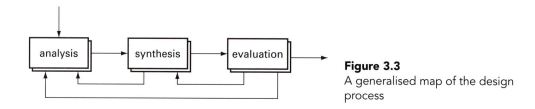

Figure 3.3
A generalised map of the design process

stages will be concerned with the overall organisation and disposition of spaces, and the later stages concerned with the selection of materials used in construction and detailing the junctions between them. In fact this turns out to be yet another example of what may seem logical from a superficial study but where reality is more messy. This is nicely put by the famous American architect Robert Venturi:

> We have a rule that says sometimes the detail wags the dog. You don't necessarily go from the general to the particular, but rather often you do detailing at the beginning very much to inform.
>
> (Lawson 1994b)

It is for this reason that Venturi is so unhappy about the increasing tendency in the United States to separate conceptual design from design development, even appointing different architects at the two stages. The use of the 'design and build' system in the United Kingdom has brought similar problems. At least one very successful and much admired architect, Eva Jiricna, has indicated that her design process is very much a matter beginning with what others would conventionally regard as detail. She likes to begin by choosing materials and drawing full size details of their junctions:

> In our office we usually start with full-size detail . . . if we have, for example, some ideas of what we are going to create with different junctions, then we can create a layout which would be good because certain materials only join in a certain way comfortably.
>
> (Lawson 1994b)

Clearly if this process works well for such a highly acclaimed architect we must take it seriously. The problem for the Markus/ Maver map, then, is just what constitutes 'outline' and what is meant by 'detail'. Experience suggests that this not only varies between designers but may well vary from project to project. What might seem a fundamental early decision on one project may seem a matter of detail which could be left to the end on another. Even if the design strategy itself is not driven by detail as in Eva Jiricna's case, it seems unrealistic to assume that the design process is inevitably one of considering increasing levels of detail.

The map, such as it is, no longer suggests any firm route through the whole process (Fig. 3.4). It rather resembles one of those chaotic party games where the players dash from one room of the house to another simply in order to discover where they must go next. It is about as much help in navigating a designer through the process as a diagram showing how to walk would be to a one-year-old child. Knowing that design consists of analysis, synthesis and

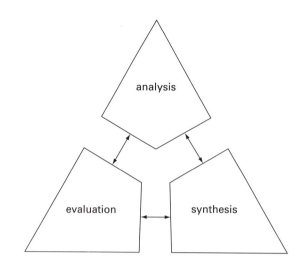

Figure 3.4
A more honest graphical representation of the design process

evaluation linked in an iterative cycle will no more enable you to design than knowing the movements of breaststroke will prevent you from sinking in a swimming pool. You will just have to put it all together for yourself.

Are these maps accurate?

We could continue to explore maps of the design process since a considerable number have been developed. Maps of the design process similar to those already discussed for architecture have been proposed for the engineering design process (Asimow 1962) and (Rosenstein, Rathbone and Schneerer 1964), the industrial design process (Archer 1969) and, even, town planning (Levin 1966). These rather abstract maps from such varying fields of design show a considerable degree of agreement, which suggests that perhaps Sydney Gregory was right all along, perhaps the design process is the same in all fields. Well unfortunately none of the writers quoted here offer any evidence that designers actually follow their maps, so we need to be cautious.

These maps, then, tend to be both theoretical and prescriptive. They seem to have been derived more by thinking about design than by experimentally observing it, and characteristically they are logical and systematic. There is a danger with this approach, since writers on design methodology do not necessarily always make the best designers. It seems reasonable to suppose that our best designers are more likely to spend their time designing than writing about methodology. If this is true then it would be much more interesting to know how very good designers actually work than to know what a design methodologist thinks they should do! One compensating factor here is that most academic writers are also involved in teaching design, and thus have many years of experience of observing their students. However, that also begs the question as to whether students might design differently to the way experienced practitioners work.

Some empirical studies

All these questions suggest that some hard evidence is required rather than just relying on logical thought. In recent years we have indeed begun to study design in a more organised and scientific way. Studies in which designers are put under the microscope have been, and continue to be, conducted and from this research we are gradually learning something of the subtleties of design as it is actually practised. We next examine some of this work, but before we begin a word of caution is necessary. Conducting empirical work on the design process is notoriously difficult. The design process, by definition, takes place inside our heads. True we may see designers drawing while they think, but their drawings may not always reveal the whole of their thought process. That thought process is not always one which the designers themselves would be used to analysing and making explicit. There are many experimental techniques we can use to overcome these problems, but any one experiment on the nature of the design process is likely to be flawed in some way. By putting all this work together, however, a general picture of the way designers think is gradually emerging.

A laboratory study of design students

Some years ago I was interested in the general question of cognitive style in the design process and how it was acquired. As first a student of architecture and then a student of psychology I began to feel that my fellow students shared some common ways of thinking but that the architects seemed to think in distinctly different ways to the psychologists. Two very specific questions then developed out of this general interest. Were these differences real or not and, if real, did they reflect the different nature of people who became architects as opposed to psychologists or did they reflect the different nature of their jobs?

A series of experimental situations was therefore devised in which the subjects would solve design-like problems under laboratory conditions with no other distractions (Lawson 1972). It was, of course, vital that no specialist technical knowledge was necessary to solve the problems to avoid giving any advantage to the architect subjects over the others. In one experiment the subjects had to complete a design using a number of modular coloured wooden blocks. They were given more blocks than they actually needed, and the design problem required a single storey arrangement of three modular bays by four bays. The vertical faces of the blocks were coloured red and blue and, on each occasion the subject was required to make the perimeter wall of the final arrangement either as red or as blue as possible (Fig. 3.5).

The task was made more complex by the introduction of some 'hidden' rules governing allowed relationships between some of the blocks. This meant that some combinations of blocks would be allowed whilst others would not. These rules were changed for each problem, and the subjects knew that some rules were in operation but were not told what they were. Thus this abstract problem is in reality a very simplified design situation where a physical three-dimensional solution has to achieve certain stated performance objectives while obeying a relational structure which is not entirely explicit at the outset.

In order not to intimidate the subjects, they were left alone to solve the problems with a computer setting each problem and

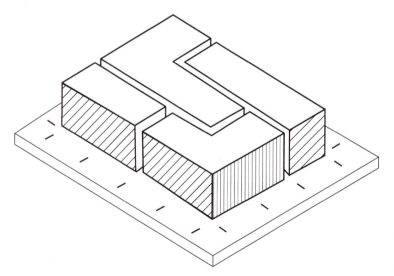

Figure 3.5
A laboratory experiment to investigate the design process

telling them, when they asked, whether their proposed solution was an allowed combination or not. In addition, unknown to the subjects the computer was able to record and analyse their problem-solving strategy. Initially two groups of subjects were used comprising final year students of architecture and postgraduate science students (Lawson 1979b).

The two groups showed quite consistent and strikingly different strategies. Although this problem is simple compared with most real design problems there are still over 6000 possible answers. Clearly the immediate task facing the subjects was how to narrow this number down and search for a good solution. The scientists adopted a technique of trying out a series of designs which used as many different blocks and combinations of blocks as possible as quickly as possible. Thus they tried to maximise the information available to them about the allowed combinations. If they could discover the rule governing which combinations of blocks were allowed they could then search for an arrangement which would optimise the required colour around the design. By contrast, the architects selected their blocks in order to achieve the appropriately coloured perimeter. If this proved not to be an acceptable combination, then the next most favourably coloured block combination would be substituted and so on until an acceptable solution was discovered.

The essential difference between these two strategies is that while the scientists focused their attention on understanding the underlying rules, the architects were obsessed with achieving the desired result. Thus we might describe the scientists as having a problem-focused strategy and the architects as having a solution-focused strategy.

Thus we had the beginnings of an answer to our first question. It does indeed look as if the cognitive style of the architects and the scientists was consistently different. To address the second question a further run of the experiment was necessary. Here the subjects were school pupils at the end of their study immediately before going to university, and university students at the very beginning of the first year of a degree in architecture. Both these groups were much less good at solving all the problems and neither group showed any consistent common strategy. The answer, then, to the second question appeared to be that it is the educational experience of their respective degree courses which makes the science and architecture students think the way they do, rather than some inherent cognitive style.

The behaviour of the architect and scientist groups seems sensible when related to the educational style of their respected courses. The architects are taught through a series of design studies and receive criticism about the solution they come up with rather than the method. They are not asked to understand problems or analyse situations. As in the real professional world the solution is everything and the process is not examined! By comparison scientists are taught theoretically. They are taught that science proceeds through a method which is made explicit and which can be replicated by others. Psychologists, in particular, because of the rather 'soft' nature of their science are taught to be very careful indeed over their methodology.

However, this is perhaps too simple an explanation. Although their performance was no better overall, both groups of design students showed greater skill than their peers in actually forming the three-dimensional solutions. They appeared to have greater spatial ability and to be more interested in simply playing around with the blocks. Is it possible that the respective educational systems used for science and architecture simply reinforce an interest in the abstract or the concrete? These experiments do not enable us to answer this question. However, they are also very limited in their ability to model the actual design process so for further progress we need to turn to more realistic investigations.

The results of this experiment also further question the division between analysis and synthesis seen in the maps of design earlier in this chapter. What is clear from this data, is that the more experienced final year architecture students consistently used a strategy of analysis through synthesis. They learned about the problem through attempts to create solutions rather than through deliberate and separate study of the problem itself.

Some more realistic experiments

In a slightly more realistic experiment, experienced designers were asked to redesign a bathroom for speculatively built houses (Eastman 1970). The subjects here were allowed to draw and talk about what they were doing and all this data was recorded and analysed. From these protocols Eastman showed how the designers explored the problem through a series of attempts to create solutions. There is no meaningful division to be found between analysis and synthesis in these protocols but rather a simultaneous learning about the nature of the problem and the range of possible solutions. The designers were supplied with an existing bathroom design together with some potential clients' criticisms of the apparent waste of space. Thus some parts of the problem, such as the need to reorganise the facilities so as to give a greater feeling of spaciousness and luxury, were quite clearly stated. However the designers discovered much more about the problem as they critically evaluated their own solutions. One of Eastman's protocols shows how a designer came to identify the problem of shielding the toilet from the bath for reasons of privacy. Later this becomes part of a much more subtle requirement as he decided that the client would not like one of his designs which seems deliberately to hide the toilet, the toilet then was to be shielded but not hidden. This subtle requirement was not thought out in the abstract and stated in advance of synthesis but discovered as a result of manipulating solutions.

Using a similar approach, Akin asked architects to design rather more complex buildings than Eastman's bathroom. He observed and recorded the subjects' comments in a series of protocols (Akin 1986). In fact, Akin specifically set out to 'disaggregate' the design process, or break it down into its constituent parts. Even given this interventionist attack on the problem, Akin failed to identify analysis and synthesis as meaningfully discrete components of design. Akin actually found that his designers were constantly both generating new goals and redefining constraints. Thus, for Akin, analysis is a part of all phases of design and synthesis begins very early in the process.

Interviews with designers

So far we have looked at the results of experiments in which designers are asked to design under experimental conditions. These conditions can never actually model the real design studio, so an alternative research method of interviewing designers about their methods allows them to describe how they work under normal conditions. Of course this research method is also flawed since we are dependent on the designers actually telling the truth! Whilst it is quite unlikely that they would deliberately mislead us, nevertheless memory can easily play tricks and designers may well convince themselves in retrospect that their process was more logical and efficient than was actually the case. One of the advantages of the interview is that we can sometimes persuade very good designers to allow us to interview them whereas, sadly, many of the laboratory experiments are carried out on students who are easily accessible to research workers!

The primary generator

Some years ago a research student and colleague of mine, Jane Darke, interviewed some well-known British architects about their intentions when designing local authority housing. The architects first discussed their views on housing in general and how they saw the problems of designing such housing, and then discussed the history of a particular housing scheme in London. The design of housing under these conditions presents an extremely complex problem. The range of legislative and economic controls, the subtle social requirements and the demands of London sites all interact to generate a highly constrained situation. Faced with all this complexity Darke shows how the architects tended to latch on to a relatively simple idea very early in the design process (Darke 1978). This idea, or primary generator as Darke calls it, may be to create a mews-like street or leave as much open space as possible and so on. For example, one architect described how 'we assumed a terrace would be the best way of doing it . . . and the whole exercise, formally speaking, was to find a way of making a terrace continuous so that you can use space in the most efficient way . . .'. Thus a very simple idea is used to narrow down the range of possible solutions, and the designer is then able rapidly to construct and analyse a scheme. Here again we see this very close, perhaps inseparable, relation between analysis and synthesis. Darke however used her empirically gained evidence to propose a new kind of map which had some parallels with a more theoretical proposition (Hillier, Musgrove and O'Sullivan 1972). Instead of analysis–synthesis Darke's map reads generator–conjecture–analysis (Fig. 3.6). In plain language, first decide what you think might be an important aspect of the problem, develop a crude design on this basis and then examine it to see what else you can discover about the problem.

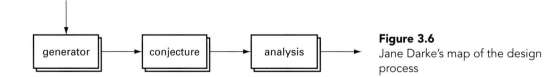

Figure 3.6
Jane Darke's map of the design process

Further evidence supporting the idea of the primary generator has been collected more recently using experimental observation and analysis of the drawings produced by designers (Rowe 1987). When reporting one of these case studies in detail, Rowe describes his analysis of a series of design drawings and detects lines of reasoning which are based on some synthetic and highly formative design idea rather than on analysis of the problem:

> Involving the a priori use of an organising principle or model to direct the decision making process.

These early ideas, primary generators or organising principles sometimes have an influence which stretches throughout the whole design process and is detectable in the solution. However, it is also sometimes the case that designers gradually achieve a sufficiently good understanding of their problem to reject the early thoughts through which their knowledge was gained. Nevertheless this rejection can be surprisingly difficult to achieve. Rowe (1987) records the 'tenacity with which designers will cling to major design ideas and themes in the face of what, at times, might seem insurmountable odds'. Often these very ideas themselves create difficulties which may be organisational or technical, so it seems on the face of it odd that they are not rejected more readily. However, early anchors can be reassuring and if the designer succeeds in overcoming such difficulties and the original ideas were good, we are quite likely to recognise this as an act of great creativity. For example, Jorn Utzon's famous design for Sydney Opera House was based on geometrical ideas which could only be realised after overcoming considerable technical problems both of structure and cladding. Unfortunately, we are not all as creative as Utzon, and it is frequently the case that design students create more problems than they solve by selecting impractical or inappropriate primary generators.

We return to these ideas again in a later section but before we leave Darke's work it is worth noting some other evidence that she presents with little comment but which even further calls into question the value of design process maps. One of the architects interviewed was explicit about his method of obtaining a design brief (stages A and B in the RIBA handbook):

> A brief comes about through essentially an ongoing relationship between what is possible in architecture and what you want to do, and everything you do modifies your idea of what is possible . . . you can't start with a brief and (then) design, you have to start designing and briefing simultaneously, because the two activities are completely interrelated.

(Darke 1978)

This must also ring very true to any architect who has designed for a committee client. I have found that one of the most effective ways of making apparent the disparate needs of groups in multi-user buildings such as hospitals is to present the client committee with a sketch design. Clients often seem to find it easier to communicate their wishes by reacting to and criticising a proposed design, than by trying to draw up an abstract comprehensive performance specification.

This discussion has oversimplified reality by implicitly suggesting that primary generators are always to be found in the singular. In fact, as Rowe points out, it is the reconciling and resolving of two or more such ideas which characterises design protocols. However, we must leave further discussion of this complication, and of the rejecting or resolving of primary generators, until a later chapter.

In summary

This chapter has examined the design process as a sequence of activities and found the idea rather unconvincing. Certainly it is reasonable to argue that for design to take place a number of things must happen. Usually there must be a brief assembled, the designer must study and understand the requirements, produce one or more solutions, test them against some explicit or implicit criteria, and communicate the design to clients and constructors. The idea, however, that these activities occur in that order, or even that they are identifiable separate events seems very questionable. It seems more likely that design is a process in which problem and solution emerge together. Often the problem may not even be fully understood without some acceptable solution to illustrate it. In fact, clients often find it easier to describe their problems by referring to existing solutions which they know of. This is all very confusing, but it remains one of the many characteristics of design that it so challenging and interesting to do and study.

Our final attempt at a map of the design process shows this negotiation between problem and solution with each seen as a reflection of the other (Fig. 3.7). The activities of analysis, synthesis and evaluation are certainly involved in this negotiation but the map does not indicate any starting and finishing points or the direction of flow from one activity to another. However, this map should not be read too literally since any visually understandable

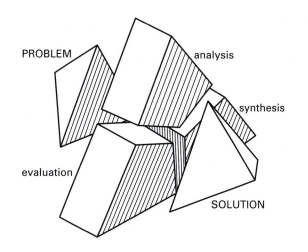

Figure 3.7
The design process seen as a negotiation between problem and solution through the three activities of analysis, synthesis and evaluation

diagram is probably far too much of a simplification of what is clearly a highly complex mental process.

In the next section of this book we explore the nature of design problems and their solutions in order to get a better understanding of just why designers think the way they do.

References

Akin, O. (1986). *Psychology of architectural design*. London, Pion.

Archer, L. B. (1969). The structure of the design process. *Design Methods in Architecture*. London, Lund Humphries.

Asimow, M. (1962). *Introduction to Design*. Englewood Cliffs, Prentice Hall.

Darke, J. (1978). The primary generator and the design process. *New Directions in Environmental Design Research: procedings of EDRA 9*. Washington, EDRA. 325–337.

Eastman, C. M. (1970). On the analysis of the intuitive design process. *Emerging Methods in Environmental Design and Planning*. Cambridge Mass, MIT Press.

Gregory, S. A. (1966). *The Design Method*. London, Butterworths.

Hillier, B., Musgrove, J. et al. (1972). Knowledge and design. *Environmental Design: research and practice EDRA 3*. University of California.

Jones, J. C. (1966). Design methods reviewed. *The Design Method*. London, Butterworths.

Jones, J. C. (1970). *Design Methods: seeds of human futures*. New York, John Wiley.

Lawson, B. R. (1972). Problem Solving in Architectural Design. University of Aston in Birmingham.

Lawson, B. R. (1979b). "Cognitive strategies in architectural design." *Ergonomics* 22(1): 59–68.

Lawson, B. R. (1994b). *Design in Mind*. Oxford, Butterworth Architecture.

Levin, P. H. (1966). "The design process in planning." *Town Planning Review* 37(1).

Markus, T. A. (1969b). The role of building performance measurement and appraisal in design method. *Design methods in Architecture*. London, Lund Humphries.

Matchett, E. (1968). "Control of thought in creative work." *Chartered Mechanical Engineer* **14**(4).

Maver, T. W. (1970). Appraisal in the building design process. *Emerging Methods in Environmental Design and Planning*. Cambridge Mass, MIT Press.

Page, J. K. (1963). Review of the papers presented at the conference. *Conference on Design Methods*. Oxford, Pergamon.

Rosenstein, A. B., Rathbone, R. R. et al. (1964). *Engineering Communications*. Englewood Cliffs, Prentice Hall.

Rowe, P. G. (1987). *Design Thinking*. Cambridge Mass, MIT Press.

PART TWO

PROBLEMS AND SOLUTIONS

4

The components
of design problems

It seemed that the next minute they would discover a solution. Yet it
was clear to both of them that the end was still far, far off, and that
the hardest and most complicated part was only just beginning.
                                    Anton Chekhov, *The Lady with the Dog*

It has long been an axiom of mine that the little things are infinitely
the most important.
                Sir Arthur Conan Doyle, *The Adventures of Sherlock Holmes*

Above and below the problem

Designers are traditionally identified not so much by the kinds of
problems they tackle as by the kinds of solutions they produce. Thus
industrial designers are so called because they create products for
industrial and commercial organisations whereas interior designers
are expected to create interior spaces. Of course, reality is not actually quite so rigid as this. Many designers dabble in other fields,
some quite regularly, but most designers tend not to be quite so
versatile as some writers on design methodology appear to think.
We have already seen that this is to some extent the result of
the range of technologies understood by the designer. Architects
for example need to understand, amongst a great deal else, the
structural properties and jointing problems associated with timber. It
seems likely, then, that most architects could turn furniture designer
to design a wooden chair, although a furniture designer would probably claim to be able to recognise architect-designed chairs. This is
because most architects are used to handling timber at a different
scale and in a different context and thus have already developed a
'timber language' with a distinctly architectural accent. The imposed
loads and methods of construction of buildings are rather different

to those found in furniture. While timber is capable of solving both problems there are many other materials, each with their own technology, which are not usually common to architecture and furniture design. Although both are possible, we do not very often see brick chairs or polypropylene buildings!

The various design fields are also often thought to be different in terms of the inherent difficulty of the problems they present. It is easy to assume that size represents complexity. This argument suggests that architecture must be more complex than industrial design since buildings are larger than products. Certainly it is possible to see the three-dimensional design fields in a tree with town planning at the roots and the trunk beginning to branch out through urban design, architecture and interior design to the twigs of industrial design, but does this really mean that town planning is more difficult than product design? (Fig. 4.1).

Difficulty is, of course, a subjective matter. What one person finds difficult may often be easy to another, so we must look at the exact nature of these various kinds of problems to discover more. Urban design solutions are obviously much larger in scale than architectural solutions, but are urban design problems also in some way bigger and more complex than architectural problems? The answer to this question must be that this is not necessarily so. What really matters

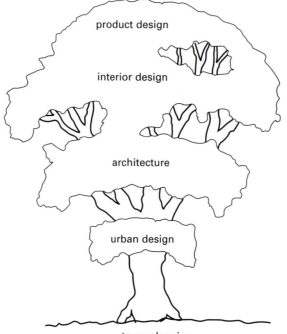

Figure 4.1
A 'tree' of three dimensional design fields

here is just how far down the hierarchy the designer must go. For example, when designing an ordinary house architects are unlikely to be greatly concerned with detailed considerations of methods of opening and closing cupboard doors. There may be some thought necessary as to whether the windows might be of the sliding sash, hinged casement or pivoting variety; but even that is not usually critical. The designer of a small caravan or boat, however, may need to give very careful thought to such matters. Even the way in which cupboard doors open in the restricted space available may be of crucial significance. Thus part of the definition of a design problem is the level of detail which requires attention. What usually seems detail to architects may be central to interior or industrial designers and so on.

The beginning and end of the problem

How, then, do we find the end of a design problem? Is it not possible to go on getting involved in more and more detail? Indeed this is so; there is no natural end to the design process. There is no way of deciding beyond doubt when a design problem has been solved. Designers simply stop designing either when they run out of time or when, in their judgement, it is not worth pursuing the matter further. In design, rather like art, one of the skills is in knowing when to stop. Unfortunately, there seems to be no real substitute for experience in developing this judgement. This presents considerable difficulties not just for students of design, but also for practitioners. Since there is no real end to a design problem it is very hard to decide how much time should be allowed for its solution. Generally speaking, it seems that the nearer you get to finishing a design the more accurately you are able to estimate how much work remains to be done. As we have seen in the last section we learn about design problems largely by trying to solve them. Thus it may take quite a lot of effort before a designer is really aware just how difficult a problem is. First impressions are rarely very reliable in these matters. Design students seem to be incorrigibly optimistic in their estimation of the difficulty of problems and the time needed to arrive at acceptable solutions. As a result students often fail to get down to the level of detail required of them by their tutors. It is all too easy to look superficially at a new design problem and, failing to see any great difficulty, imagine that there is no real urgency.

Only later, perhaps when it is too late, do the difficulties emerge in response to some effort.

One of the essential characteristics of design problems then is that they are often not apparent but must be found. Unlike crossword puzzles, brain-teasers or mathematical problems, neither the goal nor the obstacle to achieving that goal are clearly expressed. In fact, the initial expression of design problems may often be quite misleading. If design problems are characteristically unclearly stated, then it is also true that designers seem never to be satisfied with the problem as presented. Eberhard (1970) has amusingly illustrated this sometimes infuriating habit of designers with his cautionary tale of the doorknob. He suggests that there are two ways in which designers can retreat back up the hierarchy of problems, by escalation and by regression.

When faced with the task of designing a new knob for his client's office door, Eberhard's designer suggests that perhaps 'we ought to ask ourselves whether a doorknob is the best way of opening and closing a door'. Soon the designer is questioning whether the office really needs a door, or should even have four walls and so on. As Eberhard reports from his own experience, such a train of argument can lead to the redesign of the organisation of which the client and his office are part, and ultimately the very political system which allows this organisation to exist is called into question. This escalation leads to an ever wider definition of the problem. Rather like the after-image in your eye after looking at a bright light, the problem seems to follow your gaze.

We may also respond to a design problem by what Eberhard calls regression. A student of mine who was asked to design a new central library building decided that he needed to study the various methods of loaning and storing books. As his design tutor I agreed that this seemed sensible, only to discover at the next tutorial that his work now looked more as if he was preparing for a degree in librarianship than one in architecture. This trail of regression is to a certain extent encouraged by some of the maps of the design process which were reviewed in Chapter 3. This behaviour is only one logical outcome in practice of the notion that analysis precedes synthesis and data collection precedes analysis. As we have seen, in design it is difficult to know what problems are relevant and what information will be useful until a solution is attempted.

Both escalation and regression often go together. Thus my architectural student studying librarianship may also become convinced that a new central library building is no answer. The problem, he may argue, lies in designing a new system of making books more available by providing branch libraries, travelling libraries or perhaps even using new methods of data transmission by television.

While this continuous broadening of the problem can be used to avoid the issue and put off the evil day of actually getting to grips with the design, nevertheless it does represent a sensibly cautious response to unclearly stated problems. Design action, like medicine, is only needed when the current situation is in some way unsatisfactory, but which is better, to treat the symptoms or to look for the cause?

The design fix

A client once asked me to design an extension to his house. The initial brief was rather vague with various ideas of adding an extra bedroom or a study. The real purpose of this extension was difficult to understand since the house was already large enough for all the family to have their own bedrooms and still leave a room which could have been used as a study. The site was cramped and any extension had to either occupy some valued garden space or involve considerable expense in building over a single storey garage and removing a rather splendid pitched roof. It seemed that any extension was almost bound to create new problems, and was not even likely to prove a worthwhile investment. The client's thinking was still unclear and at one meeting, ideas of being able to accommodate grandparents were being discussed to the sounds of rather loud music from one of the teenage children's bedrooms. It then gradually emerged that this was the real source of the problem. In fact the house was indeed already large enough but not well enough divided up acoustically. The problem then shifted to installing some better sound insulation, but this is by no means easy to achieve with existing traditional domestic construction. I suggested the actual solution initially as a joke. Buy the children some headphones! Thus by treating the cause of the problem rather than fixing the symptoms the client kept his garden and his money. I regrettably lost some fees, but gained a very grateful client who remained a friend. This presents a rather unglamorous view of design problems. The stereotypical public image of design portrays the creation of new, original and uncompromising objects or environments.

The reality is that design is often more of a repair job. Part of the problem is in correcting something which has gone wrong in some way. A new housestyle for a commercial organisation, refitting a shop interior, extending a house, planting trees to form a shelter belt or declaring a housing action area are all design responses in different fields to existing unsatisfactory situations. For this reason design is referred to by many writers as providing a 'fix' of some kind. The designer is seen as attempting in some way to improve or fix something which is wrong. We return to this notion of design as a 'fix' again later where we shall briefly explore the argument that designing technology to fix a symptom only makes more secure the cause of that symptom. For example, designing noise barriers to screen motorways can be seen actually to weaken the case for a quieter, less energy-intensive method of transport than the internal combustion engine. The central theme of this chapter, however, is that a significant part of a design problem often lies in relating to what already exists. The definition of such problems then is a matter of deciding just how much of what already exists can be called into question. Design problems do not have natural or obvious boundaries but, rather, seem to be organised roughly hierarchically. It is rarely possible to discern precisely how far above the stated problem one should begin and how far below one should call a halt. Creatively uncovering the range of the problem is one of the designer's most important skills, and we shall look at some problem identification techniques in Chapter 12.

The multi-dimensional design problem

Design problems are often both multi-dimensional and highly interactive. Very rarely does any part of a designed thing serve only one purpose. The American architect Philip Johnson is reported to have observed that some people find chairs beautiful to look at because they are comfortable to sit in, while others find chairs comfortable to sit in because they are beautiful to look at. Certainly no one can deny the importance of both the visual and ergonomic aspects of chair design. The legs of a stacking upright chair present an even more multi-dimensional problem. The geometry and construction of these chair legs must provide stability and support, allow for interlocking when stacked and be sympathetic to the designer's visual intentions for the chair as a whole. The designer of such a chair is unlikely to succeed by thinking separately about the problems of stability, support, stacking and visual line since all must be satisfied by the same element of the solution.

In fact, the designer must also be aware of other more general problems such as cost and manufacturing limitations, the availability of materials and the durability of finishes and joints.

In design it is frequently necessary to devise an integrated solution to a whole cluster of requirements. We saw in Chapter 2 how George Sturt's dished cartwheel provided such an integrated response to structural, mechanical, and even legislative demands. In buildings the window offers an excellent example of another unavoidably multi-dimensional component (Fig. 4.2). As well as letting in daylight and sunlight and allowing for natural ventilation, the window is also usually required to provide a view while retaining privacy. As an interruption in the external wall the window poses problems of structural stability, heat loss and noise transmission, and is thus arguably one of the most complex of building elements. Modern science can be used to study each of the many problems

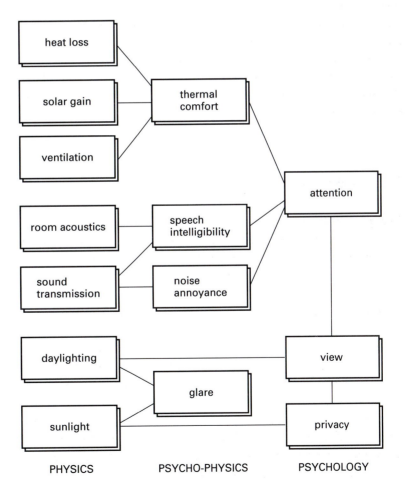

Figure 4.2
Some of the complex array of issues involved in designing a window

of window design with branches of physics, psycho-physics and psychology all being relevant. This is indeed a complex array of concepts to lay before an architect. Most courses in architecture attempt to teach most of this scientific material. However, the methods of science are perhaps surprisingly unhelpful to the designer. Modern building science techniques have generally only provided methods of predicting how well a design solution will work. They are simply tools of evaluation and give no help at all with synthesis. Daylight protractors, heat loss or solar gain calculations do not tell the architect how to design the window but simply how to assess the performance of an already designed window.

Sub-optimising

Chris Jones (1970) summarises how John Page, a professor of building science, proposes that designers should adopt what he calls a cumulative strategy for design in such a situation. This would involve setting carefully defined objectives and criteria of success for the performance of the window on all the dimensions we have identified. Page's strategy then calls for the designer to collect a variety of what he calls sub-solutions for each criterion and then discard the solutions which fail to satisfy all the criteria. Thus the window designer would produce a succession of designs, some intended to achieve a good view, others to avoid solar gain or good daylighting and so on. We are told that this strategy is intended to increase the amount of time spent on analysis and synthesis and reduce the time spent on the synthesis of bad solutions.

It is interesting that this strategy, suggested by a scientist, resembles the behaviour of the science students in the experiment described in the last chapter. Such an approach, however, does not seem born of a clear understanding of the true nature of design problems. Because design problems are so multi-dimensional they are also highly interactive. Enlarging our window may well let in more light and give a better view but this will also result in more heat loss and may create greater problems of privacy. It is the very interconnectedness of all these factors which is the essence of design problems, rather than the isolated factors themselves. In this respect designing is like devising a crossword. Change the letters of one word and several other words will need altering necessitating even further changes. Modify the dish of George Sturt's cartwheel and it may fail to support its load and the lateral thrusts unless the angle of toe-in and axle mounting are also changed. After this the cart may not fit the rutted roads unless the length of the axle and shape of the body are changed. As we have seen, the cartwheel was the result of many years of experience rather than theoretical analysis.

The integrated solution

Until the advent of modern building science this is just how windows were designed. Perhaps the finest period for window design in England was the eighteenth century. The vertical proportions of Georgian windows positioned near the outer edge of the wall and with splayed or stepped reveals gave excellent daylight penetration and distribution (Fig. 4.3). The vertical sliding sash was reasonably weatherproof and gave much more flexible ventilation configurations than the hinged casement which was to replace it.

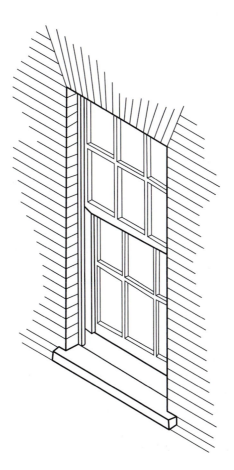

Figure 4.3
The Georgian window offers a beautifully integrated solution

The proportions of solid wall and window, so fundamental to the late renaissance, worked well structurally, gave an even light and offered privacy for those behind. Above all, of course, the Georgian window was integrated into a superb architectural language. So it seems unlikely that the eighteenth-century architect would have been distressed by a lack of expertise in building science.

Thus it is the case that good design is usually an integrated response to a whole series of issues. If there was one single characteristic which could be used to identify good designers it is the ability to integrate and combine. A piece of good design is rather like a hologram; the whole picture is in each fragment. It is often not possible to say which bit of the problem is solved by which bit of the solution. They simply do not map on to each other that way.

However if modern designers are going to abandon traditional or vernacular solutions, they cannot afford to remain so ignorant of the structure of their problems as the Renaissance architect or George Sturt. As Chermayeff and Alexander (1963) put it:

> Too many designers miss the fact that the new issues which legitimately demand new forms are there, if the pattern of the problems could only be seen as it is and not as the bromide image (of a previous solution) conveniently at hand in the catalogue or magazine around the corner.

This 'pattern of the problem' is comprised of all the interactions between one requirement and another which constrain what the designer may do. Chermayeff and Alexander (1963) again:

> every problem has a structure of its own. Good design depends upon the designer's ability to act according to this structure and not to run arbitrarily counter to it.

We can observe some general rules about the nature of this pattern of constraints in design and we discuss these in a later chapter. First, however, we need to look more carefully at the way the performance of designs can be measured against criteria of success.

References

Chermayeff, S. and Alexander, C. (1963). *Community and Privacy*. Harmondsworth, Penguin.

Eberhard, J. P. (1970). We ought to know the difference. *Emerging Methods in Environmental Design and Planning*. Cambridge Mass, MIT Press.

Jones, J. C. (1970). *Design Methods: seeds of human futures*. New York, John Wiley.

5

Measurement, criteria and judgement in design

'She can't do Substraction,' said the White Queen. 'Can you do Division? Divide a loaf by a knife – what's the answer to that?'
'I suppose-' Alice was beginning, but the Red Queen answered for her. 'Bread-and-butter of course.'

Lewis Carroll, *Alice Through the Looking Glass*

There's no such thing as a bad Picasso, but some are less good than others.

Pablo Picasso, *Come to Judgement*

Measuring the success of design

In the last chapter we saw how a design solution is characteristically an integrated response to a complex multi-dimensional problem. One element of a design solution is quite likely simultaneously to solve more than one part of the problem. But how good a response is a design solution to its complex problem? How can we choose between alternative design solutions? Is it possible to say that one design is better than another and, if so, by how much? The question before us in this chapter, then, is the extent to which we can measure the degree of success of the design process.

It is far from easy to answer this question. In order to see how difficult it is, we shall consider the design of a garden greenhouse. There are a number of features of a greenhouse which can be varied. While the body of a greenhouse must inevitably be mainly glass, we have more choice when it comes to the frame. We might at least consider wood, steel, aluminium and plastic. The actual form of the greenhouse is even more variable with possibilities of domes, tent shapes, barrel vaults and so on. In fact there are many more design variables including the method of ventilation and type of door, the floor and foundation construction and so on. What the designer has to do is to select the combination of all these features which will give the most satisfactory performance. How then do we measure the performance of our greenhouse? The primary purpose of a greenhouse is clearly to trap heat from the sun, so we can begin by measuring or calculating the thermal efficiency of a whole range of possible greenhouses. Unfortunately, we are still some way from describing how satisfactory our greenhouse will appear to individual gardeners. They may well also want to know how much it will cost to buy, how long it will last, or how easy it will be to erect and maintain, and probably, what it will look like in the garden. The greenhouse then, must satisfy criteria of solar gain, cost, durability, ease of assembly, appearance and perhaps many others.

If we imagine that we want to assess a number of design solutions so that we can put them in order of preference we would need to begin by assessing each design against each of the criteria and then somehow combining these assessments. This leaves us with three difficulties. First, the various criteria of performance are not likely to be equally important, so some weighting system is needed. Second, performance against some of the criteria can easily be measured while in other cases this is more a matter of subjective judgement. Finally, we then have the problem of combining these judgements together into some overall assessment.

The problem of numbers and counting systems!

Of course what all this means is that measurement in design involves both quantities and qualities. Somehow, then, designers must be able to balance both qualitative and quantitative criteria in their decision-making process. We shall return to this again after a small detour to examine the range of systems available to us for recording judgements.

Quantities and qualities actually turn out not to be so different from each other as we usually assume. This is because it is not sensible to talk of a quantity as if that were a single concept. We normally measure and express quantities by counting using a numerical system. This leads us to believe that all numbers behave in the same way and this is quite untrue. Actually, we commonly employ several quite distinct ways of using numbers, without really being aware of the differences. This carelessness with numbers can be fatal if we are trying to make the sort of judgements needed in design. Numerical systems differ in the extent to which they impose rules on the way the numbers work as we move along the scale.

Ratio numbers

The numerical system which has the most demanding set of rules is known as the ratio scale. It is this scale which we tend to assume is in operation whenever we see a number, and it is the numerical scale with which we are most familiar (Fig. 5.1).

When counting objects we use this ratio scale of measurement which allows us not only to say that four is twice two but also that eight is twice four. So it is normal and correct to assume that a person on their twentieth birthday is twice as old as someone who is only ten. In turn a forty-year-old will be twice as old as the person celebrating their twentieth birthday. The scale or ruler offers us the most obvious form of ratio measurement, and we can see that the ratio of three centimetres to one centimetre is exactly the same as the ratio of six centimetres to two. This way of using numbers would thus be used in comparing the lengths or sizes of our greenhouses.

Interval numbers

However, not all the scientific measurements we could make on our greenhouse rely on ratio numbers. If we consider, not the amount of light allowed in, but the temperature inside the greenhouse we must be careful! On a sunny winter's day it might be reasonable to expect our greenhouse to achieve an indoor temperature of say

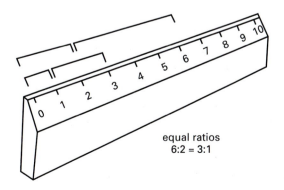

equal ratios
6:2 = 3:1

Figure 5.1
Distance is measured using the ratio numerical system

20 degrees centigrade when the outside air was only 10 degrees. Confusingly, we cannot say that the temperature inside the greenhouse is twice that outside (Fig. 5.2)!

Why this should be can be seen by using both our common temperature scales together. The outside temperature of 10 degrees centigrade can also be described as 50 degrees Fahrenheit, whilst the inside temperature of 20 degrees centigrade corresponds to about 68 degrees Fahrenheit. Thus these two temperatures give a ratio of 20 to 10 or 2 to 1 on the centigrade scale, but a ratio of 68 to 50 on the Fahrenheit scale.

This is because the zero point on these scales is not absolute but entirely arbitrary. The centigrade scale is actually defined as having one hundred equal intervals between the freezing and boiling temperatures of water. We could equally easily use the freezing and boiling temperatures of any other substance and, of course, any number of intervals between. These temperature scales are described as interval measurement. Although 20 degrees cannot be described as twice as hot as 10 degrees the difference, or interval, between 20 and 10 is exactly equal to the interval between 10 and 0.

Interval scales are frequently used for subjective assessment. Psychologists recommend that such scales should be fairly short, up to seven intervals, to retain the reliability of the interval. Thus to return to our greenhouse, we might ask a number of gardeners to assess the ease of assembly or maintenance on five-point scales. We must be careful to remember, then, that we are not justified in regarding a greenhouse assessed as four for assembly as being twice as easy to assemble as one assessed as only two.

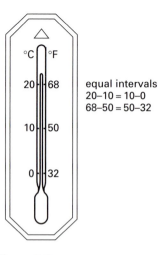

equal intervals
20–10 = 10–0
68–50 = 50–32

Figure 5.2
Temperature must be measured using the interval numerical system

Ordinal numbers

Sometimes we use an even more cautious scale of measurement where not even the interval is considered to be reliably consistent. Such scales are called ordinal, for they represent only a sequence or order (Fig. 5.3). If we take the final league table for the English Football league in 1930 (a year chosen purely at random!) we find that Leeds finished fifth, Aston Villa fourth, Manchester City third, Derby were second and Sheffield Wednesday were first. However, closer inspection reveals that the finishing positions of these teams, which are measured on an ordinal scale, are rather misleading compared to the number of points they scored, which are

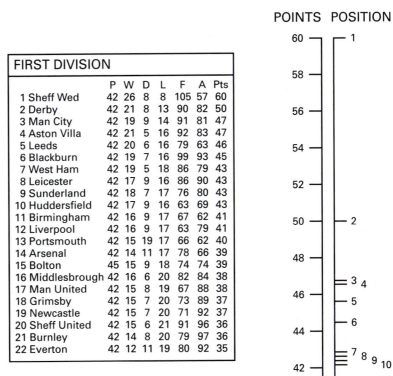

FIRST DIVISION							
	P	W	D	L	F	A	Pts
1 Sheff Wed	42	26	8	8	105	57	60
2 Derby	42	21	8	13	90	82	50
3 Man City	42	19	9	14	91	81	47
4 Aston Villa	42	21	5	16	92	83	47
5 Leeds	42	20	6	16	79	63	46
6 Blackburn	42	19	7	16	99	93	45
7 West Ham	42	19	5	18	86	79	43
8 Leicester	42	17	9	16	86	90	43
9 Sunderland	42	18	7	17	76	80	43
10 Huddersfield	42	17	9	16	63	69	43
11 Birmingham	42	16	9	17	67	62	41
12 Liverpool	42	16	9	17	63	79	41
13 Portsmouth	42	15	19	17	66	62	40
14 Arsenal	42	14	11	17	78	66	39
15 Bolton	45	15	9	18	74	74	39
16 Middlesbrough	42	16	6	20	82	84	38
17 Man United	42	15	8	19	67	88	38
18 Grimsby	42	15	7	20	73	89	37
19 Newcastle	42	15	7	20	71	92	37
20 Sheff United	42	15	6	21	91	96	36
21 Burnley	42	14	8	20	79	97	36
22 Everton	42	12	11	19	80	92	35

Figure 5.3
Rankings are an example of ordinal numbers

measured on a ratio scale. The third, fourth and fifth placed teams were only separated by one point, while Derby were three points clear of them, but Sheffield Wednesday were a massive ten points ahead of Derby. Regulations require that the materials used in buildings should not allow flame to spread across their surface in case of fire. Materials can belong to one of five surface spread of flame classes which range from class 0 to class 4. On this ordinal scale the higher the number the more rapidly flame will spread, but the difference between class 1 and class 2 is not necessarily the same as the difference between class 2 and class 3.

We also get ordinal scales when we ask people to rank order their preferences. Thus we could ask our gardeners to place a number of greenhouses in order of attractiveness of appearance. Whether ordinal or interval scales of assessment are appropriate remains a matter of judgement but, generally, ordinal scales should be used where the assessment may depend on many factors or where the factors cannot easily be defined. Thus while it seems reasonable to ask our gardeners how much easier it is to assemble one greenhouse than another, it does not seem reasonable to ask how much more attractive it may be. Academic examiners may award marks out of one hundred for a particular examination, which is really an interval scale since the zero point is rarely used. Overall degree classifications, however, are usually based on the cruder ordinal scale of first, upper and lower second, third and pass.

Nominal numbers

Finally the fourth, least precise numbering system in common use is the nominal scale, so called because the numbers really represent names and cannot be manipulated arithmetically. Staying with our football example, we can see that the numbers on the players' shirts are nominal (Fig. 5.4). A forward is neither better nor worse than a defender and two goalkeepers do not make a full back. In fact there is no sequence or order to these numbers, we could equally easily have used the letters of the alphabet or any other set of symbols. In fact, some rugby teams traditionally have letters rather than numbers on their backs as if to demonstrate this fact. The only thing we can say about two different nominal numbers is that they are not the same. This enables the referee at the football match to send off an offending player, write the number in his book, and know that he cannot be confused with any other player on the pitch. It used to be the case that the numbers on football players' shirts indicated their position on the field, with goalkeepers wearing '1' and so on.

Figure 5.4
Numbers used as names –
the nominal numerical system

The introduction of so-called 'squad numbering' removed this meaning from the numbers and was not surprisingly objected to by the traditionalist supporters.

Combining the scales

It is apparent, then, that only numbers on a true ratio scale can be combined meaningfully with numbers from another true ratio scale. We cannot combine temperatures from different scales, and certainly we cannot add together numbers from different ordinal scales of preference. Imagine that we have asked a number of people to assess several alternative designs by placing them in order of preference. These rank scores are of course ordinal numbers. We simply cannot add together all the scores given this way to a design by a number of judges. One judge may have thought the first two designs almost impossible to separate, whilst another judge may have thought the first-placed design was out on its own with all the others coming a long way behind. The ordinal numbers simply do not tell us this information. Tempting though it may be to combine these scores in this way, we should resist the temptation!

One of the most well-known cases of such a confusion between scales of measurement is to be found in a highly elaborate and numerical model of the design process devised by the industrial designer and theoretician, Bruce Archer. He, apparently somewhat reluctantly, concedes that at least some assessment of design must be subjective, but since he sets up a highly organised system of measuring satisfaction in design, Archer (1969) clearly wants to use only ratio scales. He argues that a scale of 1–100 can be used for subjective assessment and the data then treated as if it were on a true ratio scale. In this system a judge, or arbiter as Archer calls him, is asked not to rank order or even to use a short interval scale, but to award marks out of 100. Archer argues that if the arbiters are correctly chosen and the conditions for judgement are adequately controlled, such a scale could be assumed to have an absolute zero and constant intervals. Archer does not specify how to 'correctly choose' the judges or 'adequately control the conditions', so he seems rather to be stretching the argument.

In fact Stevens, who originally defined the rules for measurement scales, did so to discourage psychologists from exactly this kind of numerical dishonesty (Stevens 1951). It is interesting to note that psychology itself was then under attack in an age of logic as being too imprecise to deserve the title of science. Perhaps for this reason, many psychologists have been tempted to treat their data as if it were more precise than Stevens's rules would indicate. Archer's work seems a parallel attempt to force design into a scientifically respectable mould. Archer was writing at a time when science was more fashionable than it is today, and in a period during which many writers on the subject thought it desirable to present the design process as scientific.

Value judgement and criteria

It is frequently tempting to employ more apparently accurate methods of measurement in design than the situation really deserves. Not only do the higher level scales, ratio and interval, permit much more arithmetic manipulation, but they also permit absolute judgement to be made. If it can be shown that under certain circumstances 20 degrees centigrade is found to be a comfortable temperature, then that value can be used as an absolutely measurable criterion of acceptability. Life is not so easy when ordinal measurement must be used. Universities use external examiners to help protect and preserve the 'absolute' value of their degree classifications. It is, perhaps, not too difficult for an experienced examiner to put the pupils in rank order. However, it is much more difficult to maintain a constant standard over many years of developing curricula and changing examinations. It is tempting to avoid these difficult problems of judgement by instituting standardised procedures. Thus, to continue the example, a computer-marked multiple choice question examination technique might be seen as a step towards more reliable assessment. But there are invariably disadvantages with such techniques. Paradoxically, conventional examinations allow examiners to tell much more accurately, if not entirely reliably, how much their students have actually understood.

Precision in calculation

It is easy to fall into the trap of over-precision in design. Students of architecture sometimes submit thermal analyses of their buildings with the rate of heat loss through the building fabric calculated down to the last watt. Ask them how many kilowatts are lost when a door is left open for a few minutes and they are incapable of answering. What a designer really needs is to have some feel for the meaning behind the numbers rather than precise methods of calculating them. As a designer you need to know the kinds of changes that can be made to the design which are most likely to improve it when measured against the criteria. It is thus more a matter of strategic decisions rather than careful calculations.

Perhaps it is because design problems are often so intractable and nebulous that the temptation is so great to seek out measurable criteria of satisfactory performance. The difficulty for the designer here is to place value on such criteria and thus balance them against each other and factors which cannot be quantitatively measured. Regrettably numbers seem to confer respectability and importance on what might actually be quite trivial factors. Axel Boje provides us with an excellent demonstration of this numerical measuring disease in his book on open-plan office design (Boje 1971). He calculates that it takes on average about 7 seconds to open and close an office door. Put this together with some research which shows that in an office building accommodating 100 people in 25 rooms on average each person will change rooms some 11 times in a day and thus, in an open plan office Boje argues, each person would save some 32 door movements or 224 seconds per working day. Using similar logic Boje calculates the increased working efficiency resulting from the optimal arrangements of heating, lighting and telephones. From all this Boje is then able to conclude that a properly designed open-plan office will save some 2000 minutes per month per employee over a conventional design.

The unthinking designer could easily use such apparently high quality and convincing data to design an office based on such factors as minimising 'person door movements'. But in fact such figures are quite useless unless the designer also knows just how relatively important it is to save 7 seconds of time. Would that 7 seconds saved actually be used productively? What other, perhaps more critical, social and interpersonal effects result from the lack of doors and walls? So many more questions need answering before the simple single index of 'person door movements' can become of value in a design context.

Scientists have tended to want to develop increasingly precise tools for assessing design, but there is little evidence that this actually helps designers or even improves design standards. Paradoxically, sometimes it can have the opposite effect to that intended. For example, whilst we may all think daylight is an everyday blessing for each of us, not so when it comes to lighting calculations. A series of notional artificial mathematical sky models have been created from which the sun is totally excluded. The 'daylight factor' at any point inside a building is then calculated as the portion of one of these theoretical hemispheres which can be seen. Since the more advanced of the mathematical models do not define the sky as uniformly bright, the whole process involves highly complex solid geometry. In a misguided attempt to help architects, building scientists have generated a whole series of tools to help them calculate the levels of daylight in buildings. Tables, Waldram diagrams and daylight protractors, together with a whole series of computer programs have been presented as tools for the unfortunate architect. Now these tools all miss the point about design so dramatically as to be worthy of a little further study (Lawson 1982).

First, they all require the geometry of the outside of the building and the inside of the room in question to be defined, and the shape and location of all the windows to be known. They are purely evaluative tools which do nothing to suggest solutions, but merely assess them after they have been designed. Second, they produce apparently very accurate results about a highly variable phenomenon. Of course the level of illumination created by daylight varies from nothing at dawn to a very high level, depending on where you are in the world and the weather, and returns to nothing again at dusk. Thankfully the human eye is capable of working at levels of light 100,000 times brighter than the minimum level at which it can just work efficiently, and we make this adjustment often without even noticing! So the daylight tools indicate a degree of precision which is misleading and unnecessary. Third, the daylight tools are totally divorced from other considerations connected with window design such as heat loss and gain, view and so on as we saw in the previous chapter. Such a lack of integration makes such tools virtually useless to the design. It has been found, not surprisingly, that such tools are not used in practice (Lawson 1975a) but they are still in the curriculum and standard textbooks of many design courses.

The danger of such apparently scientifically respectable techniques is that sooner or later they get used as fixed criteria, and this actually happened in the case of daylighting. Using statistics of the actual levels of illumination expected over the year in the United Kingdom, it was calculated that a 2 per cent daylight factor was desirable in schools. It then became a mandatory requirement that all desks in new schools should receive at least this daylight factor. The whole geometry of the classrooms themselves was thus effectively prescribed and, as a result, a generation of schools were built with large areas of glazing. The resultant acoustic and visual distraction, glare, draughts, the colossal heat losses and excessive solar gain in summer, which were frequently experienced in these schools, eventually led to the relaxation of this regulation. In many areas, programmes were then put in place to fill in windows to reduce the negative effects of such a disastrous distortion of the design process.

Regulation and criteria

Unfortunately, much of the legislation with which designers must work appears to be based on the pattern illustrated by the daylighting example. Wherever there is the possibility of measuring performance, there is also the opportunity to legislate. It is difficult to legislate for qualities, but easy to define and enforce quantities (Lawson 1975b). It is increasingly difficult for the designer to maintain a sensibly balanced design process in the face of necessarily imbalanced legislation. A dramatic example of this can be found in the design of public sector housing in the United Kingdom.

The British government had commissioned an excellent piece of research completed by a committee chaired by Sir Parker Morris into the needs of the residents of family housing. The committee worked for two years visiting housing schemes, issuing questionnaires, taking evidence from experts and studying the available literature. This was to be a most thorough and reputable study which proved useful in guiding the development of housing design for several decades (Parker Morris, *Homes for Today and Tomorrow* 1961: 594, London House). The final report was in the form of a pamphlet containing over 200 major recommendations. Some of the recommendations were later included as requirements in what became the Mandatory Minimum Standards for public sector housing. It is interesting to see just which of the original Parker Morris recommendations were to become legislative requirements and why. Consider just three of these recommendations made in connection with the design of the kitchen:

1. The relation of the kitchen to the place outside the kitchen where the children are likely to play should be considered.
2. A person working at the sink should be able to see out of the window.
3. Worktops should be provided on both sides of the sink and cooker positions. Kitchen fitments should be arranged to form a work sequence comprising worktop/sink/worktop/cooker/worktop unbroken by a door or any other traffic way.

(Parker Morris 1961)

All these recommendations seem sensible and desirable. However, it seems a fair bet that most parents would rate the first as the most desirable, and probably most of us would sacrifice some ergonomic efficiency for a pleasant view. However the third recommendation is the most easily measured from an architect's drawing, and only this last recommendation became a mandatory requirement (Fig. 5.5). Thus it became quite permissible to design a family maisonette or flat many storeys above ground level with no view of any outside play spaces from the kitchen, but it would have the very model of a kitchen work surface as may not be found even in some very expensive privately built housing. It is worth noting that this legislation was introduced during the early period of what has now been called first generation design methodology. Thankfully these Mandatory Minimum Standards were later withdrawn. In a way this was also a pity as they contained other, far more sensible, requirements!

Design legislation has now rightly come under close and critical scrutiny, and designers have begun to report the failings of legislation in practice. In 1973 the Essex County Council produced its now classic *Design Guide for Residential Areas*, which was an attempt to deal with both qualitative and quantitative aspects of housing design. Visual standards and such concepts as privacy were given as much emphasis as noise levels or efficient traffic circulation. Whilst the objectives of this and the many other design guides which followed were almost universally applauded, many designers have subsequently expressed concern at the results of such notes for guidance actually being used in practice as legislation. Building regulations have come under increasing criticism from architects who have shown how they often create undesirable results (Lawson 1975b) and proposals have been put forward to revise the whole system of building control (Savidge 1978).

In 1976 the Department of the Environment (DoE) published its research report no. 6 on the *Value of Standards for the External*

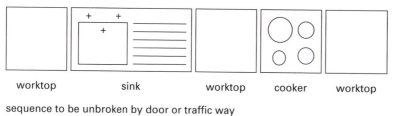

worktop   sink   worktop   cooker   worktop

sequence to be unbroken by door or traffic way

Figure 5.5
The Parker Morris recommended kitchen layout which became mandatory

Residential Environment which concluded that many currently accepted standards were either unworkable or even positively objectionable. The report firmly rejected the imposition of requirements for such matters as privacy, view, sunlight or daylight:

> The application of standards across the board defeats the aim of appropriately different provision in different situations.

This report seems to sound the final death knell for legislation based on the 1960s first-generation design methodology:

> The qualities of good design are not encapsulated in quantitative standards ... It is right for development controllers to ask that adequate provision be made for, say, privacy or access or children's play or quiet. The imposition of specified quantities as requirements is a different matter, and is not justified by design results.
>
> (DoE 1976)

Sadly, since this time legislators have not learned the lessons from their mistakes with daylight and kitchens. Legislation continues to be drawn up in such a way as to suit those whose job it is to check rather than those whose job it is to design. The checker requires a simple test, preferably numerical, easily applied on evidence which is clear and unambiguous. The checker also greatly prefers not to have to consider more than one thing at a time. The designer of course, requires the exact opposite of this, and so it is that legislation often makes design more difficult. This is not because it imposes standards of performance which may be quite desirable, but because of the inflexibility and lack of value which it introduces into the value-laden multi-dimensional process which is design.

Measurement and design methods

Reference has already been made to Christopher Alexander's famous method of design, which perhaps exemplifies the first generation thinking about the design process. We no longer view the design process in this way and in order to see why we shall pause here to fill in some detail. Alexander's method involved first listing all the requirements of a particular design problem, and then looking for interactions between these requirements (Alexander 1964). For example in the design of a kettle some requirements for the choice of materials might be as follows.

Simplicity: the fewer the materials the more efficient the factory.

Performance: each function within the kettle requires its own material, e.g. handle, lid, spout.

Jointing: the fewer the materials the less and the simpler the jointing and the less the maintenance.

Economy: choose the cheapest material suitable.

The interactions between each pair of these requirements are next labelled as positive, negative or neutral depending on whether they complement, inhibit or have no effect upon each other. In this case all the interactions except jointing/simplicity are negative since they show conflicting requirements. For example while the performance requirement suggests many materials, the jointing and simplicity requirements would ideally be satisfied by using only one material. Thus jointing and simplicity interact positively with each other but both interact negatively with performance.

Thus a designer using Alexander's method would first list all the requirements of the design and then state which pairs of requirements interact either positively or negatively. All this data would then be fed into a computer program which looks for clusters of requirements which are heavily interrelated but relatively unconnected with other requirements. The computer would then print out these clusters effectively breaking the problem down into independent sub-problems each relatively simple for the designer to understand and solve.

Alexander's work has been heavily criticised, not least by himself (Alexander 1966), although few seemed to listen to him at the time! A few years later Geoffrey Broadbent published an excellent review of many of the failings of Alexander's method (Broadbent 1973). Some of Alexander's most obvious errors, and those which interest us here, result from a rather mechanistic view of the nature of design problems:

> the problem is defined by a set of requirements called M. The solution to this problem will be a form which successfully satisfies all of these requirements.

Implicit in this statement are a number of notions now commonly rejected (Lawson 1979a). First, that there exists a set of requirements which can be exhaustively listed at the start of the design process. As we saw in Chapter 3, this is not really feasible since all sorts of requirements are quite likely to occur to designer and client alike even well after the synthesis of solutions has started. The second misconception in Alexander's method is that all these listed requirements are of equal value and that the interactions between them are all equally strong. Common sense would suggest that it is quite likely to be much more important to satisfy some requirements than others, and that some pairs of requirements may be closely related while others are more loosely connected. Third, and rather more subtly, Alexander fails to appreciate that some requirements and interactions have much more profound implications for the form of the solution than do others.

To illustrate these deficiencies consider two pairs of interacting requirements listed by Chermayeff and Alexander (1963) in their study of community and privacy in housing design. The first interaction is between 'efficient parking for owners and visitors; adequate manoeuvre space' and 'separation of children and pets from vehicles'. The second interaction is between 'stops against crawling and climbing insects, vermin, reptiles, birds and mammals' and 'filters against smells, viruses, bacteria, dirt. Screens against flying insects, wind-blown dust, litter, soot and garbage'. The trouble with Alexander's method is that it is incapable of distinguishing between these interactions in terms of strength, quality or importance, and yet any experienced architect would realise that the two problems have quite different kinds of solution implications. The first is a matter of access and thus poses a spatial planning problem, while the second raises an issue about the detailed technical design of the building skin. In most design processes these two problems would be given emphasis at quite different stages. Thus in this sense the designer selects the aspects of the problem he or she wishes to consider in order of their likely impact on the solution as a whole. In this case, issues of general layout and organisation would be unlikely to be considered at the same time as the detailing of doors and windows. Unfortunately the cluster pattern generated by Alexander's method conceals this natural meaning in the problem and forces a strange way of working on the designer.

Value judgements in design

Because in design there are often so many variables which cannot be measured on the same scale, value judgements seem inescapable. For example in designing electrical power tools, convenience of use has often to be balanced against safety, or portability against robustness. Although it may prove possible to measure designs on crude scales of satisfaction for each of these factors, they remain difficult to relate. Thus a very lightweight lawnmower while being easy to manoeuvre and push might also prove to be noisy and easily damaged. For such an item there is no one right answer since different purchasers are likely to place different values on factors such as manoeuvrability or reliability. The sensible manufacturer of such equipment will produce a whole range of alternative designs each offering different advantages and disadvantages. The problem of relative values, however, becomes much more critical when design decisions are being taken for large numbers of people who may not have the choice available to the purchasers of new lawnmowers. Examples of such design problems include public sector housing or a new school, the routeing of new roads or the siting of factories. Inherently, such projects involve varying degrees of benefit to some and losses to others. A new motorway may well save a long-distance motorist's time and relieve congestion in nearby towns but, unfortunately, it may also subject local residents to unwanted noise and pollution.

The attraction of a common metric

An attractive way out of all the difficulties we have seen in this chapter would be if we could reduce all the criteria involved in design to some common scale of measurement. Cost-benefit analysis relies upon expressing all factors in terms of their monetary value, thus establishing a common metric. Attempts have been made to apply cost-benefit analysis techniques to the kinds of design problems where there are both gainers and losers. Unfortunately, some factors are rather more easily costed than others. This is perhaps best illustrated by reference to one of the most well-known applications of cost-benefit analysis, the Roskill Commission on the siting of the third London airport. After a number of preliminary stages during which some seventy-eight sites were considered, the commission narrowed the choice down to four sites at Cublington, Foulness, Nuthampstead and Thurleigh which were then compared using cost-benefit analysis. Even the grossly simplified diagram reproduced here gives some idea of the complex array of effects which the various interested parties could be expected to have on each other as a result of such a project (Fig. 5.6). In fact there are many other much wider effects not shown which include such matters as the distortion of the national transportation network resulting

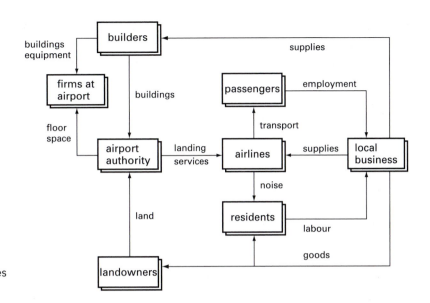

Figure 5.6
A simplified diagram of the interactions between the parties involved in a new airport

from the provision of new forms of access to the chosen site. For example, the opening of an airport at Cublington would have resulted in the closure of the existing Luton airport which would have been too close for air traffic control procedures.

Many of the benefits of the airport in terms of the profits to the various transportation authorities and other companies were reasonably easy to calculate for each site and could be set against the profits lost from the existing use of land. The costs of providing the access transportation to each site and the costs in terms of journey time were also fed into the equation. Losses in terms of reduced amenity, however, proved more difficult to assess in purely monetary terms. These effects range from otherwise unwanted expenditure resulting from people having to leave their homes, through such factors as the depreciation in value of property in the surrounding area to the noise annoyance caused by the operation of the airport.

Such a public use of cost-benefit analysis revealed many of the real dangers involved in basing decisions on the quantification of qualitative factors such as the amenity of an environment. Obviously the success of such a process is contingent upon the assumption that all the costs of amenity loss have been correctly valued. The real difficulty here is that such valuations are unlikely to be arrived at by consensus in a pluralistic society. This was demonstrated when the RIBA publicly expressed its concern at the valuations placed on both gains and losses and pointed out the many minor losses not costed which might have a large effect cumulatively:

An hour lost by an air traveller is valued very generously, taking into account business overheads as well as salary, but an hour of sleep lost by those living outside the area of major impact is given no value whatever.
(RIBA 1970)

The costing of noise annoyance or the value of quiet had proved difficult enough for the Roskill Commission, but when considerations of the conservation of wildlife at Foulness were introduced to the argument the whole decision-making process began to split at the seams. Cost-benefit analysis was clearly incapable of developing one equation to balance the profits of an airport against the loss of a totally unproductive but irreplaceable and, some would say, priceless sanctuary for birdlife. The Roskill report itself recognised the futility of attempting totally objective judgement in comparing the Cublington and Foulness sites. The choice was between the damage to the value of Aylesbury and the loss of a fine Norman church at Stewkley or the ruining of the Essex coastline and probable extinction of the dark-bellied Brent goose:

As with much else in this inquiry there is no single right answer however much each individual may believe there is. For us to claim to judge absolutely between these views (the importance of conservation of buildings or wildlife) is to claim gifts of wisdom and prophecy which no man can possess. All we can do is respect both points of view.
(Roskill Commission Report)

Even the costings of the more ostensibly easily quantifiable factors proved extremely debatable. For example the cost-benefit research team itself revised the assumptions on which total construction costs had been based. This change proved so drastic that Cublington moved from being the most costly to the least costly of the possible sites in this respect. The inquiry proceeded until it gradually became apparent that many of the fundamental underlying assumptions necessary for the cost-benefit analysis could similarly be challenged. The indecision which resulted at least in part from the discrediting of the technique led to many years of procrastination before an airport was finally built at Stanstead. Perhaps the last word here should come from Professor Buchanan, a member of the Commission who became so concerned that he published a minority report:

I became more and more anxious lest I be trapped in a process which I did not fully understand and ultimately led without choice to a conclusion which I would know in my heart of hearts I did not agree with.

Recently there has rightly been more emphasis placed on the ecological implications of design decisions. Most of the energy consumed in the developed countries is connected with the manufacturing and use of products. A very high proportion indeed is connected with the construction industry. Similarly, levels of pollution and atmospheric emissions are heavily influenced by the decisions of industrial designers, architects and town planners. All this leads us to want more information on the true impact of design decisions, not just at the stage of constructing but in terms of the full life cycle. Again legislation is increasingly setting, and then changing, limits on energy consumption and pollution. Most designers are probably very conscious of the need to improve our world in this way, but find it extremely difficult to incorporate findings and recommendations into their design process. The findings and data are seldom clearly expressed in a form which a designer can make sense of. Just as it is increasingly difficult to know what it is safe and healthy to eat, so designing in an ecologically sound way is surrounded by myths, campaigns and, sometimes, deliberately misleading data. In all this confusion, however, designers cannot usually procrastinate as did those deciding on the third London airport. They simply must get on and make the decision in as integrated and sensible a way as they can. Their decisions then remain very visible and easy to criticise as data becomes more clearly available!

Objective and subjective decisions

In the final analysis it seems unreasonable for designers to expect to find a process which will protect them from the painful and difficult business of exercising subjective judgement in situations where both quantitative and qualitative factors must be taken into account. The attempt to reduce all factors to a common quantitative measure such as monetary value frequently serves only to shift the problem to one of valuation. The Roskill Commission on the siting of the third London airport provided one further lesson of importance here. Designers and those who make design-like decisions which profoundly affect the lives of many people can no longer expect their value judgements to be made in private. Such large-scale design processes must clearly invite the participation of all those who will be substantially affected. However, we must not expect the design process to be as clear, logical and open a process as the scientific method. Design is a messy kind of business that involves making value judgements between alternatives that may each offer some advantages and disadvantages. There is unlikely to be a correct or even optimal answer in the design process, and we are not all likely to agree about the relative merits of the alternative solutions.

References

Alexander, C. (1964). *Notes on the synthesis of form.* New York, McGraw Hill.

Alexander, C. (1966). 'A city is not a tree.' *Design* **206**: 44–55.

Archer, L. B. (1969). 'The structure of the design process.' *Design Methods in Architecture.* London, Lund Humphries.

Boje, A. (1971). *Open-plan Offices.* Business Books.

Broadbent, G. (1973). *Design in Architecture.* New York, John Wiley.

Chermayeff, S. and Alexander, C. (1963). *Community and Privacy.* Harmondsworth, Penguin.

Lawson, B. R. (1975a). Heuristic science for students of architecture. University of Sheffield Department of Architecture.

Lawson, B. R. (1975b). 'Upside down and back to front: architects and the building laws.' *RIBA Journal* **82**(4).

Lawson, B. R. (1979). 'The act of designing.' *Design methods and Theories* **13**(1).

Lawson, B. R. (1982). Science, legislation and architecture. *Changing Design.* New York, John Wiley.

RIBA (1970). 'The third London airport: choice cannot be on cost alone says RIBA.' *RIBA Journal* **77**(5): 224–225.

Savidge, R. (1978). 'Revise the regs: the plan revealed.' *The Architects' Journal* **167**(14).

Stevens, S. S., Ed. (1951). *Handbook of Experimental Psychology.* New York, John Wiley.

6

A model of
design problems

As an artist I did not set out to make the public understand but to
find problems for myself of space and form, and to explore them.

Henry Moore (on his 80th birthday)

There is nothing absolute about deriving architecture from functional
manipulations. When you look at a plan by Corb, these wonderful
shapes that he has rationalised out of bathrooms and things, I mean
they are magic really, they are completely magical diagrams but
I would much rather have the magic without the spurious functional-
ity in the way.

John Outram

Analysing design problems

In this chapter we try to analyse the structure of design problems.
As with the rest of the book, this analysis is primarily directed at
those problems which are solved by three-dimensional design, but
may in many cases be sufficiently generic to apply at least in part
to graphic design and some kinds of engineering. This analysis will
be based on an investigation of the generators of design problems,
their domain of concern and their function. From this study we
shall be able to assemble the building blocks which make up a
model enabling us to understand the nature of design problems in
all their variations. This model has been found useful over many
years of teaching and researching the design process. It is presented here in order that we may further understand what makes
design problems so special and thus gain some insights into how
designers think and why.

The generators of design problems

At first sight it may seem obvious where design problems come from. Clients bring them to designers! As we shall see, whilst that is often true it is not always so, and it turns out to be only a small part of the story. It is certainly possible for designers to discover a problem without a client and much interesting design work is done under exactly these clientless conditions. We also to need to draw a careful distinction between the clients who present problems to designers and the ultimate users of the outcome. As we shall see, clients may or may not be the users of design. We have seen in the last chapter, how legislators can often pose considerable problems for the designer and they may sometimes even be in conflict with the client. Town planning legislation for example exists chiefly to protect the general public from the possible selfish excesses of individual architectural clients. Whether such development control is actually so beneficial, however, is probably debatable! However, we are in danger of getting ahead of the argument.

Clients

In design, the problem usually originates not in the designer's mind but with a client; someone in need who is unable to solve the problem, or perhaps, even fully to understand it without help. Whilst the fortunate artist may occasionally be commissioned, the designer almost always works this way. The design task, albeit ill-defined, is usually initially generated and expressed by a client. However, it is quite misleading to think that clients are a homogenous group. In many commercial situations the client may be represented by a professional, acting in that capacity more or less as a job. At the other end of the scale, many buildings are commissioned by people who have never acted as a client before. Sometimes the designer will work with an individual client, and at other times the client body may be represented by a whole committee. In the case of very large buildings commissioned by institutions or companies the programme may last several years and the membership of the client committee may change substantially.

The architects Stirling and Wilford have had considerable experience of these large institutional clients and have built many civic and educational buildings. Michael Wilford has emphasised the importance of the role of the client in the design process:

> Behind every building of distinction is an equally distinctive client, not necessarily high profile, but one who takes the time and trouble to comprehend the ideas of the architect, is supportive and enthusiastic, who is bold, willing to take risks and above all can hold his or her nerve during the inevitable crises.
>
> (Lawson 1994b)

This suggests quite firmly that Michael Wilford does not just see the client as the source of the brief but as a creative partner in the process. The architect Eva Jiricna agrees with this by suggesting 'the worst client is the person who tells you to just get on with it and give me the final product' (Lawson 1994b). The client then is the most obvious example of a source of design problems and constraints. Ideally, and frequently those constraints can be explored creatively through an interaction between designer and client. It is certainly misleading to think that a client simply presents a designer with a complete brief in which the problem is totally defined and the constraints clearly articulated. The relationship between client and designer itself actually constitutes a significant part of the design process. The way that designers perceive and understand problems is to some extent a function of the way this relationship works.

Users

A great deal of design today is commissioned by clients who are not themselves the users. Public architecture such as hospitals, schools or housing is usually designed by architects who have relatively little contact with the users of their buildings. Industrial design and graphic design are directed at a mass market and are usually commissioned by commercial clients. The traditional image of the designer establishing a personal relationship with a client/user is grossly misleading. Even architects commissioned to design new buildings for large organisations such as universities are likely to be buffered from the actual users by a client committee or even a full-time buildings department. Frequently communication between designers and their users is both indirect and, as John Page has argued, filtered by organisational politics. In his study of 'planning and protest' (Page 1972) he describes the 'people barriers' erected in many organisations to prevent too much disruptive user feedback reaching designers.

In local authorities, for example, both the politicians and administrators may attempt to establish themselves as the communication channel between the designers and the users outside in order to force through policy or maintain a powerful position in the system. On balance such organisational barriers, whatever advantages they give to the client body in terms of increased control over the designer, serve only to make the designer's task of understanding the problem more difficult. Even if there are not barriers there are what Zeisel (1984) has called 'gaps'. He referred to 'paying clients' and 'user clients'. He showed that while there might often be good communications between designers and paying clients, both have a gap in their communications with user clients (Fig. 6.1). In a more recent piece of empirical work Cairns (1996) not only demonstrated the existence of these gaps in architectural design, but also that neither architects nor their clients were always aware of these gaps.

As many young designers must have found on leaving design schools, it is one thing to design for yourself but quite another to design for a real client with personal and institutional prejudices and biases. When that client is not even the prospective user of the design, the problem becomes even more remote. This increasing remoteness of designers from those for whom they design has created the need for user requirement studies. Almost in desperation designers have turned to social and human scientists from ergonomists through architectural psychologists to urban sociologists to tell them what their users actually need. By and large this liaison between design and social science has not been as practically useful as was first hoped. Social science remains largely descriptive while design is necessarily prescriptive, so the psychologists and sociologists have gone on researching and the designers designing, and they are yet to re-educate each other into more genuinely collaborative roles. Meanwhile the communication

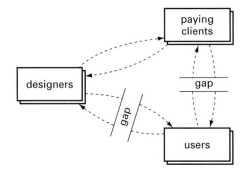

Figure 6.1
Zeisel's user-needs gap model

between the creators and users of environments often remains uncomfortably remote.

So users are generally more remote from designers than clients. Whilst the designer may be able to interact with a sympathetic and motivated client, there may be no formal access to users at all.

Designers

It is sometimes difficult to separate design from art. The products of design are frequently seen by the public as artistic, even sometimes actually as 'works of art', and designers themselves are indeed also often artists. Even the drawings generated by designers to illustrate their schemes can sometimes easily be confused with works of art. Whether or not an object can rightly be described as a 'work of art' is a matter which lies beyond the scope of this book. What is of importance here is not the product but the process. The creative process which may give rise to a work of art undoubtedly shares much in common with the design process, and many of the same talents may be needed for both. Designers, like artists, are expected not just to solve problems but to bring their issues and concerns into the process too. In this sense, however, the designer is usually rather more constrained than the artist. The artist may respond to the work in progress and is free to shift attention and explore new problems and territory. Such artistic issues are rarely clearly articulated by the artist beyond the work. It is usually critics and historians who retrospectively interpret and identify the issues which appear to them to have been uppermost in the artist's mind. When asked by a music critic to explain one of his operas, Wagner is reported to have responded rather testily 'but it is the explanation'.

The designer is usually expected to contribute problems too. In this sense designers are assumed by their clients to be artistic and their role to be at least partly interpretative. An architect's client expects rather more than just a house with rooms of appropriate sizes and relationships. The clear expectation is that an architect will consider issues of, for example, form, space and light, and through this create not just a building but what we call architecture. This client–designer relationship works both ways, for while the designer expects to be given some freedom in the definition of the design problem. It is also quite likely that the designer receiving a new commission is looking forward to being able to continue exploring problems which were identified in earlier projects. The extent to which the designer is allowed this artistic self-gratification is a function both of the nature of the problem and of the client–designer relationship. For this reason there is inherently an element of tension in the client–designer relationship. Both are dependent one upon the other and yet both in their different ways are anxious of the other exerting too much control. On the one hand the designer probably needs the fee, while on the other the designer also has a reputation which is largely the result of past work and is thus anxious to continue developing a coherent body of work for all to see. The client on the other hand cannot actually design but nevertheless may to some extent know what is wanted and is anxious lest the designer gets quite different ideas. Obviously the wise client chooses a designer who, on the basis of past work, looks likely to share an interest in the client's problems. No one could have ever expected Mies van der Rohe and Edwin Lutyens to have designed even remotely similar houses for the same client on the same site: as architects their own personal interests were too different.

It is worth noting at this point that the distinction between art and design is, like all such man-made conceptual boundaries, rather hazy and easily blurred. Students, groping to establish their role as designers are often confused by work which defies easy classification. When Peter Cook produced his highly influential 'Plug-in-City' in 1964 it at first appeared to be a piece of design; a city, admittedly imaginary and of the future, but which nevertheless looked like architecture and many of the drawings were themselves very architectural. In fact the process and intention behind such work is in some ways more akin to the artistic than the design process. 'Plug-in-City' did not solve any immediate problems, nor was it intended to be built. Rather it explored and expressed ideas, beliefs and values, and asked provocative questions about the future direction of city design and patterns of life. It is entirely appropriate that design students should be interested in, and influenced by such work, just as they might be by poetry, prose, paintings or films about similar issues. But they should not expect to approach real-world design problems posed by clients in the more introspective and personally expressive mode of the artist. Designers, unlike artists, cannot devote themselves exclusively to problems which are of interest to themselves personally.

Legislators

So far we have seen how design problems, whilst usually initiated by a client, may be contributed to by both users and designers themselves. Finally we must briefly turn our attention to another generator of design problems, perhaps the most remote of all from the designer, the legislator. Although frequently not involved in the actual design itself legislators create constraints within which designers must work. Such legislation and control may range from standards and codes of practice to guidelines and recommen-dations. Such standards may govern factors of safety, utility or appearance. They may have to be satisfied in order to sell products on the market, to allow conventional trade descriptions or to permit building construction to commence. Design legislation today may cover anything from the safety of electrical goods to the honesty of advertising or the energy consumption of buildings. In many cases complete bureaucracies exist to administer and interpret this gen-eral legislation for each specific instance. The architect today must satisfy the fire officer, the building inspector and the town planner and in addition, depending on the nature of the particular project, the housing corporation, health inspectors, Home Office inspectors, the water authority, electricity authority, the Post Office, factory inspectors, and so the list goes on. There is no point in disguising the tension which exists between designers and those who admin-ister the legislation within which society has determined they must work. The designer may, at times, see the legislator as mindlessly inflexible, while to the legislator the designer may appear wilful and irresponsible.

This conflict is exemplified in Richard Rogers's account of the problems he encountered with the Parisian Fire Department when designing the Pompidou Centre.

> As this was the first public building of grand hauteur, every regulation ever promulgated in the city of Paris since antiquity was applied in the most stringent manner conceivable to the tune of 50 million francs, some 10% of the total construction budget.
>
> (Suckle 1980)

As Rogers himself puts it, no architect would want deliberately to construct a dangerous building. However, often regulations have to be applied in situations which were not predicted when they were framed; since no designers had previously conceived such extraordinary architecture as that of Piano and Rogers, it seems unreasonable to expect this of the legislators.

The different roles of the generators of constraints

The first four building blocks of our model of design problems can now be put in place. If we stack each of the four generators of design constraints into a sort of tower, we can see that the constraints become more open for debate and discussion as we climb the tower (Fig. 6.2). Each of the generators of design problems identified here impose constraints upon the design solution but with different degrees of rigidity. The most rigid being those imposed by legislators and the most flexible those generated by the designer.

For example in designing the layout for a shop interior, constraints will be imposed by each generator. In order to ensure safety in case of fire the fire officer will require the surface materials to achieve a specified rate of resistance to flame spread, and may determine the number and position of escape doors and the width of corridors and gangways. Other legislation may control the display and storage of food, the working conditions of staff and so on. The client too will generate many design constraints connected with the primary objectives of attracting custom and selling goods. Unlike the legislator's constraints the designer is able to discuss the client's constraints and establish priorities. Conflicts between the design implications of the client's objectives are not uncommon, and here the designer is able to go back to the client and jointly they may re-appraise the client constraints. For example, on the one hand the client for our shop may want the display furniture to be designed and arranged so as to make the goods look attractive

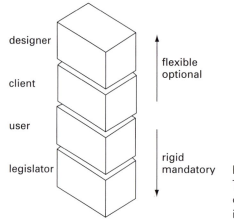

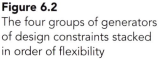

Figure 6.2
The four groups of generators of design constraints stacked in order of flexibility

and to tempt prospective purchasers. On the other hand it will certainly be important to minimise the likelihood of shoplifting or damage to unbought items. These two requirements are at least to some extent in conflict. In Alexander's terms they interact negatively. However, the exact balance of satisfaction for such requirements may not be clear to the client until the designer explores the various possibilities in physical three-dimensional terms. Our client may not be able to say exactly what degree of risk of loss from theft is acceptable in order to achieve effectiveness of display until the designer actually proposes some designs.

Clearly from the designer's point of view, client constraints are not absolute as are legislator constraints. Rather they all carry a relative value which is open to a certain amount of discussion. In this example the designer too is expected to generate constraints. Our shop designer is supposed to come up with an integrative idea, an overall concept which organises and unifies the whole interior. Thus designer-generated constraints may restrict the range of colours and materials and establish geometric and dimensional rules. The goods for sale in the shop may range from items as small as buttons through books and stationery to clothes and furniture. The shopfittings must be capable of displaying all these goods and perhaps establish a distinct but related image for each department. One design idea might be to devise a range of fittings constructed of bent plywood covered in brightly coloured laminates combined with curved chromium plated tubular frames. Having established the constraint of these materials and forms the designer would have to create actual fittings for clothes, food, jewellery and so on.

It is obvious that these designer-generated constraints are comparatively flexible. If they cause too many difficulties, or just simply do not work out the designer is free to modify or scrap them altogether. Design students often fail to recognise this simple fact but instead continue to pit their wits endlessly and fruitlessly against insuperable problems which are largely of their own making. One of the most important skills designers must acquire is the ability critically to evaluate their own self-imposed constraints and we shall return to this again in Chapter 11. For the time being it is important to recognise the different contributions to the problem made by each of the major generators of constraints. As we have seen the legislator's demand is fixed, the users may well not be around to be consulted, the client may adjust priorities as the design implications unfold and the designer may think of a new set of constraints altogether.

We should also add a word of caution here about the division between these various generators of design. The discussion so far has tended to imply the classical situation of a client commissioning a design perhaps on behalf of other users. However, this is by no means the only way design can be done. In fact, as Roy (1993) has pointed out in his study of product designers, much really creative and innovative design is initiated by designers. He studied the design of the innovative Ballbarrow, the Moulton bicycle and the Workmate® work bench. In all these cases the designer started with a personal need or involvement in the application area of the product. The designer James Dyson was fitting a cyclone air filter to his Ballbarrow factory and noticed that it worked all day without clogging. He began to wonder why his domestic vacuum cleaner was not made this way and so began the design of his highly successful revolutionary cleaner which not only maintains constant suction but also removes the need for disposable bags. In fact Dyson found it impossible to convince any British manufacturers to take on the production of his design and had to market it himself. Thus he eventually had to become his own client!

We should also note that clients come in many sizes and shapes and have many different motivations. They may be the future users of the design or may intend to exploit it financially. They may be single individuals or large committees. We shall see in a later chapter that the relationship between designer and client can be very varied, but that this relationship is more often critical to the success of the project than is usually recognised by design commentators. However, we must explore many other issues before getting involved in such a detailed examination of these roles.

The domain of design constraints

Constraints in design result largely from required or desired relationships between various elements. For example, in housing the legislator demands that there is a worktop on either side of the cooker, the client might express a wish for both the kitchen and living-room to open directly on to the dining-room and the architect may think it sensible to try to organise all the spaces around a central structural and service core.

What links all the constraints in this example is their domain of influence. All establish relationships between elements of the object being designed, in this case a house. They are entirely internal to the problem and we shall therefore call them internal constraints. Consider by contrast the following equally hypothetical, but quite likely, set of constraints. The building regulations closely define the permitted distances of windows from boundaries so as to avoid the risk of a fire spreading to adjacent properties. The client may have a strong preference for a living-room which overlooks the garden and has a sunny aspect. The architect may think it important to continue the existing street façade in terms of line and height. Here the constraints establish a relationship between some element of the house and some feature of the site. They relate the designed object to its context, and in each case one end of the relationship, the site boundary, the sun, the street, is external to the problem. We shall therefore refer to these as external constraints.

Both internal and external constraints may be generated by designers, clients, users and legislators. So far the model of design constraints appears two-dimensional, the dimensions being the generator and the domain of constraints.

Internal constraints

Internal constraints are the more obvious and easily understood in that they traditionally form the basis of the problem as most clients initially tend to express it. Thus, for an architect the internal constraints frequently comprise the majority of the brief. The number and sizes of spaces of various kinds and qualities form the most obvious client-generated internal constraints. The structure or pattern of the problem for the architect lies in the desired relationships between these spaces. These relationships may be in terms of human circulation and the distribution of services, or in the visual and acoustic connections and barriers necessary to house the various communal and private functions of the building. Architects conventionally begin to grapple with these internal constraints very early on in the process by drawing bubble diagrams and flow charts which graphically represent the required relationships. The flow of people into and around a building was a central issue of the Beaux Arts architectural design process, and this was carried into the 'functionalism' of the modern movement.

For the product designer, the internal constraints include the problems of fitting an object together. Some relationships may need to be quite close particularly where mechanics are involved. However, other items which may need linking electrically may be rather more loosely connected. Thus in the design of a power drill, the motor, gearbox and chuck are inevitably very directly connected. The switch is linked to the motor but only electrically and therefore loosely, while any reversing control is probably more likely to be mechanical thus restricting its location rather more. This central role of internal constraints is demonstrated by a study of how Mike Burrows designed the revolutionary LotusSport bicycle ridden to a gold medal by Chris Boardman in the 1992 Olympic Games (Candy and Edmonds 1996). Throughout the process, it was the relationship between front and rear wheel, saddle and handlebars which had to be resolved. Eventually Burrows discarded the traditional diamond shaped tubular frame and adopted a monocoque structure.

External constraints

For the fashion designer external constraints range from the manufacturing process, whether it be handmade or mass produced, to the human body itself. Off-the-peg clothes are obviously designed around average bodily dimensions but for the one-off high fashion designer the external constraints of a particular shape, personality and occasion provide the inspiration for the design of unique garments intended to be worn in one specific context. In theatre design, neither the play nor the stage are under the control of the designer, but a particular combination of the two might provide the inspiration for a unique set. The dramatic demands of the play together with the visual and acoustic properties and problems of the stage comprise a highly significant collection of constraints. Sometimes external constraints virtually determine the whole form of design. What makes one bridge different from another are the site conditions, the span needed, and the position and quality of supporting ground. The Severins Bridge across the Rhine in Cologne posed its own unique problems generated by external constraints. The architect's sketches show a concern about the way a conventional two-tower suspension structure would have seriously obscured the down-river view of the massively impressive cathedral which dominates the skyline (Fig. 6.3). As luck would have it there was conveniently accessible supporting ground in shallow water about a third of the way across the river. The architect's sketch shows his proposal to the engineer that they might be able to design the structure with a single tower at this point.

Figure 6.3
The architect's and engineer's sketches for a new bridge based on protecting the vista

However, not fully appreciating the engineering issues his sketch shows a catenary structure with its characteristic sagging cables. The engineer replies by changing these to taut cables and an 'A' shaped tower. Finally the junction between tower and deck is more satisfactorily resolved. Here then the external constraints, combined with the architect's concern not to destroy the Cologne skyline, have resulted in an extraordinarily distinguished and fresh solution to an age-old problem of civil engineering (Fig. 6.4).

Rowe reports several detailed studies of architects observed during a design process. In one of these experiments the designers were asked to work on a world bibliographical centre on a waterfront site in Chicago. Rowe describes how the subjects recognised the site as a major form determining influence or 'primary generator'. Rowe's designers considered 'establishing symmetry by extending out into the lake on a pier structure, similar to those (already there) adjacent to the site on the river side' (Rowe 1987). Only after this did these designers begin to explore the overall shape of their building. Then attention turned again to the site through a study of Chicago's downtown grid pattern of planning. Eventually the problem became one of resolving the two themes of creating a waterside landmark and extending the grid pattern of the surrounding city.

The scheme then developed as a linear grid-planned form terminating in a rotunda-like structure protruding into the lake. Later this was gradually altered as the actual requirements of the accommodation itself (internal constraints) were considered in detail. At

Figure 6.4
The actual bridge design of the Severins Bridge owed its unusual design to the external constraints

this point the linear grid form disappeared only to resurface again as an approach to the surrounding landscape.

    External constraints can be just as influential and inspirational at the other end of the spectrum of design. In his classic book on graphic design, Paul Rand (1970) explains how what he calls 'the given material' forms an important starting-point in advertising graphics. Rand's 'given materials' are in essence the external constraints of graphic design. The product to be promoted, the format and medium of the advertisement and the production process itself. Such factors are not under the designer's control, they already exist and the designer must work with them. On the other hand, the external constraints are the very essence of the special, and possibly unique, circumstances which make a design different. The modern movement in design has tended to play down the role of the specific and special in its search for more general, possibly even universal, solutions. In the 1990s we are returning to a period in the history of design characterised by a greater interest in external constraints. Nowhere is this more true than in architecture. The great modernist Mies van der Rohe was one of the pioneers of the modern movement international style with his clean minimalist lines. Le Corbusier called for buildings to be like ocean-going liners keeping a uniform internal environment wherever in the world they were constructed. In fact there was an alternative tradition of modernism, championed by Hans Scharoun, whose famous concert hall in Berlin demonstrated entirely site-specific architecture. Peter Blundell Jones (1995) has pointed out that Scharoun's predecessor, Hugo Haring, actually shared an office with Mies and demonstrated how they debated and contested the universal and the specific. It is interesting to note that the universalists won the debate and it is with the international style that the modern movement is associated. Perhaps this has more to do with our own laziness in terms of understanding design than with any particular merits of the argument!

The role of internal and external constraints

The essential significance of the domain of a constraint lies in the freedom available to the designer. Internal constraints generally allow a greater degree of freedom and choice since they only govern factors which are under the designer's control. Of course both internal and external constraints can be generated by designers, clients, users and legislators. We now extend our model of design problems by adding more building blocks and creating a kind of wall (Fig. 6.5).

To return to the housing example, in achieving the client's desired relationship between kitchen and dining-room the designer is able to position both. External constraints are not so simple. The client's wish to have a sunny living-room is in a sense a more demanding requirement, since much though at times they might like to, architects cannot control the movements of the sun! For this reason external constraints, although they may sometimes only constitute a

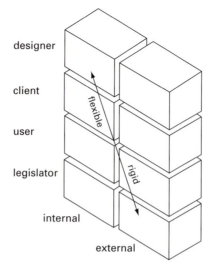

designer

client

user

legislator

flexible

rigid

internal

external

Figure 6.5
Each group can generate
internal and external constraints

small part of the total problem, are often highly significant. Such factors as the site, location, or the specific context in which a design is to be used all create external constraints which emphasise the individual and particular nature of the design. It is worth noting that when it comes to architectural design, the town planners are responsible for constraints which are located at the bottom right-hand corner of our model. This is where problems tend to be at their most demanding and challenging, and where they most restrict the options of the designer. It is perhaps not surprising, then, that architects and town planners sometimes regard each other with a certain amount of suspicion over matters of development control!

One of the most fascinating features of the design process for its would-be students seems to be the nature of the role played by external and internal constraints in the designer's mind. Clearly the balance of importance is not always the same. Perhaps one of the reasons why students of architecture find housing design so difficult is because the balance of external and internal constraints is very even. Unlike many other buildings the architect may design, the house has an internal structure which is relatively simple and easily understood. What makes the internal planning of an individual house difficult, however, is the problem of relating it to adjacent houses and other features of the site. The indications are that the experienced housing architect will use a process quite unlike that employed by the novice student. Before tackling housing for the first time architectural students are quite likely to have designed such buildings as schools or offices, where the internal planning was of paramount importance. So they have begun to develop a design process based on exploring internal constraints and thus may initially turn their attention to the house itself. By contrast the experienced housing architect already has a good grasp of the basic variations of house planning and is much more likely to concentrate on the site.

In her study of the design of six housing estates in London Jane Darke quotes several of the architects explaining their design process in just this way. Douglas Stephen was perhaps the most explicit:

> I don't think of house plans at all at the beginning . . . I think entirely of the site and of the restrictions, and there are not only spatial restrictions but also social restrictions on the site.
>
> (Darke 1978)

Other architects were less practical and more romantic about the influences of the site. Kate Macintosh thought that 'you should try to express the unique quality of the site' (ibid.) and Michael Neylan confirmed that 'we try to get the building to respond and breathe with its surroundings' (ibid.). All these architects are experienced and distinguished designers of housing and this response to a new problem is quite understandable when one remembers that the problems of a house remain fairly constant but each site is unique. As Neylan puts it: 'the whole point of good housing is the relationship between the unit (house) and what's around it' (ibid.). Perhaps it is this very close and critical interplay between internal and external constraints which makes housing such a fascinating but difficult design problem. It certainly seems likely that the balance of internal and external constraints in a design problem is of considerable significance in determining the nature of that problem and the designer's response to it. We shall return to this point again in Chapter 16.

The function of design constraints

We have seen how design problems are built up of constraints which may be either entirely internal to the system or object being designed, or may be linked with some external factor not under the designer's control. These constraints may be imposed most obviously by the client or users but also by legislators and, even, designers. The question which remains is, why are these constraints imposed? What do they achieve, what is their purpose and function? In particular can we identify and separate different types of function and study their effect on the design process?

The purpose of constraints is obviously to ensure that the designed system or object performs the functions demanded of it as adequately as possible. For this reason it is easier to develop models of the function of constraints for specific design fields such as architecture or industrial design. Hillier and Leaman have proposed such a model intended to help organise research in architecture. According to this model (Hillier and Leaman 1972) buildings can be seen to perform four functions: modifying climate, behaviour, resources and culture. Hillier and Leaman (1972) claim that 'buildings have tended to be over designed from the point of view of the relation between activity and its spatial containment, just as they have been under-designed from the point of view of climate modification'. This model has thus been used to argue for a redirection of attention in architectural research and a shift of emphasis in design. The model has been useful in exposing the argument about which functions should be allowed to dominate in the design process and why. Markus provides another example of such function models used for research in specific areas. His Building Performance Research Unit also used a four-function model (Markus 1969b) in appraising the performance of buildings. Markus sees the functions of buildings as divided between: the building system of physical components; the environmental system (which is similar to Hillier and Leaman's climate modifying function); the activity/behaviour system (which is again similar to Hillier and Leaman) and, finally, the organisational system which the building houses. Perhaps because of their very practical emphasis Markus's team failed to see buildings as contributing more widely to culture or even as symbolic entities. Markus considers the cost system not to be independent as do Hillier and Leaman but, rather, prefers to see cost, or resource, implications of achieving each of the other four groups of objectives.

Rand (1970) stresses the importance of both form and content in graphic design. The commercial designer is charged with communicating a message through a piece of two-dimensional design. Clearly then such work has a central symbolic and communicative function, but it is also important for the message, which itself might be quite ordinary, to be striking, unusual, demanding of attention and memorable. The graphic designer deals in two-dimensional composition using colour, texture, form, contrast, proportion, line, shape and so on. The manipulation of these formal materials adds style and character to the message, making it recognisable.

These two functions of form and content are obviously the essence of graphic design but they are also important in any of the environmental design fields. Whatever the designer's intentions might be we inevitably perceive design on these two levels of the formal and the symbolic. The Union Jack flag is not just a pattern of colour and form but it is also inescapably a national symbol. Cathedrals must clearly perform the very powerful symbolic function of expressing devotion to a greater being. Houses need to express the rather less dramatic but possibly just as important, message of domesticity and identity.

Portillo and Dohr (1994) investigated the criteria used by designers working on building interiors and their components. They recorded the criteria used by 41 designers in making decisions about colour and found some 107 criteria were used. Portillo and Dohr also take me to task for confusing constraints with criteria, but I shall persist with that for now and we will come to that debate later. Portillo and Dohr analysed these criteria and found they could be clustered into five categories which they call symbolic, compositional, behavioural, preferential and pragmatic. Clearly their use of 'compositional' is similar to the 'formal' we have just discussed. The behavioural and preferential were to do with the way their designers imagined the users would function and what they would prefer. The pragmatic criteria appeared to relate to cost or to the need to respect existing colour schemes or self-coloured materials which had to be used. Edmonds and Candy, writing about the design of computer interfaces, have expanded this list to include two further criteria which they call performance and contextual. Their performance criteria are to do with the basic needs of the system to deliver performance to match the tasks being performed and are, therefore, right at the root or heart of the whole design. Their contextual criteria, however, seem to belong to our second dimension, that of domain. It seems clear that what Edmonds and Candy mean here are criteria needed to satisfy external constraints such as 'the need for the system to be operable within an engineering workshop' (Edmonds and Candy 1996).

Norberg-Schultz (1963) sets up another distinction between what he calls the 'utilitarian' and the 'monumental' in architecture.

> An architecture which is determined by the need for a physical milieu, may be called 'utilitarian', while an architecture determined by the need for a symbol-milieu could be denominated as 'monumental'.

He goes on to argue for the importance of the symbolic in determining the distinction between architecture and mere building and seems, therefore, to be arguing that the purely utilitarian should not really be regarded as design in the sense we use the word in this book.

> Human values can only be preserved and mediated by means of symbolic forms, and the basic factors of a civilisation required the most articulated symbols (ibid.).

This finds an echo in the opinions of Wittgenstein who produced a considerable body of thought and writings on architecture which have been well documented (Wilson 1986).

> Where there is nothing to glorify there can be no architecture.

Heath, more recently used a similar classification of architecture into 'commodity buildings', 'systems buildings' and 'symbolic buildings' (Heath 1984). Actually none of these distinctions is realised in particular buildings, but we can still see remarkable differences in the design processes which lead to buildings towards the extremes. It is the utilitarian building types of hospitals and factories which have generally led to the main attempts at system building. No one has proposed a modularly co-ordinated standardised approach to designing churches! Of course the systematisation of the design process has crept some way across to the buildings in between such as houses and schools, and this is usually accompanied by more critical comment than when it is applied to hospitals and factories! We seem, therefore, more prepared to accept the notion of design being reduced to selecting from catalogues of components for work which is seen as heavily constrained by the practical or utilitarian or which is seen as essentially a commodity, but we recognise this to be an inappropriate methodology for more expressive value-laden and symbolic work.

There are many more models of the functions of design constraints in specific contexts which we could review and most of them have at least some useful features. However, for the purposes of this more general model we will adopt four functions, which in addition to formal and symbolic include radical and practical. While these four functions are fairly exhaustive some readers may like to add others or subdivide some to suit more specialised fields of design. Since the first edition of this book I have frequently agonised over whether to extend this range or subdivide it, but so many people have told me they find this model to be helpful in understanding design that I have left it in its original form.

Radical constraints

The radical constraints are those which deal with the primary purpose of the object or system being designed. 'Radical' is used here not in the sense of revolutionary or left-wing, but in its true meaning of 'at the root of' or fundamental. Thus, in the design of a school the radical constraints are those to do with the educational system the school is there to implement. Such constraints then can range over a tremendously wide set of issues and are generally thought to be very influential right from the very beginning of the design process.

Although these constraints are central and most critical, little need be said about them here. They are generally so important as to be obvious and reasonably well understood by the client. However, there may be conflicts between the radical constraints generated by the client and the users, or even between different groups of users. In a hospital, for example, often what is good for the patients may be inconvenient for the medical staff.

However, these radical constraints are the whole reason for having the design in the first place. In this sense they may overlap other constraints in some cases, but that will become clearer later.

Practical constraints

The practical constraints are those aspects of the total design problem which deal with the reality of producing, making or building the design; the technological problem. For the architect such problems include the external factors of the bearing capacity of the site and the internal factors of the materials used in construction. For the graphic designer there are the practical problems of printing and reprographic technology, and the media of transmission. For the product designer they most usually not only include the materials used but also the manufacturing processes.

The practical constraints are not exclusively concerned with the making of the object being designed. They also embrace the technical performance of the object during its working life. For the architect this means making a building which will continue to stand up and resist the weather and modify the internal climate as necessary. The product designer must worry about the durability of the product in use and its ability to withstand normal use, which may include such events as the object being dropped, left in direct sunlight or used under water.

Formal constraints

The formal constraints are those to do with the visual organisation of the object. They may include rules about proportion, form, colour and texture. There seems little doubt that we respond well to a certain degree of formal organisation. Music which has no rules becomes random noise whilst overly structured tunes are banal and have little lasting value. So it is with art and design in visual terms. Objects which present a totally disorganised jumble of forms, colours, textures and materials are not only difficult to understand in their own right, but hard to use in relation to other objects around them. We have a fundamental need for order and structure, whilst also appreciating variety and surprise. The trick of good design is to get an appropriate amount of order to meet the needs of the context or situation.

At their most extreme, formal rules may be based on modular systems or grids. The chief components to be found in the classical styles of architecture are based on clearly defined sets of geometrical rules. Whilst the romantic periods of design show less of a reliance on such organisation, the modern movement showed a renewed interest in geometric systems. Le Corbusier (1946) wrote of 'the necessity for order. The regulating line is a guarantee against wilfulness. It brings satisfaction to the understanding'. Formal constraints may become extraordinarily elaborate and result in the kind of visual gymnastics seen in Baroque architecture, but they can also demand extreme simplicity as exemplified by the famous aphorism of Mies van der Rohe: 'less is more'.

In the United Kingdom a whole school of ideas was developed by Sir Leslie Martin who designed with and researched geometrical rules for the organisation of space and form. His work carried on into the 'Martin Centre' at Cambridge which influenced a whole generation of architects and industrial designers. These studies of formal constraints in design can be seen in theoretical terms in major books such as *The Geometry of Environment* (March and Steadman 1974).

Symbolic constraints

The modern movement, most particularly in its international style, showed rather less interest in the symbolic properties of design. The alternative traditions of architects such as Antonio Gaudi and

Hans Scharoun show a much greater concern with the expressive qualities of design and the use of form and space to achieve specific effects rather than as an abstract assembly. Post-modern design has frequently made use of historical styles in a self-conscious attempt to reconnect contemporary life with the past and to express ideas about the contradictions of a more uncertain age.

However, we must be careful about the role of symbolism in the design process as opposed to its role in design criticism. Some designers do certainly use the generation of symbolic meaning as a central part of the process, and we shall see some examples in a later chapter. However, most of what is written about the symbolic content of design is in the form of critical analysis, as the architect and interior designer Eva Jiricna points out:

> You get an idea, but that idea is not really of a very philosophical or conceptual thought. It is really something which is an expression on the level of your experience which is initiated by the question. I don't think that great buildings have got great symbolic thinking behind them. I leave it to journalists and architectural critics to find a deep symbolic meaning because I don't think that anybody who looks at buildings can actually read the thinking behind them, and to me it's just totally useless.
>
> (Lawson 1994b)

A model of design constraints

We can now construct a fully three-dimensional block model of design problems from all the building blocks we have been exploring throughout this chapter (Fig. 6.6). The completed model of design problems now shows how, in theory, each of the generators may contribute each type of constraint. In practice, however, each tends to generate rather more of one type than another. Thus the client/user is responsible for the majority of the radical constraints and is likely to contribute some symbolic ones, while the designer is the main generator of the formal and the practical and also contributes symbolic constraints. More importantly, it is the designer's task to integrate and co-ordinate all these constraints by whatever device. We shall see more of this process in the next section but an interesting example from the work of Denys Lasdun will serve to illustrate the point here (Fig. 6.7). In his account of the National Theatre he explains how the horizontal platforms, which he calls 'strata', and which form such a dominant element throughout the building, serve as such an integrating device solving radical, formal and symbolic problems:

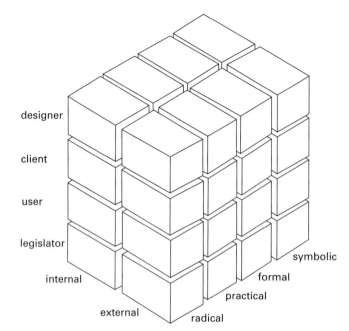

Figure 6.6
The completed model of design problems

They support the interior functions while allowing for flexible planning. They provide coherence to a large scheme which is, nonetheless, broken down to the human scale. They give visual expression to the essentially public nature of the institution: for a theatre must be a place where human contact is enriched and a common experience is shared.
(Lasdun 1965)

Just as a design is a product of the designer's approach, so it is also a reflection of the particular pattern of constraints which make up

Figure 6.7
What the architect of the National Theatre, Denys Lasdun, called 'strata' solve radical, formal and symbolic problems

the problem. We have already seen how dramatic landscape features can be major generators of architectural form, and we must all recognise the enormous influence of climate on building construction and form across the world and throughout history. The need to absorb the special constraints peculiar to a particular problem into a continuing and developing design philosophy, therefore, becomes one of the chief challenges in the practice of design. This point is acknowledged by Richard Rogers in his fascinating account of the design of the Pompidou Centre:

> It is impossible to divorce the building from its legal, technical, political and economic context. At the same time, a major part of any design approach is the way constraints may be absorbed, and whenever possible inverted into positive elements. On the one hand, new technical needs and regulations, political dicta and changing user requirements make it difficult to control the building on the other hand the way that the building overcame these constraints is a measure of the success or failure of both the building and its philosophy.
>
> (Suckle 1980)

We can now also see the overlap between the functions of constraints. For example, let us imagine we were asked to design a new flag as was the case for the European Union. Clearly the purpose of a flag is to be a symbol, so how can we sensibly separate the radical from the symbolic constraints? Thus in extreme cases one set of functions may become so important that the distinctions are blurred, but in most cases the distinctions seem to remain useful. In the design of a school the radical constraints will certainly include the need to accommodate the activities and people involved in schooling. The school will need to be composed well not only for purely formal reasons but in order that pupils and visitors can build their own mental maps of the building and navigate around it. A school must also be to some extent a symbol of the way society cares for children and, of course, the practical constraints require the designer to make not only adults but small children comfortable. Thus there are not absolutely clear distinctions between all these functions, but a designer thinking about a school might find it useful to help identify all the important problems by using these four categories of function.

The use of the model

Unlike the maps of the design process reviewed earlier in this book, this chapter has developed a model of the structure of the design problem. However, in the next chapter we shall see something of the way the process can be mapped out as designers are seen to move their attention from one part of the problem to another. Which constraints should form the starting-point of the design process, or does it matter? Which constraints are critical in determining the design form or are key factors for success? Do designers differ in the kinds of constraints they focus on and do different types of design present different balances of types of constraint? These are questions which, as yet, remain unanswered, but the model of design problems provides a structure within which we can explore these and many other issues. This model is not intended to form part of a design method but rather as an aid to the understanding of the nature of design problems, and thus only indirectly to assist in establishing a design process.

This book began with a question. How is it that we can still use the word 'design' to describe such different processes as the creation of motor cars, architecture or advertisements? Reference to the model will show that such situations differ only in the degree of importance attached to various aspects of the problem. We expect that a fashion designer will lay great emphasis on designer-generated formal and symbolic constraints. Architects are expected to take more notice of their clients and users and, because architecture is so public a matter, to respect legislative controls. Sometimes internal constraints will be dominant and sometimes the design may be largely formed by external factors.

Design situations can be seen to vary in terms of the overall degree of freedom and control available to the designer. Where the bulk of the constraints are internal and designer generated we talk of open-ended design. Where, by contrast, clients or legislators make heavy demands or there are many external factors to consider we talk of tightly constrained design. Some designers seem to prefer the open-ended situation while others are more at home with restricted problems. Gordon Murray, the successful designer of Brabham and McLaren racing cars is reported to regard the regulations imposed on Formula One cars as fundamental to the necessity to innovate (Cross 1996b). It seems for this particular designer a highly constrained problem is more interesting than the freer situations which may be more normal in other design fields.

Recognising the nature of the problem and responding with an appropriate design process seems to be one of the most important skills in design. It is very easy to neglect a set of constraints. Modern architects are often criticised for their lack of attention to the symbolic functions of design and for producing architecture which seems aggressive or inhuman. Students of design often devote too much of their time to unimportant parts of the prob-lem. It is easy for the inexperienced to generate almost impossible practical problems by slavishly following ill-conceived formal ideas which remain unquestioned but could quite easily be modified. One of the major roles of design tutors is to move their students around from one part of the problem to another and the job of the students is to learn to do it for themselves. Here again the model of design problems may be useful acting as a sort of checklist of factors to consider. Almost certainly, the skilled and experienced designer is unlikely to behave so self-consciously, but the novice student needs to learn to develop a balanced design process exploring all the important constraints, whoever generated them, whether they may be internal or external and whatever their function.

Constraints and criteria

As mentioned earlier, Portillo and Dohr have proposed a distinction between constraints and criteria in design which they thought was missing from an earlier version of this book. Their point is certainly an interesting one, although it is also partly semantic. They argue that constraints are seen as restrictive and narrowing down the designer's alternatives whereas criteria are flexible and evaluative:

> Criteria consistently reference design functions and evaluative processes based on purpose while constraints intimate design functions usually characterised as restrictive and more closely aligned with specific solu-tion requirements.
>
> (Portillo and Dohr 1994)

This is a fine point but a fair one. However I have persisted with this model of 'constraints' by which I mean issues which must be taken into account when forming the solution. Taken together these constraints form the design problem and we have seen that they may only become apparent as attempts to create the solution progress. It is rarely the case in my experience that completely clear criteria for success are mapped out in advance of attempts to produce solutions for the kinds of design being discussed here. In the end a good design is one which respects all the constraints to some degree in a balance which is thought acceptable. Of course we must also accept that some people would wish to have set more stringent criteria in some areas than others. Few of us will ever agree entirely about just how good one piece of design is.

The designer must work to negotiate a solution which meets the relative and disparate sets of criteria which are held, often implicitly, by clients, users and legislators as well as members of the design team.

Portillo and Dohr have contributed to this discussion significantly by recognising the importance of criteria in the design process. The problem with design so often is that you cannot set sensible criteria for success unless you have some appreciation of what is possible. Criteria therefore are not necessarily absolute in the design process, except sometimes when set by legislators, and we shall see in Chapter 13 that they can sometimes be very destructive as a result!

References

Cairns, G. M. (1996). 'User input to design: confirming the 'User-Needs Gap' model.' *Environments by Design* **1**(2): 125–140.

Candy, L. and Edmonds, E. (1996). 'Creative design of the Lotus bicycle: implications for knowledge support systems research.' *Design Studies* **17**(1): 71–89.

Cross, N. (1996). 'Winning by design: the methods of Gordon Murray, racing car designer.' *Design Studies* **17**(1): 91–107.

Darke, J. (1978). The primary generator and the design process. *New Directions in Environmental Design Research: proceedings of EDRA 9.* Washington, EDRA. 325–337.

Edmonds, E. A. and Candy, L. (1996). Supporting the creative user: a criteria based approach to interaction design. *Creativity and Cognition.* Loughborough, LUTCHI. 57–66.

Heath, T. (1984). *Method in Architecture.* Chichester, Wiley.

Hillier, B. and Leaman, A. (1972). 'A new approach to architectural research.' *RIBA Journal* **79**(12):

Jones, P. B. (1995). *Hans Scharoun.* London, Phaidon.

Lasdun, D. (1965). 'An architect's approach to architecture.' *RIBA Journal* **72**(4).

Lawson, B. R. (1994). *Design in Mind.* Oxford, Butterworth Architecture.

Le Corbusier (1946). *Towards a new Architecture.* London, The Architectural press.

March, L. and Steadman, P. (1974). *The Geometry of Environment.* London, Methuen.

Markus, T. A. (1969). The role of building performance measurement and appraisal in design method. *Design methods in Architecture.* London, Lund Humphries.

Norberg-Schultz, C. (1966). *Intentions in Architecture.* Cambridge, Mass, MIT Press.

Page, J. K. (1972). Planning and protest. *Design Participation.* London, Academy Editions.

Portillo, M. and Dohr, J. H. (1994). 'Bridging process and structure through criteria.' *Design Studies* **15**(4): 403–416.

Rand, P. (1970). *Thoughts on Design*. London, Studio Vista.
Rowe, P. G. (1987). *Design Thinking*. Cambridge Mass, MIT Press.
Roy, R. (1993). 'Case studies of creativity in innovative product development.' *Design Studies* **14**(4): 423–443.
Suckle, A., Ed. (1980). *By Their Own Design*. New York, Whitney.
Wilson, C. S. J. (1986). 'The play of use and use of play.' *Architectural Review* **180**(1073): 15–18.
Zeisel, J. (1984). *Inquiry by Design*. Cambridge, Cambridge University Press.

7

Problems, solutions and the design process

The only person who is an artist is the one that can make a puzzle out of the solution.

Karl Kraus, *Nachts*

Everything that is absorbed and registered in your mind adds to the collection of ideas stored in the memory: a sort of library that you can consult whenever a problem arises. So, essentially the more you have seen, experienced and absorbed, the more points of reference you will have to help you decide which direction to take: your frame of reference expands.

Herman Hertzberger, *Lessons for Students of Architecture*

Now and when

The designer has a prescriptive rather than descriptive job. Unlike scientists who describe how the world is, designers suggest how it might be. Designers are therefore all 'futurologists' to some extent. The very essence of their job is to create the future, or at least some features of it. This is obviously a rather hazardous business, and it carries with it at least two ways of being unpopular. First, the new often seems strange and therefore to some people at least unsettling and threatening. Second, of course, the designer can turn out to be wrong about the future. It is very easy with that wonderful benefit of hindsight to see design failures. The high-rise housing which was built in Britain after the Second World War now seems to be so obviously unsatisfactory, we wonder how the designers could have been so stupid!

But even on a much shorter time-scale the designer has worries and uncertainties about the future. Will the client like the design and give the final go ahead? Will it gain approval from legislators and regulators? Will it turn out to be too expensive? Will it be popular with the users? These and other similar crucial questions can only be answered by the passage of time, and the designers must hold their nerve during the process, complete the work, subject it to the test of time and wait patiently for the verdict. Such doubts and worries must have plagued the minds of many generations of designers, but now there are new and even more unsettling uncertainties facing contemporary designers.

The advanced technocratic society for which the contemporary designer works is itself changing rapidly. Unlike previous generations we live in a world with comparatively little tradition and cultural stability. The vast majority of our everyday environment has been designed and, even, invented within our own generation. The motor car and the television profoundly influence our daily lives to an extent that would probably have astonished their inventors. My father saw virtually the whole of the revolution created by the motor car and I have lived through the revolution created by the computer. My father, however, had little understanding of the implications the computer has for changing our lives. But this rate of change is now so great that it is impacting on a single lifetime. Many writers have argued that designed technology is now one of the most significant aspects of contemporary social order.

Marshall McLuhan (1967) has famously commented on the importance of the information explosion caused by printing, television and computers, and concluded that the only certainty in modern life is change. Dickson (1974) sees technology as the major determinant of the structure of society, and argued that the negative societal effects of high technology suggest we should seek alternative, less harmful forms of technology. Toffler (1970) has warned that if technology continues to advance in the present manner we shall all suffer from a cultural disorientation which he calls 'Futureshock'.

Polemical though some of these populist writers may be there is no doubt that such rapid change does result in a world which is increasingly difficult to understand and predict, so that we are simultaneously excited and fearful about the future. Perhaps we do indeed live in what Leach called a 'Runaway World':

> Men have become like gods. Isn't it about time that we understood our divinity? Science offers us total mastery over our environment and over our destiny, yet instead of rejoicing we feel deeply afraid.
>
> (Leach 1968)

All of this makes life even more difficult for the designer who now has not just got uncertainties about the design but is even unsure of the nature of the world into which it must fit. Often in recent years we have seen the design process actually outpaced by social, economic or technological change. The nature of medicine and systems of health care management have recently changed too quickly for the designers and builders of new hospitals so that new buildings are out of date or too small before they are even completed. In dense urban areas like Hong Kong, land values can change more quickly than we can construct buildings leaving projects uneconomical before they are finished. The power of the mass media can create sudden and fundamental changes of fashion and taste, leaving mass-produced items like motor cars looking outdated long before the end of their useful life. New materials and manufacturing methods can so dramatically alter the costs of items that old versions can be more expensive to maintain than the purchase of completely new ones.

How, then, can the designer respond to this uncertainty about the future? John Johansen, the American architect, describes the situation very concisely:

> Rare is the programmer or architect in a time of rapid social and techno-logical change who can truly assume that he can deal with the present alone. A developer or financier who risks the sure possibility of functional obsolescence is surely short-sighted.

(Suckle 1980)

So how can designers respond to an uncertain future? Unlike the scientist, the designer cannot apply for another research grant, and write an elegant paper describing the complexity of the situation. Designers are expected to act. There are three main ways of dealing with this in the design process, which we might call procrastination, non-committal design and throw-away design. Each seem to be more popular with particular groups of designers.

Procrastination

The first approach, procrastination, is based on the idea that somehow the future may become more certain if only we wait a little. If it is not possible to be sure of our actions now, perhaps it will be easier to take a decision next year or the year after. I regularly meet people who are tempted to follow this approach when buying a computer. If I buy now, goes the argument, they might bring out a new machine and I will be left with an out-of-date model. I try to point out that this will also be true next week, next month and next year, so it is no reason to delay. This strategy is also popular with very long time-scale decision-makers such as politicians and town planners. It is on this basis that we took so long to build the third

London airport and that we have no clear national policy on energy supply. Deep down this seems to be one of the reasons governments are following the lead of Margaret Thatcher in moving away from central strategic planning to allowing the market to decide. Design decisions taken by governments, whether regional, national or local, which can later be criticised are potential electoral millstones around the necks of the politicians. Far better, then, to be detached and free of all blame!

The real difficulty with this response to uncertainty is that once a problem has been identified it is no longer possible to avoid the consequences of making a decision. Delaying the decision itself adds to the uncertainty and may thus accelerate the problem. Once an inner city area has been identified as in need of some planning action, that area is likely to run down or become 'blighted' even more rapidly until decisions are taken about its future. Similarly if a new road is planned but the route remains under debate for any lengthy period, the property in the region of the various routes changes value. So procrastination as a strategy is deeply flawed. In many real-life design situations it is actually not possible to take no action. The very process of avoiding or delaying a decision has an effect!

Non-committal design

The second design response to uncertainty is to be as non-committal as possible whilst still actually proceeding. Thus architects have tended to design bland, anonymous and neutral buildings which are non-specific either in terms of their functions or locations. Not surprisingly there has been a reaction to such architecture which has been accused of failing to provide sufficiently positive urban environments. The notion of flexible and adaptable environments was popular for a while in schools of architecture. Habraken and his followers were highly influential and went so far as to suggest that architects should design support structures which would provide only shelter, support and services, leaving future users free to create their own homes and express their own identity by arranging the kits of parts that fit within these 'supports' (Habraken 1972).

Such ideas have remained largely theoretical and there are undoubtedly many practical and economic problems in providing buildings which are genuinely flexible and adaptable. Architects have now perhaps become slightly schizophrenic in their attitude towards flexibility. On the one hand much is said and written about designing buildings which will be able to outlast their initial function whilst, on the other hand, architects are increasingly finding that old buildings need not be demolished but can often easily be converted to new uses. John Johansen describes his approach to architectural design which he has developed in response to the uncertain future. For Johansen, this is a key aspect of his work, and he argues that 'if we assume the nature of our accommodation will change in the near future, then we must write programmes not for the present, but for the future as well'. To Johansen (Suckle 1980) it therefore seems to follow logically that he must design buildings which are themselves capable of changing.

Throw-away design

The third response to uncertainty is to design for the present only. Thus obsolescence is built in and the designed object is intended to be thrown away and replaced with a more up-to-date design. This strategy has been increasingly adopted by the designers of mass-produced goods. Everything from clothes to motor cars may be discarded in favour of new styles and images. Such an approach is particularly favoured by fashion designers with the very word 'fashion' confirming its transient nature. However, such ideas have already begun to invade more traditionally stable fields such as interior design. We are expected not only to wear this year's clothes but to prepare this year's food in this year's kitchens. Unfortunately this consumerist approach is not only wasteful of resources but also leads to short-lived goods of continually reduced quality and, thus, the need to replace things becomes not just an option but a necessity.

Design solutions creating design problems

Designing in times of rapid change is clearly more difficult than designing for a stable and predictable world. As we saw in Chapter 2 the rate of socio-technic development is itself an important influence on both the design process and the role of the designer in society. But it is important to recognise that designers are not just dependent on the future, they also help to create it. Each of the design responses to uncertain futures discussed above, themselves fashion the future, whether it be in the form of blighted inner-city areas, indecisive architecture or out of fashion motor cars. As Chris Jones (1970) puts it:

> To design is no longer to increase the stability of the man-made world: it is to alter, for good or ill, things that determine the course of its development.

So it turns out to be the case that many of our contemporary design problems are themselves substantially the results of previous design activity. This may be in the form of noise from machines or activities, or in the shape of urban decay or vandalised buildings, or in terms of dangerous and congested airports and roads. Each of these and countless other similar ailments of modern civilisation provide some of the most pressing problems facing designers, and yet to some extent at least they can 'be thought of as human failures to design for conditions brought about by the products of designing' (Jones 1970).

Finding and solving problems

It has often been suggested that design is as much a matter of finding problems as it is of solving them. In later chapters we shall discuss strategies and tactics for controlling these intermingling processes of problem identification and solution generation. At this point, however, it is important to recognise that the problems identified in any design process are not only likely to be a function of the designer's approach, but also of the time available. An interesting illustration of this may be found in Richard Rogers's account of the design of the Pompidou Centre, to which we have already referred. From an early stage Rogers tells us that he identified the need to design for flexibility. Indeed, for Rogers, the design concept, perhaps even the primary generator, caused the building to be 'conceived as a flexible container capable of continuously adapting not only in plan, but also in section and elevation to whatever needs should arise'. Rogers quickly came to view his building as a 'gigantic ever changing erector set' (Fig. 7.1). Technically, the proposed solution involved many movable components such as partitions, cladding and floors. However, Rogers had to abandon the attempt to find a technical solution to the problem of the movable floors:

> As soon as it became apparent that there was a time constraint of five years from competition to opening, we realised that it would be utterly impossible to debug the initial idea of moving floors held by friction clamps in the time allotted and consequently abandoned it.
>
> (Suckle 1980)

117

Figure 7.1
The Pompidou Centre which
Richard Rogers regarded as
'a gigantic . . . erector set'

Thus Rogers is telling us that there were more problems which had
been identified and which he would liked to have solved if he had
more time. The design process rarely has a natural conclusion of its
own, but must more often be completed in a defined period of
time. It is perhaps like writing an answer to an examination question under pressure of time. Frustratingly, you may still be thinking
of new and related issues on which to dilate as you leave the
examination hall. Certainly this seems a better model of the design
process than that conjured up by the idea of completing a crossword puzzle which has an identifiable and recognisable moment of
completion.

Design problems and design solutions are inexorably inter-
dependent. It is obviously meaningless to study solutions without
reference to problems and the reverse is equally fruitless. The more
one tries to isolate and study design problems the more important
it becomes to refer to design solutions. In design, problems may
suggest certain features of solutions but these solutions in turn
create new and different problems.

Design as a contribution to knowledge

In this chapter we have seen how the design process is affected by
the uncertainties of the future. In the last chapter we saw how the
design process could be seen to vary depending on the kind of

problems being tackled. In Chapter 3 we saw a series of attempts to define the design process as a sequence of operations, all of which seemed flawed in some way. A more mature approach was presented by Zeisel (1984) in his discussion of the nature of research into the links between environment and behaviour. He proposed that design could be recognised as having five characteristics. The first of these is that design consists of three elementary activities which Zeisel called imaging, presenting and testing. Imaging is a rather nice word to describe what the great psychologist Jerome Bruner called 'going beyond the information given'. Clearly this takes us into the realm of thinking, imagination and creativity which will be explored in the next two chapters. Zeisel's second activity of presentation also takes us into the realm of drawing and the central role it plays in the design process. This will be explored in later chapters too. Finally the activity of testing has already been explored here in Chapter 5.

Zeisel also goes on to argue that a second characteristic of designing is that it works with two types of information which he calls a heuristic catalyst for imaging and a body of knowledge for testing. Essentially this tells us that designers rely on information to decide how things might be, but also that they use information to tell them how well things might work. Because often the same information is used in these two ways, design can be seen as a kind of investigative process and, therefore, as a form of research. We currently live in a world in which it is fashionable to produce simple, some might say simplistic, measures of performance. So schools and hospitals have to summarise their performance in order that 'league tables' can be published for their 'consumers'. Similarly universities must be assessed for the quality of their teaching and research. The readers of Chapter 5 will already be alerted to the dangers of this approach. However, when it comes to assessing the research done in departments of design the problem becomes even more tricky. How on earth do we evaluate the output of artists, composers and designers in terms of their contribution to knowledge? This is a problem for those who wish to impose these simplistic global measures of performance on a complex multi-dimensional phenomena. Suffice it to say that designers are naturally able to accept these difficulties since that is just what designers have to do, but they also recognise their efforts are imperfect!

It is worth pausing briefly here to summarise some of the important characteristics of design problems and solutions, and the lessons that can be learnt about the nature of the design process itself. The following points should not be taken to represent a comprehensive list of discrete properties of the design situation; indeed they are often closely interrelated and there is thus some repetition. Taken together, however, they sketch an overall picture of the nature of design as it seems today.

Design problems

1 Design problems cannot be comprehensively stated
As we saw in Chapter 3 one of the difficulties in developing a map of the design process is that it is never possible to be sure when all aspects of the problem have emerged. In Chapter 6 we saw how design problems are generated by several groups or individuals with varying degrees of involvement in the decision-making process. It is clear that many components of design problems cannot be expected to emerge until some attempt has been made at generating solutions. Indeed, many features of design problems may never be fully uncovered and made explicit. Design problems are often full of uncertainties both about the objectives and their relative priorities. In fact both objectives and priorities are quite likely to change during the design process as the solution implications begin to emerge. Thus we should not expect a comprehensive and static formulation of design problems but rather they should be seen as in dynamic tension with design solutions.

2 Design problems require subjective interpretation
In the introductory first chapter we saw how designers from different fields could suggest different solutions to the same problem of what to do about railway catering not making a profit. In fact not only are designers likely to devise different solutions but they also perceive problems differently. Our understanding of design problems and the information needed to solve them depends to a certain extent upon our ideas for solving them. Thus because industrial designers know how to redesign trains they see problems in the way buffet cars are laid out, while operations researchers may see deficiencies in the timetabling and scheduling of services, and graphic designers identify inadequacies in the way the food is marketed and presented.

As we saw in Chapter 5 there are many difficulties with measurement in design and problems are inevitably value laden. In this sense design problems, like their solutions, remain a matter of subjective perception. What may seem important to one client or user or designer may not seem so to others. We, therefore, should not expect entirely objective formulations of design problems.

3 Design problems tend to be organised hierarchically
In Chapter 4 we explored how design problems can often be viewed as symptoms of other higher-level problems illustrated by Eberhard's tale of how the problem of redesigning a doorknob was transformed into considerations of doors, walls, buildings and eventually complete organisations. Similarly the problem of providing an urban playground for children who roam the streets could be viewed as resulting from the design of the housing in which those children live, or the planning policy which allows vast areas of housing to be built away from natural social foci, or it could be viewed as a symptom of our educational system, or the patterns of employment of their parents. There is no objective or logical way of determining the right level on which to tackle such problems. The decision remains largely a pragmatic one; it depends on the power, time and resources available to the designer, but it does seem sensible to begin at as high a level as is reasonable and practicable.

Design solutions

1 There are an inexhaustible number of different solutions
Since design problems cannot be comprehensively stated it follows that there can never be an exhaustive list of all the possible solutions to such problems. Some of the engineering-based writers on design methodology talk of mapping out the range of possible solutions. Such a notion must obviously depend upon the assumption that the problem can be clearly and unequivocally stated, as implied by Alexander's method (see Chapter 5). If, however, we accept the contrary viewpoint expressed here, that design problems are rather more inscrutable and ill defined then it seems unreasonable to expect that we can be sure that all the solutions to a problem have been identified.

2 There are no optimal solutions to design problems
Design almost invariably involves compromise. Sometimes stated objectives may be in direct conflict with each other, as when motorists demand both good acceleration and low petrol consumption. Rarely can the designer simply optimise one requirement without suffering some losses elsewhere. Just how the

trade-offs and compromises are made remains a matter of skilled judgement. There are thus no optimal solutions to design problems but rather a whole range of acceptable solutions (if only the designers can think of them) each likely to prove more or less satisfactory in different ways and to different clients or users. Just as the making of design decisions remains a matter of judgement so does the appraisal and evaluation of solutions. There are no established methods for deciding just how good or bad solutions are, and still the best test of most design is to wait and see how well it works in practice. Design solutions can never be perfect and are often more easily criticised than created, and designers must accept that they will almost invariably appear wrong in some ways to some people.

3 Design solutions are often holistic responses
The bits of design solutions rarely map exactly on to the identified parts of the problem. Rather one idea in the solution is more often an integrated and holistic response to a number of problems. The dished cartwheel studied in Chapter 2 was a very good example of this and puzzled George Sturt for exactly this reason. The single idea of dishing the wheel simultaneously solved a whole series of problems. The Georgian window studied in Chapter 4 can similarly be seen as an integrated response to a great many problems. Thus it is rarely possible to dissect a design solution and map it on to the problem saying which piece of solution solves which piece of problem.

4 Design solutions are a contribution to knowledge
Once an idea has been formed and a design completed the world has in some way changed. Each design, whether built or made, or even if just left on the drawing-board, represents progress in some way. Design solutions are themselves extensively studied by other designers and commented upon by critics. They are to design what hypotheses and theories are to science. They are the basis upon which design knowledge advances. The Severins Bridge in Cologne, which we studied in the previous chapter, does not just carry people across the Rhine it contributes to the pool of ideas available to future designers of bridges. Thus the completion of a design solution does not just serve the client, but enables the designer to develop his or her own ideas in a public and examinable way.

5 Design solutions are parts of other design problems
Design solutions are not panaceas and most usually have some undesirable effects as well as the intended good effects. The modern

motor car is a wonderfully sophisticated design solution to the problem of personal transportation in a world which requires people to be very mobile over short and medium distances on an unpredictable basis. However, when that solution is applied to the whole population and is used by them even for the predictable journeys we find ourselves designing roads which tear apart our cities and rural areas. The pollution which results has become a problem in its own right, but even the car is now beginning not to work well as it sits in traffic jams! This is a very dramatic illustration of the basic principle that everything we design has the potential not only to solve problems but also to create new ones!

The design process

1 The process is endless
Since design problems defy comprehensive description and offer an inexhaustible number of solutions the design process cannot have a finite and identifiable end. The designer's job is never really done and it is probably always possible to do better. In this sense designing is quite unlike puzzling. The solver of puzzles such as crosswords or mathematical problems can often recognise a correct answer and knows when the task is complete, but not so the designer. Identifying the end of design process requires experience and judgement. It no longer seems worth the effort of going further because the chances of significantly improving on the solution seem small. This does not mean that the designer is necessarily pleased with the solution, but perhaps unsatisfactory as it might be it represents the best that can be done. Time, money and information are often major limiting factors in design and a shortage of any of these essential resources can result in what the designer may feel to be a frustratingly early end to the design process. Some designers of large and complex systems involving long time-scales are now beginning to view design as continuous and continuing, rather than a once and for all process. Perhaps one day we may get truly community-based architects for example, who live in an area constantly servicing the built environment as doctors tend their patients.

2 There is no infallibly correct process
Much though some early writers on design methodology may have wished it, there is no infallibly good way of designing. In design

the solution is not just the logical outcome of the problem, and there is therefore no sequence of operations which will guarantee a result. The situation, however, is not quite as hopeless as this statement may suggest. We saw in Chapter 6 how it is possible to analyse the structure of design problems and in Part 3 we shall explore the way designers can and do modify their process in response to this variable problem structure. In fact we shall see how controlling and varying the design process is one of the most important skills a designer must develop.

3 The process involves finding as well as solving problems
It is clear from our analysis of the nature of design problems that the designer must inevitably expend considerable energy in identifying problems. It is central to modern thinking about design that problems and solutions are seen as emerging together, rather than one following logically upon the other. The process is thus less linear than implied by many of the maps discussed in Chapter 3, but rather more argumentative. That is, both problem and solution become clearer as the process goes on. We have also seen in Chapter 6 how the designer is actually expected to contribute problems as well as solutions. Since neither finding problems nor producing solutions can be seen as predominantly logical activities we must expect the design process to demand the highest levels of creative thinking. We shall discuss creativity as a phenomenon and how it may be promoted in Part 3.

4 Design inevitably involves subjective value judgement
Questions about which are the most important problems, and which solutions most successfully resolve those problems are often value laden. Answers to such questions, which designers must give, are therefore frequently subjective. As we saw in the discussion of the third London Airport in Chapter 5, how important it is to preserve churches or birdlife or to avoid noise annoyance depends rather on your point of view. However hard the proponents of quantification, in this case in the form of cost-benefit analysis, may argue, they will never convince ordinary people that such issues can rightly be decided entirely objectively. Complete objectivity demands dispassionate detachment. Designers being human beings find it hard to remain either dispassionate or detached about their work. Indeed, designers are often distinctly defensive and possessive about their solutions. Perhaps it was this issue above all else that gave rise to the first generation of design methods; designers were seen to be heavily involved in issues about which they were making subjective

value judgements. However, this concern cannot be resolved simply by denying the subjective nature of much judgement in design. Perhaps current thinking tends more towards making the designer's decisions and value judgements more explicit and allowing others to participate in the process, but this path too is fraught with many difficulties.

5 Design is a prescriptive activity
One of the popular models for the design process to be found in the literature on design methodology is that of scientific method. Problems of science however do not fit the description of design problems outlined above and, consequently, the processes of science and design cannot usefully be considered as analogous. The most important, obvious and fundamental difference is that design is essentially prescriptive whereas science is predominantly descriptive. Designers do not aim to deal with questions of what is, how and why but, rather, with what might be, could be and should be. While scientists may help us to understand the present and predict the future, designers may be seen to prescribe and to create the future, and thus their process deserves not just ethical but also moral scrutiny.

6 Designers work in the context of a need for action
Design is not an end in itself. The whole point of the design process is that it will result in some action to change the environment in some way, whether by the formulation of policies or the construction of buildings. Decisions cannot be avoided or even delayed without the likelihood of unfortunate consequences. Unlike the artist, the designer is not free to concentrate exclusively on those issues which seem most interesting. Clearly one of the central skills in design is the ability rapidly to become fascinated by problems previously unheard of. We shall discuss this difficult skill in Part 3.

Not only must designers face up to all the problems which emerge they must also do so in a limited time. Design is often a matter of compromise decisions made on the basis of inadequate information. Unfortunately for the designer such decisions often appear in concrete form for all to see and few critics are likely to excuse mistakes or failures on the grounds of insufficient information. Designers, unlike scientists, do not seem to have the right to be wrong. While we accept that a disproved theory may have helped science to advance, we rarely acknowledge the similar contribution made by mistaken designs.

References

Dickson, D. (1974). *Alternative Technology and the Politics of Technical Change*. London, Fontana.

Habraken, N. J. (1972). *Supports: An alternative to mass housing*. London, The Architectural Press.

Jones, J. C. (1970). *Design Methods: seeds of human futures*. New York, John Wiley.

Leach, E. (1968). *A Runaway World*. London, BBC Publications.

McLuhan, M. (1967). *The Medium is the Massage*. Harmondsworth, Penguin.

Suckle, A., Ed. (1980). *By Their Own Design*. New York, Whitney.

Toffler, A. (1970). *Futureshock*. London, Bodley Head.

Zeisel, J. (1984). *Inquiry by Design*. Cambridge, Cambridge University Press.

PART THREE

DESIGN THINKING

8

Types and styles
of thinking

The highest possible stage in moral culture is when we recognise
that we ought to control our thoughts.

Charles Darwin, The Descent of Man

The art of reasoning consists in getting hold of the subject at the right
end, of seizing on the few general ideas that illuminate the whole, and
of persistently organising all subsidiary facts around them. Nobody
can be a good reasoner unless by constant practice he has realised
the importance of getting hold of the big ideas and hanging onto
them like grim death.

*A. N. Whitehead, 1914 Presidential address to the London
Branch of the Mathematical Association*

Thinking about thinking

So far in this book we have concentrated on the nature of design
as a process and on the characteristic qualities of design problems
and good solutions. Now it is time in this third part of the book to
turn our attention to the thought processes which are required to
identify and understand those design problems and create design
solutions. In subsequent chapters we will need to consider the
principles, strategies and tactics which designers use in this mental
process. We study the traps and pitfalls that frequently beset them
and examine how designers use drawings, work in groups and with
computers. After all designers are not philosophers for whom the
thought process itself is centre of study, nor does the designer
resemble Rodin's 'Thinker' who sits in solitary mediation. Essentially
the designer's thinking is directed towards some physical end
product the nature of which must be communicated to others who
may help to design it and to construct it.

To begin with, however, we need to study thinking itself and, in the next chapter, that precious and wonderful phenomenon of creativity which is so central to design. The history of cognitive psychology reveals many conflicting views about the nature of thought and the thought process from the most mechanistic to the most mythical. We begin with a problem familiar to those who study design. The word 'thinking', like the word 'design', is used in so many ways in everyday language that we need to specify exactly which versions of it we are examining.

There is the sort of thinking we do when we say are trying to think where we left something. This is essentially remembering and is obviously vital to design but again not the central task. There is the use of the word 'think' which we apply to the act of concentrating or simply paying attention, as when we say 'think what you are doing'. There is the use of the word to mean belief as when someone says what they 'think'. There is the thinking which psychologists would label 'autistic' but which ordinary people might describe as day-dreaming. This leads to a sort of uncontrolled stream of consciousness which in itself can be useful to designers but is certainly not their main tool. There is the sort of imaginative thinking we do which might be described as fantasy anchored in reality. Here we might 'think' through some scenario which is possible but not actual. Clearly this is very much what designers do. Finally there is the sort of thinking which we might call 'reasoning'. This is self-consciously done with a deliberate attempt to control the direction of thought towards some intended end product but where some obstacles have to be overcome. This is reflective thought and problem-solving.

In Chapter 9 we explore creative and imaginative thinking, but it is the last of these many forms of thinking that we are primarily studying here. The great British philosopher and student of thought, Ryle (1949) described even this last version of thinking as being 'polymorphous'. Just as two farmers might do quite different things, with one rearing sheep and another reaping crops, Ryle famously explained, we still recognise them both as farmers. So it is with thinking.

Theories of thinking

This subject is not an easy one since it takes us quickly into the psychology of thinking and to some extent of feeling and emotion. So much has been written about the phenomenon of thought and the business of thinking by philosophers and psychologists that we cannot possibly do justice to the subject here. However, this chapter attempts the almost impossible, which is a brief survey and summary of the key points from these debates which seem important to the study of design.

Cognitive psychology is one of the most problematic fields of science since it involves investigation of something we cannot see, hear or touch. We know it is going on, and we all think throughout our lives without worrying about it too much, but thinking about thinking is another matter. In terms of modern western psychology, the earliest theories of thinking were very basic indeed. In fact the 'behaviourist' theories of thinking hardly admitted that thinking was any more than very mechanistic behaviour which just happened to go inside the head. The Gestalt psychologists were more interested in how we solved problems, and more recently the cognitive science approach has tried to study humans as information processors.

The behaviourists

The behaviourist Thorndike (1911) believed that human intelligence comprises only one basic process, the formation of associations. In fact the behaviourists were reluctant to admit that humans could be distinguished from other species by our abilities to think at a high level. Following Thorndike's early writings many behaviourist psychologists tried to explain thinking purely in terms of direct associative links between stimuli and responses. They even went so far as to argue that thinking is really only sub-vocal speech or 'talking to ourselves'. Indeed some experimenters found evidence of peripheral muscular activity during thinking but, of course, they failed to show that this was actually the thinking itself. Eventually the idea was modified suggesting that the muscular activity was so small as to have no effect save to act as feedback to the thinker. The idea behind such an apparently curious notion was that in this associationist model of thought, each of our responses could be fed back to act as another stimulus eliciting yet a further response. Writers such as Osgood and Berlyne eventually abandoned the search for 'muscular thought' and introduced the notion of purely cortical responses. For Berlyne (1965), patterns of thought result from us choosing from a variety of responses which we associate with each stimulus. The choice is made simply by selecting the strongest associative link although these links can be strengthened or weakened by our experience of life.

In essence the behaviourist view is that it is unnecessary to hypothesise a complex mental mechanism where behaviour can be explained without one. This follows the sound scientific principle of not inventing complex theories when simple ones will do, but can the behaviourists adequately explain intelligent thought? Their theories have appeared most successful in explaining behaviour such as learning and the acquisition of physical skills. The rat in the psychologist's maze can be seen as learning to associate the response 'left' or 'right' with the stimulus of each junction. Thorndike expanded this simple idea by placing cats in puzzle boxes where a variety of bolts or catches needed to be released to open the cage. The cats escaped by trial and error and thus apparently learned to solve a problem. Behaviourists have thus tended to explain problem-solving or goal-directed thinking in terms of successive mental trial and error. Actually the associationist model of thought seems more applicable to imaginative thought or daydreaming. Here the thinker is not wilfully controlling direction but, rather, is allowing the thought stream to wander. However this must wait until the next chapter.

The Gestalt school

However satisfactory or not their theories may be the behaviourists have contributed little which may be used by designers wishing to improve their thinking skills. It was not until the arrival of the Gestalt school of psychology that we begin to find material useful for explaining design thinking. The Gestalt school established a tradition of studying problem-solving which is continued today by such writers as Edward de Bono. Gestalt theories of thinking concentrate on processes and organisation rather than mechanisms. Wertheimer (1959) saw problem-solving as grasping the structural relationships of a situation and reorganising them until a way to the solution is perceived. This already begins to sound more like designing than Thorndike's cats, but Wertheimer went even further. He maintained that this mental reorganisation of the situation is achieved by applying various mental modes of attack which still persist today in creativity tools such as those advocated by popularist writers. These mental tricks include trying to redescribe the problem in another way and the use of analogy as a way of shifting the mental paradigm. As we shall see later this forms the basis of a number of quite recently proposed design techniques. Whereas the behaviourists used animals to explain thought, the Gestaltists used animals to show the absence of human-like thought. The Gestaltists were also very interested in perception and, therefore, stressed the importance of context in thought. De Groot's use of words in describing Kohler's experiments with apes is most revealing:

> We humans are struck by the inability of these otherwise quite intelligent animals to take a ring off a nail; a possibility that we immediately see. Due to our experience with nails and rings and their usage, we see the situation in a totally different way than the ape does. Similar examples can be given touching upon the relation between adults and children.
>
> (De Groot 1965)

Thus for De Groot thinking depends upon acquiring the ability to recognise relationships, patterns and complete situations. In his study of chess De Groot shows how experienced chess players 'read' situations rather than 'reason them out' as do the less experienced. Thus chess masters can play so many games simultaneously simply because each time they see a board they are able to recognise the pattern of the game. This 'schooled and highly specific way of perceiving' combined with a 'system of reproductively available methods in memory' (De Groot 1965) produces a rapid and inscrutable response which, to the uninitiated observer, looks like an intuitive flash of genius. Paradoxically, chess masters may also spend far longer examining a situation than their less experienced counterparts simply because they can see more problems, perhaps further ahead, than the average player. Anyone who has watched an experienced designer at work will recognise this description. The designer may appear to be drawing in a very natural and relaxed manner as if no effort were involved at all. As Bruner puts it the designer must 'go beyond the information given' and see possibilities which others may fail to discover for themselves but still recognise as useful, appropriate and beautiful when they are presented.

Markus listed four basic sources of information available in a design decision-making situation: the designer's own experience, others' experience, existing research and new research (Markus 1969a). It is perhaps the inevitable mixing of these sources which contributes to designers' seemingly random behaviour, sometimes apparently intuitively leaping to conclusions whilst at other times making very slow progress.

The Gestalt psychologists paid particular attention to the way we represent the external world inside our heads. Most notably Bartlett in his now classical studies of thinking (Bartlett 1958) and remembering (Bartlett 1932) developed the notion of an internalised mental image which he called the 'schema'. The schema represents an active organisation of past experiences which is used to structure and interpret future events. In a series of experiments in which Bartlett asked subjects to remember drawings and reproduce them perhaps several weeks later, he showed how such memory is dependent on the drawings being meaningful. That is, we must have already formed the appropriate schemata in advance to interpret and appreciate events. The developmental psychologists such as Bruner and Piaget have shown how human thought processes develop in parallel with the child's formation of such basic and fundamental schemata.

I have for many years tried to teach first year architectural students to remember how they 'see' architecture before they develop the sophisticated concepts which architects use to debate the subject. A real problem for designers is that they have so many more concepts or schemata for describing the objects they design that they genuinely do 'see' them differently to those for whom they design. This can easily lead to a result known as 'architects' architecture', which can only be appreciated and enjoyed by other architects!

The cognitive science approach

The advent of electronic communication devices and information processing machines such as computers has generated a new perspective on human thought. Information theory has provided a metric which allows the amount of information processed during a problem to be measured. Psychologists have attempted to uncover the mechanisms with which we think by measuring our performance on simple tasks against the amount of information processed. Such writers as Posner appear to bridge the gap between the behaviourists and Gestaltists by concentrating on mechanisms while still viewing thinking as a strategic skill. Garner's (1962) influential book on cognitive psychology reports experiments in short-term memory, discrimination, pattern perception, and language and concept formation all using information theory to provide the yardstick for human performance. Other workers in this field have proposed theories of human problem-solving based on the model of the computer program. The most famous application of this technique being the GPS (general problem solver) program of Newell, Simon and Shaw (1958). Such programs cause the computer to exhibit behaviour resembling such hitherto peculiarly human characteristics as 'purpose' and 'insight'. This has the potential to shatter some of the mystique surrounding work on thought processes by showing how sequences of very elementary information transformations could account for the successful solution of complex problems. Whether such simple processes are actually the basis of human thought is, of course, still open to considerable doubt. Unfortunately there are limitations to the usefulness of such computer programs as models since they rapidly become as complex as the processes they model.

The new cognitive approach to human thinking sees human beings as much more adaptable and genuinely intelligent organisms than the early behaviourist approach. It deals with process and operational function rather than physical mechanism, and it stresses the influence of the context in which problems are perceived on the thought process itself. The cognitive psychologists, while building on the Gestalt tradition, also follow on from the first flush of enthusiasm shown by psychologists for applying information theory to human thought, but are less fanatical about its potential. In his brilliant treatise on cognitive psychology Neisser (1967) points out that humans are different from machines from the very beginning of the perceiving and thinking process:

> Humans . . . are by no means neutral or passive towards incoming information. Instead they select some parts for attention at the expense of others, recording and reformulating them in complex ways.
>
> (Neisser 1967)

As we shall see in later chapters this phenomenon of our selective perception of problems has exercised the minds of many design methodologists who seek to devise ways of broadening designers' perceptions.

Perhaps the most important feature of the cognitive psychology approach to thinking is the new recognition of the existence of some kind of executive controlling function in the mind. Since cognitive psychology accepts that information is actively reorganised and reconstructed in memory rather than passively recorded and recalled, it follows that something must control this process. The existence of such an executive function was denied not only by classical association theory but also by the Gestaltists, however, more recent work on artificial intelligence has shown how executive routines in computer programs can control the order in which a very complex sequence of operations are performed in extremely flexible and responsive ways. There is not space here to do justice to this profound and fascinating subject but the interested reader will find brilliant and readable discussions of the matter in *Plans and the Structure of Behaviour* (Miller, Galanter and Pribham 1960) and the *Ghost in the Machine* (Koestler 1967). More recently the notion of a single executive has tended to become replaced by the idea of 'agents'. These mental agents look after our thinking just as the human agents we use in everyday life look after our affairs. We employ an estate agent, for example, to find people interested in buying our house, or perhaps to find houses we might like to buy. They thus work purposefully towards a relatively simple goal. A butler is perhaps the ultimate personal agent who operates by really understanding the wishes and aspirations of the master and who almost certainly then subcontracts work to a series of more specialised agents. If the cognitive psychologists prove to be right about executives and agents then we may expect to discover much more about the way we design. If we could understand the forces and operations which are responsible for switching our attention from one part of a problem to another or allowing us to reorganise our perceptions in new ways, we should be well on the way to understanding the design process.

The cognitive theorists' approach to thinking is also attractive to those who seek to understand the design process because it draws many parallels between thought and perception. Both primary and secondary processes are postulated, the primary thought process being a multiple activity like parallel processing in computers. These crudely formed thoughts are similar to the preattentive processes in vision or hearing being only drawn to our conscious attention if selected for detailed and deliberate elaboration by the secondary processes. It is in the secondary processes where all the real work is done. These processes have to be acquired and developed, and are dependent upon what is already memorised and the way material has been organised in primary processing. The cognitive theories thus lay great emphasis upon the way we organise perceived infor-mation and store it. Failure to recall is seen as analogous to a failure to notice something in a visual scene. Attention in perception and thought is seen as responsible for directing our thoughts and thus crucial to problem-solving. This theme will be taken up again in a rather less theoretical and more practical way when we consider methods of stimulating creativity and improving problem-solving skills in design.

However, there remain many problems with what has now become known as the cognitive science approach to thought. The actual per-formance of artificial intelligence remains so far behind that of human thought in so many ways that there must be doubts as to whether the two can ever be comparable. The cognitive science approach is strongest when dealing with well-ordered problem-solving situations rather than the ill-defined 'wicked' problems which are so characteristic of design. The 'computational theory of mind' underpins the whole of the cognitive science by assuming that thought can ultimately be reduced to a computation process. Now for a such a process to be possible there must be information on which to work. For that information to be capable of being processed it must conform to some rules akin to those of languages which determine the range of symbols and the allowed relationships. The cognitive scientist Jerry Fodor (1975) summarises this problem for us:

> If our psychological theories commit us to a language of thought, we had better take the commitment seriously and find out what the language of thought is like.
>
> (Fodor 1975)

In a book rather neatly entitled *Sketches of Thought*, Vinod Goel (1995) begins to confront these problems. He analyses the sketches produced by designers and finds it impossible to define a language sufficiently rigorously for the demands of the theory. In a later chapter we shall ourselves try to understand the central role of drawing and sketching in design. It is interesting, however, now to find that cognitive scientists are increasingly interested in design for the very reason that explaining it tests their theories to, and possibly beyond, their limits.

Types of thinking

At the beginning of this chapter we saw many types of thinking and concluded that reasoning and imagining were probably the most important to designers. Reasoning is considered purposive and directed towards a particular conclusion. This category is usually held to include logic, problem-solving and concept formation. When 'imagining', on the other hand, the individual is said to draw from his or her own experience, combining material in a relatively unstructured and perhaps aimless way. Artistic and creative thought as well as daydreaming are normally considered imaginative.

This kind of simplistic taxonomy is perhaps as misleading as it is apparently helpful. If reasoning and imagining were truly independent categories of thought, one should not be able to speak sensibly of 'creative problem-solving' or a 'logical artistic development', which are both quite meaningful concepts. Many kinds of problems, even in such apparently logical disciplines as engineering, can be solved creatively and imaginatively. Certainly art can be logical and have a well-developed structure. It is even possible to study the structure of art forms using the logic of information theory (Mueller 1967). Only rarely can one find an instance in the real world outside the psychologist's laboratory when one kind of thought is employed in isolation. The mode of thinking employed is obviously very much dependent on the nature of the situation. Most writers have concentrated on two main related factors, the thinker's relation to the external world, and the nature of the control exercised over those thought processes.

Murphy (1947) suggested that mental processes are bipolar, being influenced both by the external world and by inner personal needs. In his study of personality he was particularly interested in the individual's susceptibility to these two influences, and the resultant predominance of certain thinking styles which could be observed in the individual. The normal person is rarely entirely preoccupied by either one of these influences for any amount of time but, rather, alternates between the two. It is, however, possible to identify conditions under which one would expect the normal person to attend more to one influence than the other.

Problem-solving obviously requires more attention to the demands of the external world than to inner mental needs. In imaginative thinking, on the other hand, the individual is primarily concerned with satisfying inner needs through cognitive activity which may be quite unrelated to the real world. This seems to offer a psychological distinction which parallels that between design and art discussed earlier. Design is directed towards solving a real-world problem while art is largely self-motivated and centres on the expression of inner thoughts. This does not mean that imaginative thought can be excluded from the design process but that its product will probably always need evaluation by rational thought in order that the designer's work should be relevant to the real-world problem. The control and combination of rational and imaginative thought is one of the designer's most important skills and we shall discuss this crucial issue further in Chapter 9.

Thought and personality

A very popular approach to the study of human intelligence is represented by the factorial school. This work holds that human intelligence is not a simple factor but rather a whole series of related factors each of which may be present to greater or lesser extents in any individual. In his review of such work Guilford (1956) concluded that intellectual factors could be divided into the two major groups of thinking and memory. The thinking factors, which are of most interest here, Guilford further subdivided into cognition, production and evaluation.

The cognition factors of human thought have to do with becoming aware of and understanding classes of objects or ideas. This analytic ability to classify and recognise is of the utmost importance in everyday thought. For example, it would not be possible to study the differences between the structural systems employed in Romanesque and Gothic churches unless one could first recognise and classify such buildings. Guilford maintains that there are three ways of developing such a class system depending on whether the figural, structural, or conceptual content is used. Thus one might recognise a class by its figural properties. Children may initially recognise all four-legged animals as cows and only later look for further detail such as horns or tails. The second system of class recognition, by structural content, requires some functional relationship to exist between class members such as in the 'complete the series of symbols' type of IQ test question. Finally, one might recognise a class conceptually, such as architects or lawyers as being a group of people having passed certain examinations. For Guilford, then, these cognition factors influence our ability to define and understand problems whether they are to do with the appearance, function or meaning of objects. As Guilford himself points out, problems of figural and structural types abound in design and the ability to discriminate figural and structural classes is likely to be important to the designer.

Guilford's second group of thinking factors is concerned with the production of some end result. 'Having understood a problem we must take further steps to solve it' (Guilford 1967). Just as Guilford's cognition factors deal with the ability to recognise figural, structural and conceptual order, so the production factors hypothesise our ability to generate or produce these three kinds of order, but he found that the reality was not quite as neat as the model suggested:

> In the investigation of planning abilities it was hypothesised that there would be an ability to see or to appreciate order or the lack of it, as a feature of preparation for planning. It was also hypothesised that there would be an ability to produce order among objects, ideas or events, in the production of a plan. A single ordering factor was found.
>
> (Guilford 1967)

Thus Guilford found not two abilities to handle structure or order, but one which seemed to belong amongst the production factors rather than the cognition factors. This is a most interesting observation in the light of my own experiments quoted earlier which tended to show that architects discover about the structure of their problems by attempting to generate order in their solutions, and lends more weight to the argument that analysis and synthesis in design should not be regarded as entirely separate activities (Lawson 1972). Unfortunately, few psychologists seem to have considered both the recognition and production of order at the same time so for the time being we must accept the distinction since the literature on productive thinking has several useful concepts to offer the student of design.

Of course we must not assume that all architects are the same in their thinking style, and certainly not that all designers think in exactly the same way. In an interesting set of experiments Anton van Bakel (1995) has identified what he considers to be a series of identifiably different 'styles of architectural thinking', which he links to personality variations. His experiments and interviews with designers identified the sequence and emphasis of attention to various clusters of factors. Van Bakel chose to map out what he called the solution space as a triangle with the Program (or brief), the Concept (or design principle) and the Site. His categories do not map neatly on to the model of design problems used in this book, but we can see that his Program category of issues are in reality client-generated constraints, his Concept category are designer-generated constraints and his Site category are the chief source of external constraints for architects. These results clearly suggest some consistent variation of approach which could be a matter of personal preference linked with personality factors. However, more work needs to be done to see to what extent this varies with time and types of project before we can be sure just how these various factors really interact to determine the approach a particular designer will take to a particular project.

Productive thinking and design

When Wertheimer (1959) introduced the notion of 'productive thinking' he was primarily concerned with the directional quality of thought: 'what happens when, now and then, thinking forges ahead?' He showed with a whole series of small experiments how, when in a problem situation, thinking can be productive if it follows an appropriate direction. There are at least two fundamental questions which the experimental psychologist can ask here. Is the thinker trying to control the direction of his thinking and, if so, is the direction productive or not?

It is clear that mental processes are bipolar in their directional quality just as in their relation to the external world. The thinker can wilfully control the direction of his or her thought or he/she can allow it to wander aimlessly. Normally people do not solely engage in either one kind of thought, but rather they vary the degree of directional control they exercise. Here, then, is another distinction between design and art. Designers must consciously direct their thought processes towards a particular specified end, although they may deliberately use undirected thought at times. Artists, however, are quite at liberty to follow the natural direction of their minds or to control and change the direction of their thinking as they see fit. Bartlett's (1958) classification could be used to support this argument distinguishing as it does between the artist's thinking and that of the designer:

> There is thinking which uncovers laws of finished structure or of relations among facts of observation and experiment. There is thinking which follows conventions of society or of the single person, and there is other thinking still which sees and express standards.

Clearly the search for, and expression of, standards forms an important part of artistic thought. Designers must primarily indulge in Bartlett's first kind of thinking in order that they can appreciate the relationships between the given elements of the problem. The amount of purely expressionistic thinking that may take place is largely a function of the degree to which there is room for designer-generated constraints. As we have seen this varies considerably from problem to problem and there will thus inevitably be many instances when design and art are indistinguishable by using only this test.

Bartlett goes on to suggest two main modes of productive thinking which he calls 'thinking in closed systems' and 'adventurous thinking'. A closed system, in Bartlett's definition, has a limited number of units which may be arranged in a variety of orders or relations. Formal logic is such a closed system as are arithmetic, algebra and geometry. Closed system thinking can be highly creative as in the case of discovering new mathematical proofs or making anagrams. Bartlett identifies two processes in closed system thinking, interpolation and extrapolation. Here again we see the concept of the directionality of the thought process:

> Genuine thinking is always a process possessing direction. In interpol-
> ation the terminal point and at least some evidence about the way
> there are given, and all that has to be found is the rest of the way. In
> extrapolation what provided is some evidence of the way; the rest of
> the way and the terminal point have to be discovered or constructed.
> So it is in extrapolation that directional characters or properties are
> likely to become most prominent.
>
> (Bartlett 1958)

Although these two processes of interpolation and extrapolation are attractive concepts, when we consider real-world design conditions the situation loses some of its clarity. Rarely in design does one know or not know the terminal point but, rather, one has some information about it; it is a matter of degree. In some kinds of design one knows exactly where one will end up, in others one has very little idea.

Bartlett's other mode of productive thought, adventurous think-ing, is less clearly defined than thinking in closed systems. In this mode of thought the repertoire of elements which can be con-sidered is not prescribed. Indeed, adventurous thinking often depends for its success upon elements not normally related being brought together in a new way, hence its adventurous nature. Yet again, however, the distinction between adventurous thinking and thinking in closed systems becomes blurred when applied to design situations. It is certainly possible to find examples of closed system problems in design if we look for them. The problem of arranging tables and chairs in a restaurant certainly requires thinking in closed systems. Often, however, such examples do not bear too close an examination for rarely does the designer work exclusively with a kit of parts. If a particular arrangement of tables will not fit, the designer may often be free to try different sizes or shapes of tables or even alter the shape of the restaurant! Thus the ensemble of ele-ments in design problems is usually neither entirely closed nor entirely open. In fact we often recognise a creative response to a design problem as one where the designer has broken free of a conventionally restricted set of elements. Thus the rigid imposition of closed systems as in the case of system-building is seen by many designers as a threat to their creative role.

Throughout much of the literature on productive thought we find a variety of closely related binary divisions between, on the one hand, rational and logical processes and, on the other hand, intu-itive and imaginative processes. These two major categories have become known as convergent and divergent production (Fig. 8.1).

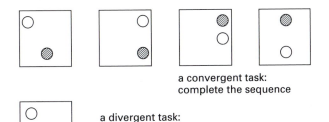

a convergent task:
complete the sequence

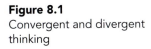

a divergent task:
what might this
represent?

Figure 8.1
Convergent and divergent
thinking

Typically the convergent task requires deductive and interpolative skills to arrive at one identifiably correct answer. Convergent ability is measured by many of the conventional IQ test problems and has been associated with ability in science. The divergent task demands an open-ended approach seeking alternatives where there is no clearly correct answer. Divergent ability can be measured by tests mistakenly called creativity tests such as 'how many uses can you think of for a brick' and divergent ability has been associated with skill in the arts. As we shall see in the next chapter these two ideas have frequently been grossly oversimplified and variously confused with intelligence and creativity. Guilford and others treat convergent and divergent thinking as separate and independent dimensions of ability which can occur in any proportions in an individual. Guilford (1967) maintains that, although few real-world tasks require exclusively convergent or divergent thought, the distinction is still valid and useful.

From our analysis of the nature of design problems it is obvious that, taken as a whole, design is a divergent task. Since design is rarely an optimisation procedure leading to one correct answer, divergent thinking will be required. However, there are likely to be many steps in any design process which themselves pose convergent tasks. True, such steps may eventually be retraced or even rejected altogether, but it would be absurd in the extreme to pretend that there are no parts of design problems which are themselves amenable to logical processes and have more or less optimal solutions. Design clearly involves both convergent and divergent productive thinking and studies of good designers at work have shown that they are able to develop and maintain several lines of thought in parallel (Lawson 1993a). However, the relationship between diverging, converging and parallel lines of thought is something we must leave until much later.

References

Bartlett, F. C. (1932). *Remembering*. Cambridge, Cambridge University Press.

Bartlett, F. C. (1958). *Thinking*. London, George Allen and Unwin.

Berlyne, D. E. (1965). *Structure and Direction in Thinking*. New York, John Wiley.

De Groot, A. D. (1965). *Thought and Choice in Chess*. The Hague, Mouton.

Fodor, J. A. (1975). *The Language of Thought*. Cambridge, Mass., Harvard University Press.

Garner, W. R. (1962). *Uncertainty and Structure as Psychological Concepts*. New York, John Wiley.

Goel, V. (1995). *Sketches of Thought*. Cambridge, Mass, MIT Press.

Guilford, J. P. (1956). 'The structure of intellect.' *Psychological Bulletin* **53**: 267–293.

Guilford, J. P. (1967). *The Nature of Human Intelligence*. New York, McGraw Hill.

Koestler, A. (1967). *The Ghost in the Machine*. London, Hutchinson.

Lawson, B. R. (1972). *Problem Solving in Architectural Design*. University of Aston in Birmingham.

Lawson, B. R. (1993). 'Parallel Lines of Thought.' *Languages of Design* **1**(4): 357–366.

Markus, T. A. (1969). 'Design and research.' *Conrad* **1**(2).

Miller, G. A., Galanter, E. et al. (1960). *Plans and the Structure of Behaviour*. New York, Holt Rinehart and Winston.

Mueller, R. E. (1967). *The Science of Art (the cybernetics of creative communication)*. London, Rapp and Whiting.

Murphy, G. (1947). *Personality: a biosocial approach to origins and structure*. New York, Harper and Row.

Neisser, U. (1967). *Cognitive Psychology*. New York, Appleton Century Crofts.

Newell, A., Simon, H. A. et al. (1958). 'Elements of a theory of human problem solving.' *Psychological Review* **65**(3).

Ryle, G. (1949). *The Concept of Mind*. London, Hutchinson.

Thorndike, E. L. (1911). *Animal Intelligence*. London, Macmillan.

van Bakel, A. (1995). *Styles of Architectural Designing: empirical research on working styles and personality dispositions*. Eindhoven, Technical University of Eindhoven.

Wertheimer, M. (1959). *Productive Thinking*. New York, Harper and Row.

9

Creative thinking

It is a well known fact that all inventors get their first ideas on the back of an envelope. I take a slight exception to this, I use the front so that I can incorporate the stamp and then the design is already half done.

Roland Emett

Genius is one per cent inspiration and ninety-nine per cent perspiration.

Thomas Alva Edison

What do we mean by creativity?

Most people would describe design as one of the most creative of human pursuits. The so-called creative arts include musical composition, painting, sculpture and the various forms of two- and three-dimensional design. However, creativity and creative thought can be applied just as much in science, medicine, philosophy, the law, management and many other fields of human endeavour. In the creative arts, including design, the whole point of the business is to create something which other people will experience and which is in some way or other original and new. No book on the thinking processes involved in design could be complete without some examination of the fundamentals of creativity and creative thought.

There is now a huge body of literature on creativity which has been studied extensively not only by psychologists but by philosophers and, more recently, by cognitive scientists and computer scientists. Some of our most profound insights into creativity also come from some famous and outstandingly creative people who have described and reflected on the processes involved. Then there are those who write about how to enhance or increase our creativity offering us techniques to use either as individuals or in groups.

Margaret Boden (1990) has proposed that it is useful to distinguish between what she calls H-creativity and P-creativity. H-creativity is that which results in novel and fundamentally new ideas in the history of the world. Thus Einstein's discovery of relativity or the moment when Archimedes leapt from his bath shouting 'Eureka!', are both moments of H-creativity. P-creativity, whilst less glamorous is none the less important to us here. For Margaret Boden rightly points out that an idea which is fundamentally novel to the individual mind is still of great significance, even though it may not necessarily be new to the world. Actually, in design there are often many developments of great significance for which it is quite hard to be sure just who had the H-creative idea and when. History tends to credit such developments to individuals as if they worked in splendid isolation from their colleagues and other designers.

When Alec Issigonis turned the internal combustion engine sideways, compressed the engine compartment, removed the traditional boot and styled the famous Mini, he created more than just another design for a car. By combining a number of new ideas together, he made us look at the car differently. Suddenly a motor car could become almost a fashion accessory, an extension of our clothes that could also transport us around cities. This was surely one of the most creative moments in the history of the automobile. Hundreds, perhaps thousands, of cars have been designed, but only occasionally does a design 'break the mould'. Other designs may be interesting, attractive, even exciting, but only occasionally is a design truly innovative. When Mario Bellini designed the famous Golfball typewriter for Olivetti he enabled us to see fundamentally new possibilities. The design replaced the traditional moving carriage carrying the paper from side to side, and instead kept the paper still, except for its feed, and moved the printing head. The further revolutionary idea of putting all the characters on a ball-shaped device which could rotate enabled the user to replace it and thus change fonts.

Many other examples can be found through the history of design which are innovative and mould breaking, and they often become what are regarded as 'classics' of design having a kind of timeless quality (Forty 1986). What these designs have in common is not just that they brilliantly solved the problems posed, but they changed the world irrevocably. They are the one-way valves of design history equivalent to the great discoveries of science. Once you have the Mini, a whole series of small, highly manoeuvrable, mass-produced city cars are possible. Small is no longer poor, but chic, fashionable and clever. Once you have the Barcelona Pavilion designed by Mies van der Rohe in 1929 a whole new generation of buildings become possible in which the relationship between walls, the means of supporting the roof and the spaces they define become changed in fundamental ways.

However, let us begin at the beginning, which is something that the creative mind may often not do, but on this occasion it seems necessary!

Some accounts of the creative process

The mathematician Henri Poincaré (1924) reflected on his own considerable creative achievements in mathematical thought and has left us with some insights about the processes involved. Typically he describes a process divided into phases of quite different kinds of thought. First a period of initial investigation of the problem in hand, followed by a more relaxed period of apparent mental rest. Next, an idea for the solution appears almost unbidden by the thinker probably at the most unexpected time and in the most unlikely place. Finally the solution needs elaboration, verification and development. Thus Poincaré describes his work for his first memoir on a series of mathematical functions known as Fuchsian. He talks of working hard for two weeks to prove that such functions could exist. During this period he sat at his desk for at least one or two hours each day trying out combinations without any positive result. However, one evening he unusually drank black coffee and could not sleep and records that 'ideas rose in crowds' (Poincaré 1924). By morning he had established a class of Fuchsian functions which he could then write down. Needing to take his ideas further to understand the relationship between these functions and some others he had discovered, his work was interrupted by a trip away from home on a geological excursion. He records how the travel made him forget his work but that later on the trip he was about to board a bus when 'at the moment I put my foot on the step the idea came to me' (Poincaré 1924).

This 'eureka' moment, as it is often called, seems quite characteristic of great creative moments. We have all heard how Archimedes is supposed to have leapt out of his bath crying 'Eureka' having solved a problem he had been working on for some time. Others such as Helmhotz and Hadamard offer similar descriptions, with the latter claiming to have woken with solutions in mind that were not there before sleep. More well known are the accounts of the famous chemist Friedrich von Kekule who discovered the ring structure of the benzene molecule while half asleep in front of the fire.

It is not just scientists and mathematicians who report the sudden unexpected emergence of ideas. Painters, poets and composers seem to have similar experiences. Mozart wrote in a letter: 'When I am, as it were, completely myself, entirely alone, and of good cheer – say travelling in a carriage, or walking after a good meal, or during the night when I cannot sleep; it is on such occasions that my ideas flow best and most abundantly.' The poet, Stephen Spender, talks of a 'stream of words passing through my mind' when half asleep. Famously Samuel Taylor Coleridge reported having the vision which led to the extraordinary images of Xanadu in Kubla Khan, after having taken opium. So it goes on.

We must, however, not get too carried away with the romantic notion of the creative leap into the unknown. Creative thinkers also characteristically work very hard. True the great geniuses seem to find life fairly easy, but for most of us ideas come only after considerable effort, and may then require much working out. It is generally recognised that although Mozart would write down music almost as he saw it in his mind's eye, Beethoven felt the need to work over his ideas time and time again. Musical scholars have expressed astonishment at the apparent clumsiness of some of Beethoven's first notes, but of course we are all astonished by what he eventually did with them.

Thus great ideas are unlikely to come to us without effort, simply sitting in the bath, getting buses or dozing in front of the fire is unlikely to be enough. This is what Thomas Edison means when he talks of the 'ninety-nine per cent perspiration' in the quotation at the start of this chapter. The general consensus is that we may identify up to five phases in the creative process (Fig. 9.1) which we will call 'first insight', 'preparation', 'incubation', 'illumination', and 'verification' (Kneller 1965).

The period of 'first insight' simply involves recognising that a problem or problems exist and making a commitment to solve them. Thus the problem situation is formulated and expressed either formally or informally in the mind. This period is normally quite short, but may last many years. In design situations, the problem is rarely clearly stated at the outset and this phase may require considerable effort. It is interesting that many experienced designers report the need for a clear problem to exist before they can work creatively. The architect/engineer Santiago Calatrava has produced some of the most imaginative and innovative structures of our time, but all in response to specific problems: 'It is the answer to a particular

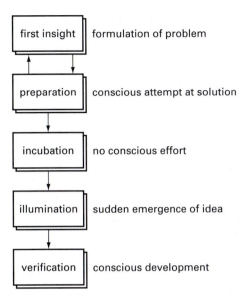

first insight | formulation of problem

preparation | conscious attempt at solution

incubation | no conscious effort

illumination | sudden emergence of idea

verification | conscious development

Figure 9.1
The popular five-stage model
of the creative process

problem that makes the work of the engineer . . . I can no longer design just a pillar or an arch, you know I need a very precise problem, you need a place' (Lawson 1994a). A similar statement is attributed to Barnes Wallis: 'There has always been a problem first. I have never had a novel idea in my life. My achievements have been solutions to problems' (Whitfield 1975). Of course Barnes Wallis had many novel and innovative ideas, but he and Calatrava seem to be telling us that they are most creative when the problem is imposed upon them from outside. This might seem in conflict with some recently fashionable views on design education that students should be given free and open situations in order to develop their creativity!

The next phase of 'preparation' involves considerable conscious effort in the search for a solution to the problem. As we have seen, in design at least, there is likely to be some coming and going between this and the first phase as the problem may be reformulated or, even, completely redefined as the range of possible solutions is explored. What seems common ground amongst those who write about creativity, however, is that this period of intense, deliberate, hard work is frequently followed by the more relaxed period of 'incubation'.

We have already heard how Poincare's incubation came from a journey, but such a possibility does not always present itself to the practising designer. Alexander Moulton is famous for the innovative bicycle which carries his name and the rubber cone spring suspension system employed by Issigonis on the Mini which later gave rise to the Hydrolastic and eventually Hydragas systems. Moulton (Whitfield 1975) advises: 'I'm sure from a creative point of view that it's important to have one or two dissimilar lines of thought to follow. Not too many, but just so that you can rest one groove in the mind and work in another.' Thus the practising designer and the design student alike need several things to work on in order not to waste time while one 'incubates'.

We have already documented the apparently magical moment of 'illumination' earlier in this chapter and little more needs to be said. Quite how and why the human mind works in this way is not certain. Some argue that during the incubation period the mind continues to reorganise and re-examine all the data which was absorbed during the intensive earlier periods. In a later chapter we shall examine some of the many techniques recommended for improving creativity. Most rely upon changing the direction of thinking, since it is generally recognised that we find it easier to go on in the same direction rather than start a new line of thought. The incubation period may also bring a line of thought to a stop, and when we return to the problem we find ourselves freer to go off in a new direction than we were before.

Finally we come to the period of 'verification' in which the idea is tested, elaborated and developed. Again, we must remind ourselves that in design, these phases are not as separate as this analysis suggests. Frequently the verification period will reveal the inadequacy of an idea, but the essence of it might still be valid. Perhaps this will lead to a reformulation of the problem and a new period of investigation, and so on.

Speed of working

We can see from the previous section that the creative phases of the design process are likely to involve alternating periods of intense activity and more relaxed periods when little conscious mental effort is expended. This is characteristic of the descriptions we have from many good designers about their working methods. An excellent example of this comes again from Alexander Moulton:

> Thinking is a hard cerebral process. It mustn't be imagined that any of these problems are solved without a great deal of thought. You must drain yourself. The thing must be observed in the mind and turned over and over again in a three-dimensional sort of way. And when you have gone through this process you can let the computer in the mind, or whatever it is, chunter around while you pick up another problem.

Moulton also talks of a 'fury of speed so that the pressure of creativity is maintained and doubt held at bay'. Philippe Starck talks of working intensively in order to 'capture the violence of the idea'. Starck famously claims to have designed a chair on an aircraft flight during the period of take-off while the seatbelt signs were on! In describing this intensive period of investigation a number of architects have likened it to juggling. Michael Wilford uses this analogy of a

> juggler who's got six balls in the air . . . and an architect is similarly operating on at least six fronts simultaneously and if you take your eye off one of them and drop it, you're in trouble'.
>
> (Lawson 1994a)

Richard MacCormac (Lawson 1994) echoes this idea and also points out that 'one couldn't juggle very slowly over a long period'. This explains the particular feature of being creative in design. It is rarely a simple problem with only one or two features, but more normally a whole host of criteria must be satisfied and a multitude of constraints respected. The only way to keep them all in mind at once, as it were, is to oscillate very quickly between them like a juggler. This of course may well not bring the solution immediately, as we have seen, that may come after a more relaxed incubation period.

The creative personality?

Already in this chapter we have studied the words of a number of famously creative people who are scientists, mathematicians, composers, poets or, of course, designers. This raises the question as to whether or not some people are naturally more creative than others. Is creativity correlated with intelligence or are there some relationships between creativity and personality? Psychologists have studied highly creative people in the search for answers to these questions.

One study of exceptionally creative scientists (Roe 1952) found that they were characteristically very intelligent, but also persistent and highly motivated, self-sufficient, confident and assertive. Designers have been a popular subject group for such studies. Mackinnon has conducted a whole series of studies of the creative personality and he explains his choice of architects:

> It is in architects, of all our samples, that we can expect to find what is most generally characteristic of creative persons . . . in architecture, creative products are both an expression of the architect, and thus a very personal product, and at the same time an impersonal meeting of the demands of an external problem.
>
> (Mackinnon 1962)

He found his creative architects to be poised and confident, though not especially sociable. They were also characteristically intelligent, self-centred, outspoken and, even, aggressive and held a very high opinion of themselves (Mackinnon 1976). Disturbingly it was the group of architects judged as less creative who saw themselves as more responsible and having a greater sympathetic concern for others!

Intelligence does seem to play some part in creative talent. Mackinnon recorded that while 'no feeble-minded subjects have shown up in any of our creative groups', this does not mean that very intelligent people are naturally highly creative. The kinds of tests used by psychologists to measure creativity normally differ from the traditional intelligence test. The typical intelligence test question asks the subject to find a correct answer, usually through logical thought, whereas the creativity test question is more likely to have many acceptable answers.

Getzels and Jackson in a famous and rather controversial study, compared groups of children who scored highly on creativity tests with those who performed well at the more conventional intelligence tests. They claimed to have identified many differences between these two groups of gifted children, not least of which was the image the children had of themselves which was largely shared by their teachers (Getzels and Jackson 1962). The so-called 'intelligent' children were seen as conforming and compliant and tending to seek the approval of their elders, while the 'creative' children were more independent and tended to set their own standards. The so-called 'creative' children were less well liked by their teachers than the 'intelligent' children. This, together, with Mackinnon's descriptions of creative architects tends to confirm the often held view that highly creative people may not be easiest to get on with, and are not generally bothered by this.

More recently, the differences between the 'intelligent' and 'creative' groups has been seen as a tendency to excel in either convergent or divergent thinking. Hudson has conducted a whole series of studies of groups of schoolboys measured to have high performance at these two types of thinking skills. He has shown that, generally, high convergent ability schoolboys tend to be drawn to the sciences while their more divergent counterparts show a preference for the arts (Hudson 1966). In fact, science is no more a matter of purely convergent production than the arts are exclusively a matter of divergent thought (Hudson 1968). This concentration on convergent or divergent thought may therefore prove something of a red herring in developing our understanding of creativity.

This rather popular tendency to regard divergent thinking as the core skill in the arts does not stand up to examination. A visit to the Clore Gallery at the Tate in London will reveal just how persistent and single-minded was the great British painter J. M. W. Turner. Painting after painting reveals an obsession with the problem of portraying light on the solid canvas. There is no great flight of ideas here, but rather a lifetime of trying to perfect a technique. A glorious and wonderfully expressive technique.

Conversely, we have already seen how successful scientists may be regarded as highly creative and how their ideas generate a complete shift in the way we see things. A dramatic demonstration of this can be found in a most revealing account of the work of James Watson and Francis Crick who discovered the beautiful double helical geometry of DNA (Watson 1968). The structure of DNA as we know it today simply could not be logically deduced from the evidence available to Watson and Crick. They had to make a leap into the unknown, a demonstration of divergent thought *par excellence*!

Creativity in design

Whilst we have seen that both convergent and divergent thought are needed by both scientists and artists, it is probably the designer who needs the two skills in the most equal proportions. Designers must solve externally imposed problems, satisfy the needs of others and create beautiful objects. Herman Hertzberger points this out when he describes what creativity means to him in architecture. He was discussing the problem of designing an entrance stair for a school:

> For me creativity is, you know, finding solutions for all these things that are contrary, and the wrong type of creativity is that you just forget about the fact that sometimes it rains, you forget that sometimes there are many people, and you just make beautiful stairs from the one idea you have in your head. This is not creativity, it is fake creativity.
>
> (Lawson 1994a)

These comments from Hertzberger suggests that we must be careful to draw the distinction between originality and creativity in design. In the competitive and sometimes rather commercial world of design, the novel and startlingly different can sometimes stand out and be acclaimed purely for that reason. But being creative in design is not purely or even necessarily a matter of being original.

The product designer Richard Seymour considers good design results from 'the unexpectedly relevant solution not wackiness parading as originality' (Lawson 1994a). The famous architect, Robert Venturi has said, for a designer, 'it is better to be good than to be original' (Lawson 1994a). Hertzberger, Seymour and Venturi all seem to be cautioning us against the recent trend to value the purely original-looking design without testing it to see if it really can fulfil the demands placed on it.

So we are beginning to get a picture of the creative process in design. It probably follows the phases of creativity outlined earlier, it involves periods of very intense, fast working rather like juggling, and the relating of many, often incompatible or at least conflicting demands. We have seen at the very beginning of this book how good design is often a matter of integration. George Sturt's cartwheels relied on the single idea of dishing to solve many totally different problems. This idea however is rarely easily found and often comes in a moment of 'illumination' after a long struggle.

It is hardly surprising then, that good designers tend to be at ease with the lack of resolution of their ideas for most of the design process. Things often only come together late on towards the end of the process. Those who prefer a more ordered and certain world may find themselves uncomfortable in the creative three-dimensional design fields. Characteristically designers seem to cope with this lack of resolution in two main ways: by the generation of alternatives and by using 'parallel lines of thought'.

Some designers seem to work deliberately to generate a series of alternative solutions early on, followed by a progressive refinement, testing and selection process. Others prefer to work on a single idea but accept that it may undergo revolution as well as evolution. Either way round, simply waiting for one idea to appear seems unlikely to prove very successful. It often seems to be the case that our thought processes have a will of their own. Once we have had an idea or started to look at a problem in a particular way it requires real effort to change direction. Creative thinkers in general and designers in particular seem to have the ability to change the direction of their thinking thus generating more ideas. We will discuss techniques for doing this as part of the design process in Chapter 12.

It is also clear that good designers characteristically have incomplete and possibly conflicting ideas as a matter of course, and allow these ideas to coexist without attempting to resolve them too early in the process. These 'parallel lines of thought' will also be discussed in detail in Chapter 12.

Education for creativity

In design at least, we have seen that there are a number of skills which experienced designers seem to have acquired that assist in releasing their creative potential. True, we have also seen that designers judged to be creative seem to share some common personality characteristics. The evidence is thus confusing, as it often is in psychology. Are we creative because we are born that way, or are we creative because we have learnt to be? We simply do not have a reliable answer to such a question, which in any case is not really the business of this book. Suffice it to say here that there is enough evidence that we can improve our creativity to warrant careful attention to the educational system through which designers pass.

In particular an issue here is the extent to which we should make design students aware of previous design work. One school of thought may suggest that students should be allowed a free and open-ended regime in which free expression is encouraged. Another might argue that designers have to solve real-world problems and they should pay attention to the acquisition of knowledge and experience.

Certainly there is much evidence on the side of the open, free and expressive school of thought. Many studies have, for example, demonstrated the mechanising effect of experience. Quite simply, once we have seen something done in a certain way, or done it ourselves, this experience tends to reinforce the idea in our minds and may block out other alternatives. In one of the most dramatic demonstrations of this phenomenon subjects were asked to perform simple arithmetic by pouring water between three jugs of different capacities. For each problem the actual size of the three jugs was varied, but for several problems in sequence the solution remained essentially the same. Later, a problem with an alternative and much simpler solution was presented, the subjects typically failed to notice and continued to use the more complex answer (Luchins and Luchins 1950).

An engineering lecturer once told me that he enjoyed teaching undergraduates because 'they didn't know certain things were difficult'. Consequently he found students occasionally came up with novel solutions to problems which had already been thought to be well understood. Whilst he may have been right, what he failed to point out was that this was actually very rare, and much more normally his students suggested solutions which were already known not to work or be satisfactory. One tends to remember student successes rather than their failures!

By comparison Herman Hertzberger in his excellent book *Lessons for Students of Architecture* suggests the importance of gaining knowledge and experience:

> Everything that is absorbed and registered in your mind adds to the collection of ideas stored in the memory: a sort of library that you can consult whenever a problem arises. So, essentially the more you have seen, experienced and absorbed, the more points of reference you will have to help you decide which direction to take: your frame of reference expands.
>
> (Hertzberger 1991)

It remains the case, however, that design education all over the world is largely based on the studio where students learn by tackling problems rather than acquiring theory and then applying it. Learning from your own mistakes is usually more powerful than relying on gaining experience from others! The popularity and success of the studio system has more recently led some design educationalists to assume that all learning can be this way. There are, however, problems with such a system, for the student is not only learning through the studio project, but is also usually performing and being assessed through it. What might have made a good learning experience may not necessarily have generated a high mark. Unfortunately, too, the emphasis in such studios tends to be on the end product rather than the process. Thus students are expected to strive towards solutions which will be assessed, rather than showing a development in their methodology. Often, too, the inevitable 'crit' which ceremoniously concludes the studio project tends to focus on retrospective condemnation of elements of the end product rather than encouragement to develop better ways of working (Anthony 1991).

A study of design education in schools (Laxton 1969), concluded that children cannot expect to be truly creative without a reservoir of experience. Laxton developed a rather elegant model of design learning using the metaphor of a hydroelectric plant (Fig. 9.2). He argued for a three-stage model of design education in which major skills are identified and developed. The ability to initiate or express ideas, Laxton argued, is dependent on having a reservoir of knowledge from which to draw these ideas. This seems similar

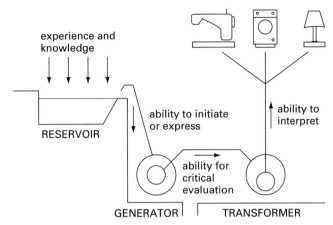

Figure 9.2
Laxton's ingenious hydro-electric
model of design learning

to Hertzberger's exhortation to students of architecture to acquire knowledge. Laxton's second skill is the ability to evaluate and discriminate between ideas. Finally, the transformation or interpretative skill is needed to translate ideas into the appropriate and relevant context. Kneller (1965) in his study of creativity makes a similar point:

> One of the paradoxes of creativity is that, in order to think originally, we must familiarise ourselves with the ideas of others . . . These ideas can then form a springboard from which the creator's ideas can be launched.

Design education, then, is a delicate balance indeed between directing the student to acquire this knowledge and experience, and yet not mechanising his or her thought processes to the point of preventing the emergence of original ideas.

References

Anthony, K. H. (1991). *Design Juries on Trial: the renaissance of the design studio*. New York, Van Nostrand Reinhold.

Boden, M. (1990). *The Creative Mind: Myths and Mechanisms*. London, Weidenfeld and Nicolson.

Forty, A. (1986). *Objects of Desire: design and society since 1750*. London, Thames and Hudson.

Getzels, J. W. and Jackson, P. W. (1962). *Creativity and Intelligence: Explorations with gifted children*. New York, John Wiley.

Hertzberger, H. (1991). *Lessons for Students in Architecture*. Rotterdam, Uitgeverij 010.

Hudson, L. (1966). *Contrary Imaginations: a psychological study of the English schoolboy*. London, Methuen.

Hudson, L. (1968). *Frames of Mind: ability, perception and self-perception in the arts and sciences.* London, Methuen.

Kneller, G. F. (1965). *The Art and Science of Creativity.* New York, Holt, Rinehart and Winston.

Lawson, B. R. (1994). 'Architects are losing out in the professional divide.' *The Architects' Journal* **199**(16): 13–14.

Lawson, B. R. (1994). *Design in Mind.* Oxford, Butterworth Architecture.

Laxton, M. (1969). Design education in practice. *Attitudes in Design Education.* London, Lund Humphries.

Mackinnon, D. W. (1962). *The nature and nurture of creative talent.* Yale University.

Mackinnon, D. W. (1976). 'The assessment and development of managerial creativity.' *Creativity Network* **2**(3).

Poincaré, H. (1924). *Mathematical creation.* Creativity. London, Penguin.

Roe, A. (1952). 'A psychologist examines sixty-four eminent scientists.' *Scientific American* **187**: 21–25.

Watson, J. D. (1968). *The Double helix: a personal account of the discovery of the structure of DNA.* London, Wiedenfield and Nicolson.

Whitfield, P. R. (1975). *Creativity in Industry.* Harmondsworth, Penguin.

10

Guiding principles

Working in philosophy – like work in architecture – is really more a working on oneself.

Wittgenstein

'Why,' said the Dodo, 'the best way to explain it is to do it.'

Lewis Carroll, *Alice in Wonderland*

Introduction

The designer does not approach each design problem afresh with a *tabula rasa*, or blank mind, as is implied by a considerable amount of the literature on design methods. Rather, designers have their own motivations, reasons for wanting to design, sets of beliefs, values and attitudes. In particular, designers usually develop quite strong sets of views about the way design in their field should be practised. This intellectual baggage is then brought by a designer into each project, sometimes very consciously and at other times rather less so. For some designers this collection of attitudes, beliefs and values are confused and ill formed, for others they are more clearly structured and for some they may even constitute something approaching a theory of design. Ultimately, some designers even go so far as to lay out these thoughts in books, articles or lectures. There is perhaps more of a tradition of publishing arguments and positions in some design fields than others. Architects, for example, seem more easily tempted to go into print than industrial designers! We might call these ideas 'design philosophies', although perhaps in many cases this would seem rather too grand a title. Whether they represent a collection of disjointed ideas, a coherent philosophy or even a complete theory of design, these ideas can be seen as a set of 'guiding principles'. This collection of principles is likely to grow and change as a designer develops. Sometimes they may be defended with considerable vigour and become highly personal territory. Their impact on the design process may be quite considerable.

We can explore the significance of these guiding principles in several ways. First, some designers seem able to articulate these principles very clearly and to hold them with great conviction, whilst others are less certain of their 'rightness'. Second, some designers seem to allow their guiding principles to dominate the process, whilst for others they are more in the background. Finally, we can examine the content of the ideas themselves and see how they relate to the model of design problems which we have already mapped out.

Morality and design

Design in general can be seen to pass through phases of relative certainty and doubt. Right now we seem to be in a post-modern period of pluralist confusion with no one widely held set of design theories. However, only relatively recently during the modern movement could design ideas be seen to be fairly generally accepted across the various design disciplines. Walter Gropius (1935) who was largely responsible for the creation of the Bauhaus, itself a cross-disciplinary school of design, announced this period of confidence by claiming that 'the ethical necessity of the New Architecture can no longer be called in doubt'. The great architect, James Stirling (1965) was to reflect that as a student he 'was left with a deep conviction of the moral rightness of the New Architecture'.

Such high levels of confidence were not new amongst architects. Roughly a century earlier Pugin had famously defended the Victorian Gothic revival not only as structurally honest, but as an architectural representation of the Roman Catholic faith. He saw the pointed arch as true and pure, and deprecated the use of its rounded counterpart: 'If we view pointed architecture in its true light as Christian art, as the faith itself is perfect, so are the principles on which it is founded' (Pugin 1841). All this is a little curious since some four centuries before that Alberti had studied Vitruvius and published his *De Re Aedificatoria*. Here he commended to Pope Nicholas V the whole idea of the Renaissance, rejecting the authority of the medieval stonemasons and therefore, of course, their Gothic arches! He too implied support from the 'ultimate authority' by advocating the use of proportions and design principles which he based on the human body! We come full circle back to the twentieth century to find Le Corbusier advancing his own variation on this theme in his famous treatise *The Modulor.* (Fig. 10.1) He proposed a proportional system based on numbers which he claimed could be derived from the ratios of parts of the human body and which, therefore, had some deep significance and rightness (Le Corbusier 1951).

It is not our purpose here to debate the rightness or otherwise of these ideas and others have covered the various theories of design far more thoroughly. What is of interest here is the apparent need to create an underpinning theory of design based on some kind of moral certainty. The moral stance in design has been explored by David Watkin (1977) who illustrates a series of such currently held positions and shows how they 'point to the precedent of Pugin when they suggest that the cultural style they are defending is an inescapable necessity which we ignore at our peril and that to support it is a stern and social duty'.

I have been privileged to study the work and process of a considerable number of leading architects and find none of them think of themselves as working within a 'style', and yet all have strong

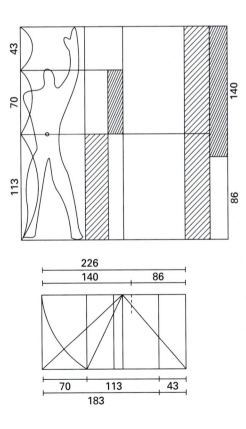

Figure 10.1
Le Corbusier claimed a higher level of authority for his proportional system by relating it to the human frame

intellectual programmes behind their work. This again seems to reflect Pugin's position since he regarded his work as based on 'not a style but a principle'. Many architects today regard the styles of architecture more as inventions of the critics than as sets of rules which they themselves follow. Robert Venturi was surely making this point when he said:

> Bernini didn't know he was Baroque . . . Freud was not a Freudian and Marx was not a Marxist.
>
> (Lawson 1994b)

However, the word 'style' is used comfortably and with enthusiasm in other design fields, most notably in fashion. The word 'fashion' itself has come to stand for something temporary and passing. Perhaps because buildings are more permanent and costly, architects feel the need to describe their work as supported by more lasting ideas. We have already seen how design may even be used to create a throw-away or disposable consumerist approach to artefacts (Chapter 7). Principles thus are seen to confer greater authority of correctness than styles!

Perhaps at this point it is worth remembering a definition of design which we saw in Chapter 3. 'The performing of a very complicated act of faith' (Jones 1966). Perhaps this helps us to understand the almost religious fervour with which designers will sometimes defend the 'principles' which underpin their work. It is indeed difficult to sustain the effort to bring complex design to fruition with having some inner belief and certainty. If anything is possible, how can a design be defended against those who may attack it. With the sophisticated technology available today almost anything is possible so it is perhaps comforting to have some principles which suggest fairly unequivocally that some ideas are more right than others!

But there are dangers here. The comfort of a set of principles may be one thing, but to become dominated by a doctrinaire approach is another. The architect Eric Lyons (1968) spoke out against this even whilst the modern movement was still in full swing:

> There is far too much moralising by architects about their work and too often we justify our ineptitudes by moral postures . . . buildings should not exist to demonstrate principles.
>
> (Lyons 1968)

This has been reflected more recently by Robert Venturi who has argued that:

> The artist is not someone who designs in order to prove his or her theory, and certainly not to suit an ideology . . . any building that tries

merely to express a theory or any building that starts with a theory and works very deductively is very dry, so we say that we work inductively.

(Lawson 1994b)

So we begin to get a picture that the design process is essentially experimental. Design theories, philosophies, call them what you will, are not usually too well defined. Each design can therefore be seen simultaneously not only to solve a problem but to gain further understanding of these more theoretical generic ideas. Herman Hertzberger, the great Dutch architect has described his famous Centraal Beheer office building as a 'hypothesis':

Whether it can withstand the consequences of what it brings into being, depends on the way in which it conforms to the behaviour of its occupants with the passing of time.

(Suckle 1980)

In fact, this building is remarkable and seminal in its attempt to deal with the social and personal lives of the people working in it, rather than seeing its occupants as cogs in some office machine. Hertzberger had already written extensively on his structuralist theory of architecture. Here he contrasted the design of tools with the design of instruments. The latter, he argued, are less specific and encourage people to take possession of them and become creative with them:

I try to make a building as an instrument so that people can get music out of it.

(Hertzberger 1991)

Some designers seem to see their whole career as a journey towards the goal of ultimate truth, whereas others seem more relaxed and flexible in their attitudes to the driving forces behind their work. The famous architect Richard Rogers tells us that:

One is constantly seeking universal rules so that one's design decisions do not stem from purely arbitrary preferences.

(Suckle 1980)

However, not all designers find it necessary to strive consciously for some underlying theory to their work. The architect Eva Jiricna, is well known for her beautiful 'High Tech' interiors which show a consistently thorough attention to the choice and jointing of materials, but she explains this very pragmatically:

It's not an abstract process. I think that if you are a painter or a sculptor then it's all very abstract but architecture is a very concrete job. I really think that all that philosophy is a false interpretation of what really happens. You get an idea, but that idea is not really of a very philosophical or conceptual thought. It is really something which is an expression on the level of your experience which is initiated by the question.

(Lawson 1994b)

This echoes something that I have often found to be the case when investigating the process of well-known designers. Critics have written explaining how we should interpret their work and often this has become received wisdom. However, the designers themselves claim not to have intended such an interpretation. In Eva Jiricna's case this has amusingly even extended to the symbolic intentions behind her clothes which are almost invariably black. In fact Eva herself explains this as practical rather than symbolic, allowing her to her to 'go to the office in the morning, to site in the afternoon, and to the theatre in the evening, so it's extremely practical'.

Critics, then, may infer what the designer has not implied and we must be very wary of reaching conclusions about the process which created the object that is being criticised!

Decomposition versus integration

Designers vary in the extent to which they portray their work as driven by a limited portfolio of considerations and in the extent to which they wish to make this explicit. We have seen earlier in this book how good design is often an integrated response to a whole series of issues. The cartwheels made in George Sturt's wheelwright's shop were dished for a whole range of reasons. However it is also possible to view the designed object as a deconstruction of the problem. Even before the idea of deconstruction as a philosophical game became popular some designers had a preference for articulating their work in a technical sense. Richard Rogers prefers to 'clarify the performance of the parts' and thus he separates functions so that each part is an optimum solution to a particular problem and plays what he calls 'a single role'. Such a design process was very much implied by Christopher Alexander's famous method reviewed in an earlier chapter which depended on breaking the problem down into its constituent parts. By contrast Herman Hertzberger (1971) actually advocates the more integrated approach where ambiguity and multiplicity of function are deliberately designed into objects. He shows, for example, in a housing scheme, a simple concrete form outside each dwelling can carry a house number, serve to house a light fitting, act as a stand for milk bottles, offer a place to sit, or even act as a table for an outdoor meal. In this case

Hertzberger is far from trying to optimise this object to any one particular function but rather seeing it as a sort of compromise.

As time passes different issues are inclined to come into the spotlight and assume a foreground role in design. In some cases this may simply be a matter of fashion and style, but in other cases this may result from the wider social, economic or political agenda of the time. One such issue in recent years is undoubtedly the question of 'green' design. Some designers have written books and even designed almost as a form of propaganda in order to promote a change of attitude more widely. For example, Robert and Brenda Vale have written many papers and books following on from their famous 'autonomous house' (Vale and Vale 1975) and they have constructed a number of houses for themselves and others demonstrating these principles. By contrast Richard Burton (1979), who established the first ever energy policy for the RIBA was careful to issue a caveat:

> Energy in building has had something of a fanfare lately and maybe it will have to continue for some time, but soon I hope the subject will take its correct place among the twenty other major issues a designer of buildings has to consider.
>
> (Burton 1979)

Perhaps, in the context of this book, Richard Burton is warning us that we must look carefully indeed at a process which from the outset seeks to demonstrate the importance of a limited range of problems. In general the design process needs to be more balanced and almost by definition less focused than some polemical work might require.

The future

We have already seen how design is prescriptive rather than descriptive. Any piece of design contains, to some extent, an assertion about the future. As Cedric Price puts it in relation to architecture:

> In designing for building every architect is involved in foretelling what is going to happen.
>
> (Price 1976)

Designers then are guided in their work by both their own vision of the future and their level of confidence in this vision. The strongest visions can easily become rather frightening, especially when in the minds of designers such architects can have such a significant impact on peoples' lives. The futurist movement in art in the early part of the twentieth century became confused with architecture in the mind of the Italian architect Sant-Elia. In his 1914 *Manifesto of Architecture* Sant-Elia declared that:

> We must invent and rebuild ex novo our modern city like an immense and tumultuous shipyard, active mobile and everywhere dynamic, and the modern building like a gigantic machine.

Sant-Elia's future vision was a highly technological one with the citizens of his cities rarely to be seen in his images. (Fig. 10.2) This confidence and assertion of architecture as social engineering were to take the Futurists down the road to fascism and we must be thankful that their confident vision remained largely unrealised. This link between a confident belief in the future and technology is also often to be found associated with right-wing political ideology. In his book, *Man Made Futures*, Weinberg (1974) is quite explicit about this connection:

> Technology has provided a fix – greatly expanded production of goods – which enables our capitalist society to achieve many of the aims of the Marxist social engineer without going through the social revolution Marx viewed as inevitable.

(Weinberg 1974)

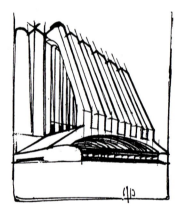

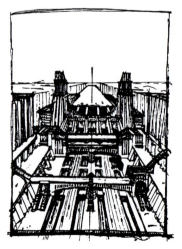

Figure 10.2
A confident set of futuristic images by Sant-Elia from which people are entirely excluded

Weinberg argued that the 'fixes' provided by technology included 'fixing' the problems of poverty and even 'fixing' the problems of war through the nuclear deterrent. As one of the editors of the book, Nigel Cross, comments several years later, 'Weinberg is apparently suggesting that a belief in technology is demonstrably superior or more effective than either Marxism or Christianity'.

More recently we have become less confident both about the future and about the power of technology to solve our problems. These are not, therefore, generally times in which we find designers having Utopian dreams. Such as they are, today's Utopias are actually nostalgic such as the romantic village of Poundbury designed by Leon Krier to demonstrate the architectural theories of the Prince of Wales, laid out in his 'Vision of Britain'.

Content

The content of designers' guiding principles is as varied as the designers themselves. It is hardly the purpose of this book to attempt some comprehensive tour of all the guiding principles at work in the minds of the designers of today or of the past. However, such a review might itself form the basis of an interesting history of the various design fields. In fashion, for example, clothes not only change in style but also the underpinning ideas which give rise to those styles can be seen to change too. Clothes cannot be entirely separated from the social mores of their times, particularly with regard to the extent to which the body is revealed, concealed, disguised or even distorted. At times fashion can be seen to be primarily about image, and at other times about practicality. At times there is an obsession with colour and there are phases of interest in materials or textures.

So it is with industrial design, architecture, interior design and the graphic design fields. In order to explore these ideas a little further we will use the model of design problems developed earlier in the book as a way of structuring this investigation.

Client

The attitude towards client-generated constraints varies from designer to designer. Two well-known twentieth century British architects illustrate this variation. Sir Denys Lasdun clearly sees the architect as having a responsibility to lead the client forward:

> Our job is to give the client not what he wants but what he never even dreamt he wanted . . . what I have previously said about the client affects the methodology of design.
>
> (Lasdun 1965)

By contrast at around the same time, Sir Basil Spence was to portray the architect as a 'tailor who measures the thin chap and the fat chap and makes them both comfortable'. For Spence the architect was most definitely not a reformer.

I have found that one of the characteristics which many very good designers share in common is the extent to which they focus on the client and see the client playing a role in the very design process itself. Certainly a supportive and understanding client can make an enormous difference to the success of a project, as Michael Wilford has pointed out:

> Behind every building of distinction is an equally distinctive client, not necessarily high profile, but one who takes the time and trouble to comprehend the ideas of the architect, is supportive and enthusiastic, who is bold, willing to take risks and above all can hold his or her nerve during the inevitable crises.
>
> (Wilford 1991)

A heartfelt plea to the client for this understanding comes from Denise Scott Brown who talks of the client 'letting you be on their side'. Her partner, Robert Venturi explains how important and yet delicate this can be:

> you need not to worry about saying something stupid . . . you need sometimes to think out loud and be free to say stupid things . . . and if the client has faith this can often lead to something . . . we think that architecture has to derive from collaboration and we learn a lot from the client . . . we get some of our best ideas from clients, we love collaborating with them.
>
> (Lawson 1994)

Perhaps only the best designers have the confidence to allow their clients into what is a delicate and easily disturbed creative process.

Users

As we have already seen, the needs of the clients of design and the users of design are not always exactly the same. If a designer is lucky, the client will express a single clear view on all matters relating to the brief, although this is by no means always the case. Users, however, are all different and likely to make differing demands on the final design. The different kinds of users involved in buildings often makes this extremely complex. In designing hospitals for example, I often found that what seemed to be convenient for the nursing staff was rather disliked by the patients. In investigating buildings in use I have found that what students think makes a good lecture theatre can be almost diametrically opposed to the views of their lecturers (Lawson and Spencer 1978). Herman Hertzberger positively revels in this mass of conflicting demands since his guiding principles are built around a general concern for the inhabitants of buildings as people rather than as representatives of the roles they play (Fig. 10.3). Resolving the potential conflicts between these roles appeals to him:

> I prefer, for instance, to make a school over making a house, because the house I feel has too much of a constraint just to follow the particularity and idiosyncrasy of just one person or couple. I prefer to have a school where you have a board, you have teachers, you have parents and you have children, and the users are all of them.
>
> (Lawson 1994b)

In architecture, then, there are sometimes opportunities to involve the users of buildings in the design process. One of the most

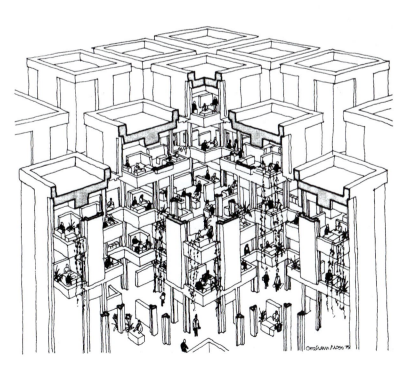

Figure 10.3
Herman Hertzberger's famous office building for Centraal Beheer at Appledorn in Holland is an example of a user-centred approach to architecture

notable attempts to explore the implications of this is to be found in the housing work of the Dutch architect Habraken who believed that 'the process simply does not work if the occupants are not involved'. This led Habraken to write his famous treatise, *Supports*, in which he advocated the deliberate separation of those parts of the solution which he thought must be determined by the architect from those which he felt must be more capable of being determined by the users. This leads to a design process which consciously allocates responsibilities between designer and user (Habraken 1972).

Practical

The practical constraints offer fertile ground for guiding principles. For those designers who are fascinated by the materiality and process of making things, these practical constraints can offer major generative design ideas. The so called 'high-tech' school of design depends on the glorification of the technology and the expression of the technology in a very self-conscious way.

In architectural design, the business of making buildings stand up, span large spaces and withstand the forces of nature offer a whole range of structural ideas. For some designers the structural elements should describe how they do their job. Thus Richard Rogers tells us that he designs each structural member to be efficient and reflect the nature of the loads imposed upon it:

> Tension chords become the thinnest of solids, compression members are steel tubes; the differing diameters describe the various loads each member must carry.
>
> (Suckle 1980)

By contrast, Arthur Erikson tells us that:

> I have long preferred in spite of structural inefficiency, the visual ambiguity of columns and beams being the same size. Logically the beams should be narrow and deep for bending moments and the columns in compression proportionally smaller, but this makes for a great deal of visual tension.
>
> (Suckle 1980)

The great architect and engineer Santiago Calatrava studied moving folding structures for his doctorate. To this day he retains a keen interest in the idea of 'dynamic equilibrium' in which structures balance but in rather more athletic ways than the more normal, rather static forms used in architecture. Calatrava is fascinated by the human body and in particular its ability to move and thus take up a variety of

configurations each of which is stable and suitable for resisting a particular set of forces. The exhibitions of his work show how he explores
these ideas in abstract sculptures as well as in realised designs:

> It is very good to do a sculpture because you can have it at home and
> look at it every night, you can meditate on it and turn it. This is the only
> quiet moment in the whole process to bring a project to realisation . . .
> this focus is very important because it gives you a certain authority . . .
> you can also show it to people and they understand.
>
> (Lawson 1994b)

Calatrava is also fascinated by the properties of materials rather
than just the structural configuration of his work:

> For me the antagonism between materials, especially materials like steel
> and a material like concrete or stone creates a simple dualism which you
> can see sometimes in the sculptures. I have done this with two or three
> materials hitting each other.

Often we find the design ideas are not as new as they first seem,
and in this case Calatrava himself readily acknowledges the historical influence of Violet-le-Duc on his work. The interior designer
and architect Eva Jiricna also uses a design process very much
driven by decisions about materials:

> In a way material dictates the concept . . . and materials are not inter-
> changeable . . . to me the material really is the starting point of the
> story.
>
> (Lawson 1994b)

Keeping engineering and technology in the background can be a
guiding principle as much as expressing it. The product designer,
Dick Powell considers that they 'should simply be slaves of the
market place':

> It's people who determine what products are. We've been entrusted
> with the task of trying to reflect what people want. We have to bend
> technology to suit that purpose . . . our work is a constant compromise,
> a half-way point between artistic creation and a logical engineering
> approach to design.
>
> (Gardner 1989)

This difficult balancing act is referred to by the architect Ian Ritchie
who has something of a 'high-tech' reputation but who nevertheless does not feel that technology is a design generator for him:

> When people ask me this question I use an analogy. I describe this
> beautiful parrot sitting on my shoulder – multi-coloured, very beautiful –
> called 'technology'. Very often he leaps off the shoulder and onto the

paper and shits all over it before we've actually started thinking and you have to get hold of him and stick him back up there. He is tame, he does behave himself and he doesn't always end up in the project at all, but he's there and we talk to him all the time.

(Lawson 1994)

Radical

The radical constraints may offer the most obvious source for a set of guiding principles in design, but actually it turns out not to be so. The very central purpose and reason for existence of the object being designed will inevitably be at the centre of the attention of any good designer, and so hardly needs any further focus. Of course such constraints are also often so specific and local to the problem that they rarely offer a opportunity for more generic investigation. Some designers, however, do become known for specialising in certain kinds of problems and, thus, sets of radical constraints. Some architects certainly have reputations for designing certain types of buildings such as hospitals, offices or housing.

Of all the constraints, however, perhaps the radical issues are those which most 'get under the skin' of designers. To hear the architect Frank Duffy lecture about office design is to become aware of his depth of study and interest in the subject. This interest has led to a series of publications which have a wider concern than normally expected of an architect (Duffy 1993). Duffy has for many years worked on the design of office buildings but his experience has taken him beyond the mere building to the socio-economics of the workplace itself. The product designers Seymour Powell have been responsible for a growing list of new motorcycles working for Norton, Yamaha, MZ and BSA. The work is innovative and much admired, but a visit to their design practice reveals a deeper interest. The studios are housed in a converted chapel which is set back slightly from the road and usually displays a wide range of motorcycles belonging to the members of the practice. Richard Seymour talks about these machines with an enthusiasm and dedication which makes it clear that they are not just part of his job, but part of his life!

Thus, when Duffy talks about a particular office design or Seymour about a specific motorcycle, it is clear that there is a passion which has underpinned the design process and a set of attitudes which informed it but which transcends any one design.

Formal

The visual composition of objects, and in particular designed objects, is usually of interest to most designers. For some, however, formal constraints can be assembled into geometric and proportional rules which form continuing sets of guiding principles. We have already discussed the work of the classical architects such as Vitruvius and the Renaissance architects such as Palladio and Alberti who studied their systems. We have seen even a modernist architect like Le Corbusier laying down proportional systems, albeit less rigid ones. The use of geometric principles in design has more recently found a new lease of life in the work of some of those interested in the application of computers to design. Here it is possible to introduce these rules in the form of 'shape grammars' to a computer so that it may produce designs which follow the underlying principles of a particular designer or stylistic period.

The power of formal geometry to offer guiding principles to architects was studied for many years at the Martin Centre in Cambridge (March and Steadman 1974). These studies showed how geometry may be used to understand both abstract and concrete formal possibilities. Such branches of mathematics as topology and Boolean algebra and, more recently, fractal geometry can offer designers powerful tools for describing and generating form. In some cases such studies have led to an understanding of how traditional designs work, whilst others simply offer pattern books of ideas. A recent interest in the tesselations and other patterns of Islamic and oriental art has opened up new possibilities, especially for decoration which is beginning to reappear after a period of minimalism.

The use of these geometrical ideas as guiding principles is evident in the work of the architect Richard MacCormac, once a student at the Martin Centre, and famous for a series of highly admired domestic scale buildings often involving some element of repetition such as university halls of residence:

> We look for a clear geometric analogy for the content of the problem. All our schemes have a geometric basis, whether it is the pinwheel arrangement of Westoning, the courtyard system of Coffee Hall flats and Robinson College, the specific tartan grid of the Blackheath houses or the circle-based geometry of Hyde Park Gate . . . Geometry is used as a means of making distinctions between one kind of place and another so that different activities take place in situations which have their own identity and, through use, can increase their distinctiveness.
>
> (MacCormac and Jamieson 1977)

Richard MacCormac describes how his practice has built up what he calls a 'repertoire of tricks' which seem to draw heavily not only on his time at the Martin Centre but also on his study of the work of the great English architect Sir John Soane. In the catalogue which accompanied the exhibition of the work of James Stirling and Michael Wilford, at the RIBA in 1996, Michael Wilford wrote of the 'series of interlocking strategies' which they had developed over three decades of work:

- The expression of the primary functional activities of the building through a rich, hierarchical composition of formal geometries.
- Incorporation of coherent circulation patterns to provide clear routes and connections in and around the building.
- Development of spatial sequences to reinforce the circulation patterns and functional activities.
- Articulation of spaces in and around the building to enhance the public realm.
- Subordination of structure and systems to formal and spatial objectives.
- Use of solid and void, light and shade, colour, texture, a limited pallet of materials and landscaping in support of formal and spatial objectives.

This can be seen as a remarkably clear description of a set of guiding principles mainly centred around developing formal constraints to organise and express the radical functions and circulation of people. There is also a clear wish to relegate the practical constraints to a lower level. Elsewhere in the same catalogue Michael Wilford claims that 'architecture, as a pragmatic art, cannot be about style'. Critics have noted over the years how the work of Stirling, first with Gowan and then with Wilford, went through a series of phases. Perhaps the critics would do better to concentrate less on the superficial apparently stylistic changes and pay more attention to these guiding principles which can be seen to have an increasingly consistent influence on Wilford's work with Stirling, and since.

Symbolic

In general the modern movement in design was a period of emphasis on the formal rather than the symbolic and, in this sense can be interpreted as another cycle in the historical tendency for periods of formalism and expressionism or classicism and romanticism to alternate. Even the explicitly expressive and communicative design fields such as graphic and stage design went through periods which might be thought to be austere or, even, brutal. The product designer, Richard Seymour makes this point in describing the approach of Seymour/Powell who try to give their designs a 'personality':

> Unfortunately it doesn't lend itself to methodology, though many designers try . . . back in the 1960s and 1970s the idea was that if you got the ergonomics right, the moulding right, the material right and usability and function correct, then in a mysterious way it would make itself into a good design . . . but we don't do that, we start with the total product.
>
> (Gardner 1989)

Typefaces without serifs were popular and theatrical sets became indicative rather than an attempt faithfully to recreate the scene. Richard Buckle, describing the work of the famous ballet designer Sophie Fedorovitch, 'believed in cutting down the decor and dresses of a ballet to the minimum'. However, such minimalism still had its symbolic job to do and Buckle explains how Fedorovitch achieved this trick in her acclaimed set for *Nocturne*:

> She only used a few pillars stuck with posters, framing a ground-row and a well-lit sky cloth yet we knew we were on the Butte Montmarte, with Paris sleeping below. Her dresses were often mere wisps of colour without any pattern: her sets were sometimes hardly there at all.
>
> (Buckle 1955)

Similarly in her final design for *Veneziana*, only to be produced posthumously, Fedorovitch maintained this almost stubborn refusal to use the obvious symbols:

> How many designers could have resisted introducing a suggestion of the Salute, the Rialto, the Campanile or St Mark's, one of the famous Venetian landmarks? She contented herself with an empty looming, thunder coloured sky over the lagoon, framed by pink walls and gilded lattices. The revellers wore clashing yellows, pinks and reds; there was a white Punchinello, a tremendous tragic courtesan in black and diamonds. At the end four lanterns on poles were carried in. Nothing could have been more romantically Venetian.

Such a consistent body of work clearly suggests that Sophie Fedorovitch had some guiding principles about the minimal use of symbolic material in theatre design. Of course, a member of the audience for Fedorovitch's ballets knew only too well where they were set, and one suspects this game of seeing how little purely symbolic material was needed could become a highly intellectual one. Even so it is by no means unknown to hear boos at the opera or ballet when a designer goes further with this game than some of the audience feel is acceptable.

The product designer Richard Seymour talks about the 'X-factor' in the work of Seymour/Powell:

> The X-factor in a product is its essential personality, its desirability quotient . . . We're constantly searching for that elusive product iconography, the psychological bridge between consumers as they are and consumers as they'd like to be.
>
> (Gardner 1989)

This idea of creating a product with a 'personality' to express some features of the lifestyle of its owner is demonstrated by a whole series of designs by Seymour/Powell including their remarkable Blackhawk Stutz electric guitar designed in 1986 which is intended for the rock performer, and departs radically from the traditional form inspired by the need for an acoustic enclosure (Fig. 10.4). In graphic design things need to be even more direct:

> It is in symbolic, visual terms that the designer ultimately realises his perceptions and experiences; and it is in a world of symbols that man lives. The symbol is thus the common language between artist and spectator.
>
> (Rand 1970)

In architectural design, the symbolic is less directly necessary than for theatre and graphic design, but none the less important

Figure 10.4
The Blackhawk Stutz Electric Guitar designed by Seymour/Powell expresses the rock performer for whom it was intended

according to some writers who have warned against the danger of architects only attending to formal constraints:

> Spatial structure is not a goal in itself, but is only relevant if it concretises the spatial implications of a character.
>
> (Norburg-Schultz 1975)

The great philosopher Wittgenstein, who became something of a student of architecture through his friendship with Adolf Loos went so far as to insist that this was an essential distinguishing feature of architecture as opposed to mere building. He wrote in a private notebook that:

> Architecture immortalises and glorifies something. Hence there can be no architecture where there is nothing to glorify . . . Architecture is a gesture. Not every purposive movement of the human body is a gesture. And no more is every building designed for a purpose architecture.
>
> (Wilson 1986)

Conclusions

Designers do not work or think in the sort of mental strait-jacket implied by the analysis used in this chapter to map out the range of influences on guiding principles. The Malaysian architect, Ken Yeang has attracted considerable attention for his approach to building in the tropical countries of south-east Asia. A review of his own books reveals the guiding principles behind this growing and consistent corpus of work. Ken investigated the ecological issues involved in architectural design for his doctorate at Cambridge somewhat before such ideas became fashionable. He started to lecture and write about these ideas, and began his architectural practice in Kuala Lumpur where he inevitably found himself contributing to the increasingly vertical skyline of that city. Concerned to develop a sense of regional identity in the face of unthinkingly imported western architectural ideas, he began to study the locally traditional forms and construction of buildings. Such a study led him to the conclusion that one of the strongest influences on traditional architecture was a response to the climate. The hot, wet tropical climate of south-east Asia suggested

DESIGN PRINCIPLES & AGENDA

• Generally, the service-core position is of central importance in the design of the tall building. The service-core not only has structural ramifications. It's location can affect the thermal performance of the building, its views and determines what parts of the peripheral walls will have openings and glazing. Core positions in buildings can be classified into three types: the 'centre core', the 'double core' and the 'single core'. In the tropics, the cores should preferably be located on the hot-sides of the building being the east and the west sides. It is evident that a double core has many benefits. By placing each of the two cores on the sides, they provide buffer zone as insulation to the internal floor spaces. Studies have shown that the minimum air-conditioning load results from using the double-core configuration in which the window openings run from north to south, and the cores are placed on the east and the west sides. These also applies to buildings in the temperate climatic zone.

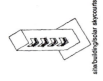

central core

side core

end core

cores at hot sides

• The lift lobbies, stairways and toilets zone are areas that should be given natural ventilation and a view out where possible. This means that they inevitably should be placed at the periphery of the useable floor-space as against being placed in the central-core position. External periphery placements of these parts of the building result in energy savings since these areas would not require mechanical ventilation, and require reduced artificial lighting besides eliminating the need for additional mechanical pressurisation ducts for fire-protection purposes. Aesthetically, by placing these on the periphery of the building, these areas receive natural sunlight and provide views to the outside which with a central core position would not be possible. In this way the building user on leaving an elevator at the upper floor can see out and be aware of the place (instead of entering an artificially lit lobby that could be anywhere in the world.

• Tall building is exposed more directly to the full impacts of external temperatures and radiation heat. Accordingly, the overall building's orientation has important bearing on energy conservation. In general, arranging the building with its main and broader openings facing north-south shows the greatest advantage with regard to reducing the building's solar insolation (and its air-conditioning load). As frequently happens, the geometry of the site would not coincide with the north-south geometry of the sun. In which case, the other built-elements of the building may if expedient for planning purposes follow the geometry of the site (e.g. to optimise upon basement carparking layouts, etc.). The typical floor window openings should generally face the direction of the least direct solar insolation (i.e. north-south in the tropics). Some corner shading adjustments or shaping may need to be made for those site locations which lie further north or south of the tropics or for non-conformity of building plan to the solar path. Generally the window openings should orientate north-south unless important views require other orientations or openings. If required for aesthetic reason, curtain-wall may be used on these non-solar facing facades. On the other building faces, some for of solar shading is required while also taking into consideration the quality of light entering the spaces. In temperate zones, these transitional space can have adjustable glazing at the outer face so that the balcony or recesses can act as 'sun-spaces' to collect solar-heat positively like green-houses, conservation, sun-room, etc.

side/building adjustments

• Deep recesses may be used at the building's hot sides to give shading. A window can be totally recessed to become balconies or become small-sky-courts' that can synergistically serve a number of other functions besides sun-shading. Placing balconies at the hot-elevations permit the glazing to these areas to be full-height clear panels. These can be

recessed sun-spaces

view out from lobby

awareness of place

sliding openable panels to give access to these balcony spaces. The balcony spaces can serve as evacuation spaces in case of emergencies, as large terraces for planting and landscaping, as a flexible zone for the addition of future executive wash-rooms or kitchenette facilities.

• Large multi-storey transitional spaces might be introduced in the central and periphery parts of the building such as air-spaces and atriums. These serve as "in-between" zones located between the insides and the outside of the building. These should be designed to function in a similar to that of the traditional 'verandahway' in the old shop-houses or of the porches in the early 19th century masonry houses in the tropics. Atriums should not be totally enclosed but should be placed in this in-between space between the insides and the outsides and whose tops could be shielded by a louvred-roof to encourage wind-flow through the inner areas of the building. These may also be designed to function as wind-scoops to bring and to control natural ventilation to the inner parts of the building.

transitional spaces

• The external walls of the building should be regarded more as a permeable environmentally-interactive membrane with adjustable openings (rather than as a sealed-skin). in temperate climate, the external wall has of course, to serve both very cold winters as well as hot summers. In which case, the external wall should be filter-like and have variable parts that provide good insulative functioning in the cold periods and be operable in the hot seasons. Where in the tropics, the external wall should have moveable parts that control and enable good cross-ventilation for internal comfort, provide solar protection from the sun, regulate any wind-swept rain besides facilitating the rapid discharge of any heavy rain-fall.

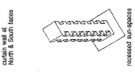

environmentally-interactive wall

• The building plan in addition to responding to the commercial intentions of the building (e.g. enabling single, double or multiple tenancies situations) should be reflective of the pattern of life and culture of the place and climate. Partly this involves an understanding of the spatial modalities of people, the way they may work, the way culture arranges privacy and community. This can be reflected in the plan's configuration, its depth, the position and configuration of the entrance and exits, the means of movement through and between spaces, the orientation and external views as interpreted in the plan, and others. At the same time, the plan should also reflect the air-movements through the spaces and provision of sunlight into the building. The space for work even in a high-rise commercial structure has to have some degree of humanity, some degree of interest and some degree of scale. For instances, the use of large terraces and skycourts might serve as communal spaces as well as ventilating spaces into the upper parts of the tall building.

site/building/solar skycourts

balconies & terraces

plan/use pattern/ventilation

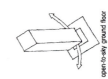

• The ground floor in the tropics should preferably be open to the outside and be a naturally ventilating space. The ground floor relation to the street is also important. The introduction of the internalised indoor atrium at the ground floor may mean the demise of street-life. Free-standing fortress-like buildings also tend to separate the building from the pavement and further alienate the street. By being set back, it eliminates pedestrian movement and reduces the communication and movement into and around buildings from traffic and access points. Free-standing buildings become isolated buildings on isolated plots depicting an 'island site'.

open-to-sky ground floor

Figure 10.5
Some of Ken Yeang's principles for designing the ecologically sound tropical skyscraper

a different approach to the external skin of the building to that employed in the more northern climes of Europe and the USA:

> Climate, viewed in the overall perspective of human history and built settlements, is the single most constant factor in our landscape, apart from its basic geological structure. While socio-economic and political conditions may change almost unrecognisably over a period of, say, one hundred years as may visual taste and aesthetic sensibility, climate remains more or less unchanged in its cyclical course.
>
> (Yeang 1994)

Thus here we see Ken Yeang resolving his interests in ecological architecture, the climate of the tropics and his concern to develop new forms of regionally expressive architecture. Finally he combines this with his interest in a particular building type, the commercial skyscraper commonly found in the central business districts of Asian cities. These interests then range across practical, symbolic and radical constraints but can be absorbed into an overarching set of guiding principles with which Ken Yeang designs. So well resolved are these principles that he has now drawn them up quite explicitly into a sort of guide for use by members of his design practice (Fig. 10.5). After designing many notable tall buildings Ken Yeang was able to refine and extend these ideas sufficiently to publish them in book form (Yeang 1996).

Here again we see the way these guiding principles have been formed over a number of years of practising design. There is clearly a two-way process. On the one hand the guiding principles influence and set the mental context for each design process. On the other hand, each design problem enables the designer to learn more about the guiding principles and express them ever more clearly, eventually resulting in books and lectures. In this sense, design is also a form of research, it offers an action-based method of advancing knowledge. In the next chapter we shall see how important these guiding principles are during the design process and how they operate in practice.

References

Buckle, R. (1955). *Modern Ballet Design*. London, A & C Black.
Burton, R. (1979). 'Energy in buildings.' *Architects' Journal* 170(44): 922.
Duffy, F. (1993). *The Responsible Workplace*. London, Butterworth Heinemann.

Gardner, C. (1989). 'Seymour/Powell: a young British design team with international flair.' *Car Styling* **70**: 110–132.

Gropius, W. (1935). *The New Architecture and the Bauhaus*. London, Faber and Faber.

Habraken, N. J. (1972). *Supports: An alternative to mass housing*. London, The Architectural Press.

Hertzberger, H. (1971). 'Looking for the beach under the pavement.' *RIBA Journal* **78**(8).

Hertzberger, H. (1991). *Lessons for Students in Architecture*. Rotterdam, Uitgeverij 010.

Jones, J. C. (1966). Design methods reviewed. *The Design Method*. London, Butterworths.

Lasdun, D. (1965). 'An architect's approach to architecture.' *RIBA Journal* **72**(4).

Lawson, B. R. (1994). *Design in Mind*. Oxford, Butterworth Architecture.

Lawson, B. R. and Spencer, C. P. (1978). 'Architectural intentions and user responses: the psychology building at Sheffield.' *The Architects' Journal* **167**(18).

Le Corbusier (1951). *The Modulor*. London, Faber and Faber.

Lyons, E. (1968). 'Too often we justify our ineptitudes by moral postures.' *RIBA Journal* **75**(5).

MacCormac, R. and P. Jamieson (1977). 'MacCormac and Jamieson.' *Architectural Design* **47**(9/10): 675–706.

March, L. and P. Steadman (1974). *The Geometry of Environment*. London, Methuen.

Norburg-Schultz, C. (1975). *Meaning in Western Architecture*. London, Studio Vista.

Price, C. (1976) 'Anticipatory design.' *RIBA Journal* **84**(7).

Pugin, A. W. N. (1841). *The True Principles of Pointed or Christian Architecture*. London,

Rand, P. (1970). *Thoughts on Design*. London, Studio Vista.

Stirling, J. (1965). 'An architect's approach to architecture.' *RIBA Journal* **72**(5):

Suckle, A., Ed. (1980). *By Their Own Design*. New York, Whitney.

Vale, B. and R. Vale (1975). *The Autonomous House: design and planning for self-sufficiency*. London, Thames and Hudson.

Watkin, D. (1977). *Morality and Architecture*. Oxford, Clarendon Press.

Weinberg, A. M. (1974). Can technology replace social engineering? *Man Made Futures*. London, Hutchinson Educational/Open University.

Wilford, M. (1991). 'Inspired patronage.' *RIBA Journal* **98**(4): 36–42.

Wilson, C. S. J. (1986). 'The play of use and use of play.' *Architectural Review* **180**(1073): 15–18.

Yeang, K. (1994). *Bioclimatic Skyscrapers*. London, Artemis.

Yeang, K. (1996). *The Skyscraper Bioclimatically Considered*. London, Academy Editions.

11

Design strategies

The act of making an architectural decision can perhaps be stripped of its mystique, while some far more viable set of operations is seen to add up to something – not a style, not even a discipline, but some indefinable aggregate of operations which have been intelligent and appropriate and have given a situation its fourth dimension.

Peter Cook, *Architecture Action and Plan*

I would be the voyeur of myself. This strategy I employed for the rest of my captivity. I allowed myself to do and be and say and think and feel all the things that were in me, but at the same time could stand outside observing and attempting to understand.

Brian Keenan, *An Evil Cradling*

Theory and practice

In the last chapter we saw that it is common for designers to carry some set of guiding principles with them through their working lives. This intellectual baggage is most frequently gathered during that career, with each project contributing to it in some way. We saw some examples of sets of guiding principles and many others could have been presented. The intention was simply to suggest that it is not necessary to include revolutionary or fringe ideas about design in order to find considerable variation in approach to the design process. This hopefully acts as a counterbalance to the earlier part of the book when emphasis was laid on the more theoretical writings of design methodologists. If we are to gain any real insight into the complexities of the design process then we must study not only what theoreticians say but also what practitioners do.

The early years of the design methodology movement were characterised by a tendency to look for common features in the design process or at least to classify design strategies. Earlier in this book we examined some maps of the design process which it is assumed will be taken up by all designers. The message from the practitioners is rather different. They speak less of clearly defined routes and rather more of their own individual interests, approaches and strategies. Our earlier examination of some maps of the design process suggested that, whilst many seemed quite logical, none were really all that useful. The writings of practitioners confirm the view that there is not one route through the design process but many. However, it is not enough to rely entirely on designers' accounts of what they do. If we could accurately describe what goes on in our head when we design, then there would be no need for any books such as this!

Begin at the beginning

We know that the process starts with some sort of problem and finishes with some sort of solution, but how do designers get from the first to the second? We have explored maps of the design process and generally found them wanting, since they are neither accurate nor helpful. So just how do designers begin their work?

We know that design problems are rarely, if ever, fully described at the start of the design process. We have also seen empirical evidence suggesting that designers use what we might call solution rather than problem-focused strategies. That is to say their emphasis is more on reaching a solution rather than on understanding the problem. Our examination of the nature of design problems and solutions perhaps now shows this to be rather more logical than it might have at first seemed. We saw that design problems cannot be comprehensively formulated and that solutions cannot be logically derived from them. However, most design problems are also far too complex for the designer to hold all the factors in mind at once. So where do designers begin and what sort of strategies do they employ to proceed?

The brief

Conventionally a design begins with a brief, which we may imagine a designer is given by a client. However, since design problems cannot be comprehensively stated this begs the question of what is in the brief and what is not! This itself can vary considerably. The brief may be quite complete in a design competition. In, for example, architectural competitions there may be a site, a schedule of accommodation and a set of requirements all laid out quite explicitly. This is necessary in the case of the competition where the designer is probably allowed little or no contact with the client before submission. In the more normal design process our question is not so easy to answer. A common complaint from designers is that their clients do not involve them early enough in the process. Perhaps clients feel that they must have a clear definition of the problem before they commission a designer, but this is not so. In a study of architects and their clients, most of the architects argued that they preferred to be involved with the project from the very beginning (Lawson and Pilling 1996).

Some clients are experienced at their job, and may even be acting in that capacity professionally. It is also increasingly the case that large clients for buildings may take on their own architects to help them develop a brief which may later be given to quite different architects. However, many clients for design are less experienced at preparing design briefs. The architect and interior designer Eva Jiricna tells how, in her experience, 'we never, ever get a brief from a client which we can start working on' (Lawson 1994). Now this might seem problematic for designers, but when asked about this most of them are quite happy to receive briefs which are very brief indeed! The Malaysian architect Ken Yeang, even prefers to start with what might be called a 'mission statement' of just a few sentences. (Lawson 1994). The view expressed by Michael Wilford describing his work with James Stirling, is reflected by many architects and designers:

> We have found over the years that the ideal brief is probably one or two pages even for the most complex project. Many clients think they have got to produce something that is two inches thick before an architect can even put pen to paper. We prefer it the other way round, we prefer the thinnest possible information so that we can get a grasp on the whole thing and gradually embellish it with detail later.
>
> (Lawson 1994)

Protocol studies

To find out how the design process actually begins to develop the brief and formulate a solution we need to turn to some of the many studies on design process protocols. These protocols have been gathered under a wide range of conditions, but all share in common a rather more controlled environment than the design studio normally provides. The process studied usually has quite a short duration measured in a few hours and often is completed within one session. Such conditions are, of course, highly artificial so we must be careful how we analyse the findings of such studies.

Not surprisingly, most design strategies seem to begin with a brief scanning of the problem as it appears initially. However, it is also common to find that elements of solutions rather than problems begin to emerge very early on in the process. In one of the earliest of these studies, subjects were asked to design a new bathroom, and they invariably began drawing solutions almost immediately (Eastman 1970). One experimental technique used to externalise and reveal design thinking is to use groups of subjects and record their conversations. One such study of architectural students designing a nursery school was video-recorded and then analysed for both words and actions. It was rarely very long in these protocols before the subjects began to use such phrases as 'this suggests' or 'we could try'. It was found here that different aspects of the problem were examined to see what they might suggest in terms of ideas about the solution, rather than analysed in their own right (Agabani 1980).

There are many ways of analysing the data from such design process protocols. A notable contribution to the field has been made by a conference at which all the contributors had analysed the same two video-recorded design protocols. Both were industrial design problems, in one case tackled by an individual who was asked to think aloud and in the other case was worked on by a group (Cross, Christiaans et al. 1996). Some researchers tried to break down the process into sequences, others looked to classify the kinds of cognitive activity they thought to be revealed. Others still tried to link the events on the path to the solution with phases of thinking, while yet others concentrated on the cognitive style of the designers. Finally, researchers concentrated on the inadequacies of the protocols themselves to properly represent real design activity (Lloyd, Lawson et al. 1995). Thus there was sufficient material here to publish a book larger than this one just on two design protocols!

Heuristic strategies

An examination of protocols obtained from such closely observed design sessions reveals that most designers adopt strategies which are heuristic in nature. The essence of this approach is that it is simultaneously educational and solution seeking. Heuristic strategies do not so much rely upon theoretical first principles as on experience and rules of thumb.

To illustrate this principle let us look at two methods of sizing timber floor joists. In the first, theoretical method, calculations are performed using the known compressive and bending stress capabilities and elasticity of the timber. The calculations give a depth of timber which will not deflect more than 0.003 of the span and will not cause the bending and sheer stresses to exceed the permitted levels. The calculations are based on established theories of structural mechanics and would be performed by structural engineers and required for building regulation approval. The alternative to this precise but laborious procedure is to use our second, rule of thumb or heuristic, method. There are many possible rules such as 'the depth of 50 mm wide joists at 400 mm centres is 25 mm for every half metre of span'. Such a method is by no means precise but will never be very far out. However, not only does the method go straight to the solution, but it is educational in the sense of clearly identifying the critical relationship between depth and span of the joist. The rule of thumb is also much more practical in that timber does not come in an infinite range of depths but is commonly available in multiples of 25 mm.

This rule of thumb provides a good model of the heuristic strategy so commonly employed by designers. A rough idea is quickly developed for the most significant elements of the solution which can then be checked by more precise methods and adjusted as necessary. Such rules as those relating depth and span clearly cover the critical aspect of the problem of sizing a joist. However, in more complex design situations it is by no means so easy to decide what is critical. Indeed what is important or critical is likely to be a matter of opinion. Here designers need rather more sophisticated heuristic strategies.

Three early phases of working on the same problem

To see how this might actually work in practice we shall briefly consider the approach taken by three groups of architecture students towards a competition to design a large new county authority office building. After a fairly short period of work the groups presented their ideas and thoughts so far. Here, then, rather than working on protocols we can analyse the presentations made by the design students at an early interim criticism session with their tutors.

The first group started by describing how they felt that the environmental requirements of the office space were the critical factors (Fig. 11.1). They had done a literature review of all the research they could find on office space and had arrived at a sketch design of a 'typical bay' showing the structural and service systems for providing shelter, power, comfort and light while maintaining a relatively uninterrupted floor space to give flexibility of layout. The building, they thought, could be assembled by replicating these bays as desired and as the site permitted.

By contrast the second group took the view that office space itself was not difficult to design and they had focused their attention on some rather unusual features of the site. (Fig. 11.2) The sub-urban parkland site was located between two major radial roads connected by a footpath. This group had noticed that the competition brief had stressed the importance of not presenting a remote or forbidding image to the ratepayers. They decided to build their office around a covered mall which followed the line of the footpath and thus brought the public right through the building. Taken together with the banks of trees, south-facing slope and considerations of screening noise from the busy roads this enabled our second group to develop proposals for the siting and massing of their building. The next phase, they explained, would be to fit the various departments into the building adjusting the envelope where necessary.

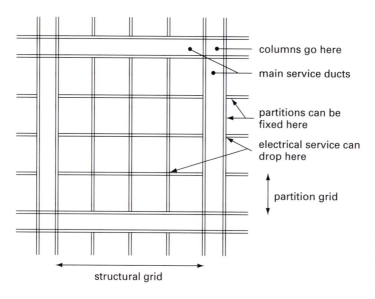

columns go here

main service ducts

partitions can be fixed here

electrical service can drop here

partition grid

structural grid

Figure 11.1
A student group present their early work in designing an office building

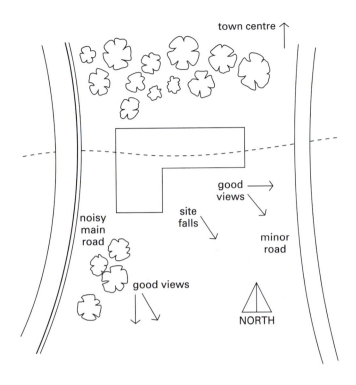

town centre ↑

good ——→
views ↘

noisy
main
road

site
falls ↘

minor
road

good views
↓ ↘

NORTH

Figure 11.2
The second group seem to be
concentrating on quite different
problems

The third group had focused more on the visitors rather than just the regular inhabitants of the building (Fig. 11.3). This group were anxious to avoid what they saw as the usual failings of such buildings, that is, presenting large inscrutable façades with unclearly structured interiors in which it is easy to get lost. For them the whole structure of the organisation provided the stimulus to building form. Each section and department were to be clearly articulated using a hierarchy of open spaces linked by well-defined routes to a central entrance court.

It is difficult to decide whether any of these approaches are better than the others and it is certainly not possible to declare any to be either right or wrong. Although at first sight these three approaches may seem rather different, in fact they share basically the same overall strategy. In each case a group of sub-elements of the overall problem have been clustered together and elevated to the role of form generator.

What differentiates the three is simply the kind of constraint which has been used in this focal role. The first and last group concentrated on the way the building should be organised by focusing on internal constraints while the second group looked at the external constraints imposed by the site. The first and second groups looked at constraints generated by two different types of

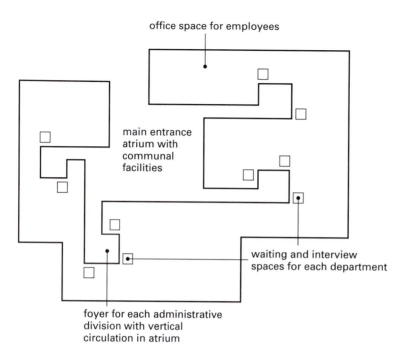

office space for employees

main entrance
atrium with
communal
facilities

waiting and interview
spaces for each department

foyer for each administrative
division with vertical
circulation in atrium

Figure 11.3
The third group add to the
variety of approaches possible

user, the employee and the local taxpayer. The first group gave
priority to the efficient control of the working conditions and thus
recognised mainly radical constraints. By contrast, the second
group thought that the quality of the place was more important
and they recognised more symbolic constraints. The third group,
when questioned, saw no conflict between these and felt that the
physical expression of the organisation achieved in their building
would not only be easy for the taxpayer to relate to but would also
lend a sense of identity and belonging to the employees, thus
creating a good social working environment.

The primary generator

We have seen how the range of possibilities can be restricted by
initially focusing attention on a limited selection of constraints and
moving quickly towards some ideas about the solution. In essence
this is the 'primary generator' idea which we first introduced in
Chapter 3, but where does the primary generator come from and
how does it work?

Obviously it is highly desirable that the primary generator
involves issues likely to be central or critical to the problem.
However, what is central and what is critical may turn out to be two

quite different things as we shall see. The student architects designing a building for a county administrative authority used a variety of generators relating to the radical functions, user constraints and external constraints of the site. The first and obvious source of a primary generator, then, is the problem itself. Finding those issues most likely to be central is a matter of common sense and some experience, and these students were all demonstrating a growing sense of judgement in these matters.

What is used as a primary generator is also likely to vary to some extent between the different design fields and problems. Mario Bellini the designer of the Olivetti golf-ball portable typewriter, emphasises the difference between designing static artefacts such as furniture, and mechanical or electrical goods in this respect (Bellini 1977). Obviously, the product designer must learn to adapt the design process to the situation.

We have seen in the last chapter that designers develop their own sets of guiding principles and these often set the direction for the primary generator in any one design project. Thus the architect/engineer Santiago Calatrava with his guiding principles of dynamic equilibrium is likely to use practical constraints about the structure of his building. However, he has himself noted that this is not enough, and that it is the highly specific and local external constraints which often help him to create form:

> I can no longer design just a pillar or an arch, you need a very precise problem, you need a place.
>
> (Lawson 1994)

For the experienced designer, then, the guiding principles when set against the local external constraints may often create the material for the collection of issues which primarily generate the form of the solution. The designer uses this initial attempt at the solution gradually to bring in other considerations, perhaps of a more minor or peripheral nature.

The central idea

These primary generators, however, often do much more than simply get the design process started. Good design often seems to have only a very few major dominating ideas which structure the scheme and around which the minor considerations are organised. Sometimes they can be reduced to only one main idea known to designers by many names but most often called the 'concept' or 'parti'.

In 1994 Jonathan Miller made his Covent Garden debut as an opera director, having also designed the sets. In the programme he wrote that 'the formal artificiality of the work is part of its essential mechanism, for it demonstrates reality without slavishly representing it. It is an argument as opposed to a report – an epigram rather than a memo'. His production of *Così fan tutte* was set in modern times and relied upon costumes exclusively designed by Giorgio Armani. The public is well used to Armani's own restricted palette of plain-coloured fabrics in soft textures and colours largely restricted to fawns, beiges and browns. This simple idea was carried through into the colours and textures of the set, itself very simply arranged using a large backdrop wall with an opening surrounded by a suggestion of a classical architrave. With all the technical and financial power of the Royal Opera behind him, Miller chose this simple and consistent message which effectively conveyed his interpretation of 'demonstrates reality without slavishly representing it'. It was surely the determination with which he resisted any temptation to depart from this one simple single idea which made this production so memorable visually.

The industrial designer James Dyson is famous for a number of innovative domestic products and is perhaps most well known for his revolutionary 'Ballbarrow'. Dyson had experience of using a traditional barrow and found it frequently got stuck in the muddy ground of a garden (Fig. 11.4). He transferred the idea of using a spherical wheel from some previous experience and adapted the shape of the body of the barrow to make it more suitable for mixing cement and for tipping. As Roy (1993) says, throughout the design process was 'an essential generating idea . . . a ball-shaped wheel'. Roy documents this and other cases where the whole design process is driven by one single, relatively simple, but revolutionary idea.

Another dramatic example of this is reported by Nigel and Anita Cross in a fascinating study of the successful racing-car designer Gordon Murray. It was Murray, when working for the Brabham formula one team, who first introduced the idea of refuelling pit stops since adopted by all his competitors. Murray describes how he was thinking logically how to make the car lighter in order to make it faster. The idea of running with a half empty fuel tank became the central driving force behind a huge development programme. At that time pit stops were only used in emergencies and to change tyres. Murray worked out the gains in time from the lighter load and calculated the maximum time he could allow for refuelling whilst still gaining an advantage. From this came the need to design a way of

Figure 11.4
According to Robin Roy,
James Dyson created his
revolutionary 'Ballbarrow' by
working throughout the design
process with an 'essential
generating idea'

injecting the fuel much faster and a way of heating up the new tyres to racing temperature before fitting them. Both have become common and accepted practice.

These examples from very different design fields all offer very good examples of the creative process studied in Chapter 9. A moment of inspiration leading to a central or big idea combined with dogged determination and single-mindedness. Gordon Murray's own description of the pleasure he gets from his job reveals this process:

> That's what is great about race car design, because even though you've had the big idea – the 'light bulb' thing, which is fun – the real fun is actually taking these individual things, that nobody's ever done before, and in no time at all try and think of a way of designing them. And not only think of a way of doing them, but drawing the bits, having them made and testing them.
>
> (Cross 1996b)

This central generative idea may become very important to the designer for whom it sometimes becomes like a 'holy grail'. Characteristically designers become committed to, and work for, the 'central idea'. The architect Ian Ritchie explains the importance of this to the whole process:

> Unless there is enough power and energy in this generative concept, you will actually not produce a very good result, because there is this three years or so of hard work to go through and the only sustenance, apart from the bonhomie of the people involved, is the quality of this idea, that is the food. It's the thing that nourishes, that keeps you, you know every time you get bored or fed up or whatever, you can go back and get an injection from it, and the strength of that idea is fundamental. It has to carry an enormous amount of energy.
>
> (Lawson 1994b)

Just as a commitment to the idea can be seen to 'nourish' the designer, as Ritchie puts it, so can the search for it in the first place. The central idea does not always appear easily and the search for it may be quite extensive. The architect Richard MacCormac describes this search:

> This is not a sensible way of earning a living, it's completely insane, there has to be this big thing that you're confident you're going to find, you don't know what it is you're looking for and you hang on.
>
> (Lawson 1994b)

The central idea may not always be understood immediately it begins to appear. Richard MacCormac has described this in the development of the design for his acclaimed chapel at Fitzwilliam College in Cambridge. (Fig. 11.5) Very early in the design process the idea was established of the worship space being a round object at the first floor in a square enclosure: 'At some stage the thing became round, I can't quite remember how.' Eventually the upper floor began to float free of the structure supporting it. However, it was not until the design team were considering such detailed problems as the resolution of balcony and staircase handrails that

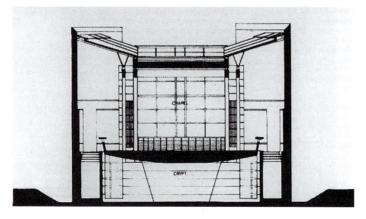

Figure 11.5
Richard MacCormac's chapel at Fitzwilliam College, Cambridge, shown in section with the worship space at the first floor

the team finally understood the idea and made explicit the notion of the congregational space being a 'vessel' (Fig. 11.6). This was then to work its way right through to inform the detailing of the constructional junctions which articulate the upper floor as if it were a boat floating (Fig. 11.7). Richard MacCormac has convincingly argued that this quality of design would have been extremely unlikely to emerge if the designers had changed between the outline and detailed design stages as is now common in some methods of building procurement.

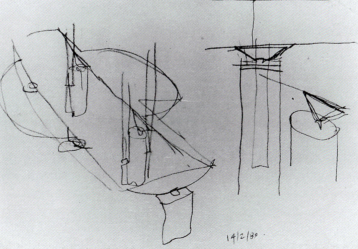

Figure 11.6
Two of Richard MacCormac's sketches as he explored the idea of the worship space as a 'vessel'

Figure 11.7
The worship space showing the influence of the 'vessel' idea coming right through into the choice of materials and junction details

Sources of primary generators

In the examples considered so far those constraints have been mainly radical in function, that is to say, they are considerations of the primary purpose of the object being designed. The architectural student groups designing a county administrative building focused their attention on providing satisfactory working conditions and internal communications. In general there seem to be three main sources for primary generators or central design ideas. First, and most obviously as we have seen, the programme itself in terms of the radical constraints involved. Second, we might reasonably expect any particularly important external constraints to impact significantly on the designer's thoughts. The design of the Severins Bridge across the

Rhine in Cologne, which was illustrated in Chapter 6, is a very good example of a central design idea emerging from external constraints. Third, we may expect designers to bring their own continuing programme or 'guiding principles' (see Chapter 10) to bear on the specific project. This deserves further illustration here.

As we saw in the last chapter many architects have some guiding principles based around practical constraints. One area particularly popular during the modern movement was that of structure, with the notion of 'structural honesty' forming an important part of many architects' guiding principles. Bill Howell (1970) described how his practice of Howell, Killick, Partridge and Amis developed a philosophy of building they called 'vertebrate architecture' in which 'the interior volume is defined and articulated by actual, visible structure'. Howell showed how this led to a design process in which architect and engineer worked in close dialogue to develop the anatomy of each building. At first glance this approach seems rather wilful and, indeed, Howell (1970) admits that 'we do it, because we like it'. This suggests a design process which is guided by a general set of principles about the role of structure, and in which the primary generator is likely to be the structural form of the building. The sequence of drawings shown here, drawn during the design process for Howell's University Centre building in Cambridge, rather tend to confirm this (Fig. 11.8). Of course, such a design process cannot exclude all other considerations, it is just that they are organised around the primary generative ideas. Howell describes exactly such a process in his own words:

> While thinking about structural economy, the relationship of internal partitioning to downstanding beams, the relationship of cladding to the structure, and so on, you are taking decisions which affect the relationship of the anatomy of the building to its site and to its neighbours.
>
> (Howell 1970)

Of course this strategy is not in some way 'right' or 'wrong'. It simply worked for this particular designer and created an architecture of a certain kind which has been much admired (Fig. 11.9). By way of illustrating this we might consider how Arthur Erikson, who has a very different set of guiding principles about structure, describes his design process for his Museum of Anthropology in Vancouver:

> As with all my buildings, the structure was not even considered until the main premises of the design, the shape of the spaces and the form of the building, had been determined . . . It is only when the idea is fully rounded and fleshed out, that structure should come into play and bring its discipline to give shape and substance to the amorphic form. In that sense it is afterthink.
>
> (Suckle 1980)

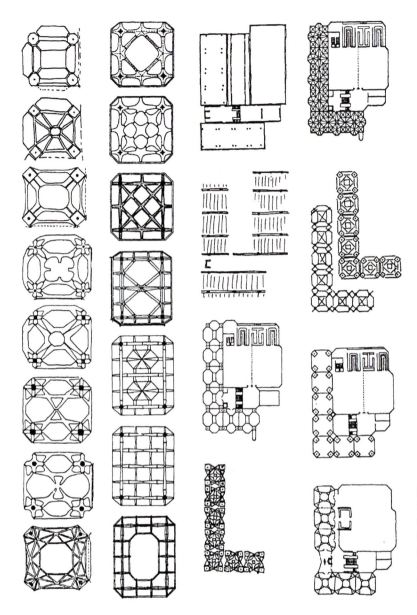

Figure 11.8
Bill Howell called his
approach to design 'vertebrate
architecture', with the form
generated mainly from the
structure. This sequence of
drawings shows the process
operating

The primary generator and crucial constraints

At this point we should examine the importance of the concept of
constraints. It may not always be obvious that what is important to
a client or a user is not always critical during the design process.
In Agabani's (1980) study of the way architectural students perceive
design problems one experiment required pairs of students to
design a children's nursery. After reading the brief and watching a

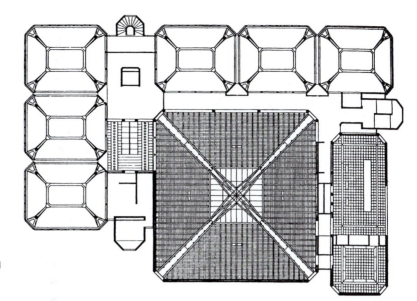

Figure 11.9
The final design of this building
by Bill Howell shows the
influence of his process

video-recording of the site the students were themselves recorded as they discussed the problem. The very first recorded comment from one pair of subjects was to the effect that: 'the most important thing is that we are going to have children playing outside' (Agabani 1980). Now while playing outside is certainly a requirement for nursery design it hardly seems to be 'the most important thing'. However, the same designer continued: 'so which way round do you put all the playing areas so that they can wander around?' (Agabani 1980). This can now be seen as an assessment not of what is most important to the client or user but what is critical to the designer. In this case, orientation of major spaces towards the protected and sunny side of the site followed by a consideration of vehicular access was quite fundamental in organising the overall form. In this sense these constraints are seen by the designer as crucial in determining form and, therefore, worthy of becoming primary generators. Making sound judgements on such things must surely be a matter of experience and perhaps one of the central skills of good designers.

The life of the primary generator

So far we have seen how both empirical research and the anecdotal evidence gathered from practising designers suggest that the early phases of design are often characterised by what we might call analysis through synthesis. The problem is studied not in minute detail but in a fairly rough way as the designer tries to identify not the most important (to the client) issues, but the most crucial in determining form. Once a solution idea can be formulated, however nebulous it may be, it can be checked against other more detailed problems. In the experimental studies mentioned earlier both Eastman's and Agabani's results show the combined use of evolutionary and revolutionary modifications of early solutions. In the evolutionary phase the designer is really following his or her nose, gradually modifying the embryonic design as it is tested to see if it satisfies constraints and is found wanting. Eventually, unless the design proves totally successful, one of two things happens to halt this evolutionary phase. Either the general form of the solution reveals itself incapable of solving enough problems, or so many modifications have to be made that the idea behind the solution is lost and abandoned. In either case the designer is likely to choose the revolutionary step of starting a completely new train of thought.

This is the point where creativity is required rather than ingenuity. The train of thought is broken and no longer sequential. Some effort has to be made to look for a new set of problems or a new angle. In fact the whole primary generator may be scrapped in favour of a new focus. I have overheard many conversations between design students discussing their progress, where one will tell the other that they 'have just started again'. Such a thing is impossible, the design process can only begin once, and lessons learned, attitudes developed and understanding acquired cannot be denied. In this context, then, 'starting again' means looking for a new set of generative ideas around which to build the next onslaught on the problem. This brings us as close as we can get, so far, to the centre of design thinking, for the way in which the designer chooses to shift attention from one part of the problem to another is central to the design strategy. In experimental studies we have observed many variations. Some designers only shift attention when they come to a dead end, while others seem to deal with several ideas in parallel and we discuss this further in the next chapter.

References

Agabani, F. A. (1980). *Cognitive Aspects in Architectural Design Problem Solving*. University of Sheffield.

Bellini, M. (1977). 'The typewriter as 'just another limb'.' *Design* **348**(December).

Cross, N. (1996). 'Winning by design: the methods of Gordon Murray, racing car designer.' *Design Studies* **17**(1): 91–107.

Cross, N., Christiaans, H. et al., Ed. (1996). *Analysing Design Activity*. Chichester, Wiley.

Eastman, C. M. (1970). On the analysis of the intuitive design process. *Emerging Methods in Environmental Design and Planning*. Cambridge Mass, MIT Press.

Howell, W. G. (1970). 'Vertebrate buildings.' *RIBA Journal* **77**(3).

Lawson, B. R. (1994). *Design in Mind*. Oxford, Butterworth Architecture.

Lawson, B. R. and Pilling, S. (1996). 'The cost and value of design.' *Architectural Research Quarterly* **4**(1): 82–89.

Lloyd, P., Lawson, B. et al. (1995). 'Can concurrent verbalization reveal design cognition?' *Design Studies* **16**(2): 237–259.

Roy, R. (1993). 'Case studies of creativity in innovative product development.' *Design Studies* **14**(4): 423–443.

Suckle, A., Ed. (1980). *By Their Own Design*. New York, Whitney.

12

Design tactics

Part of the art of dealing with wicked problems is in the act of not knowing too early which type of solution to apply.
Rittel and Webber, *Dilemmas in a General Theory of Planning*

That sudden fits of inadvertancy will surprise vigilance, slight avocations will seduce attention, and casual eclipses of the mind will darken learning; and that the writer shall often in vain trace his memory at the moment of need, for that which yesterday he knew with intuitive readiness, and which will come uncalled into his thoughts tomorrow.
Samuel Johnson, *Dictionary of the English Language*

Methods and tactics

We have already seen in earlier chapters of this book that there is no one correct 'method' of designing, nor one route through the process. In this chapter we turn our attention to ways in which designers choose to control their thoughts, either consciously or not, during the design process. It is one of the infuriating characteristics of our minds that they tend to display directional inertia. How many of us have tried in vain to remember some vital piece of knowledge, perhaps in an examination, only to have it appear, as if to poke fun at our efforts, when we no longer need it? How many of us have lain awake at night turning a problem over and over in our mind and yet somehow managing to retrace exactly the same steps, only to have a completely different idea appear just when we had set the matter aside to concentrate on other things? These characteristics and the distinctively creative mind were identified in Chapter 9. Here we turn our attention to overcoming the obstacles to productive and creative thought in the design process.

Of course these characteristics of the human mind are not just an issue for designers they must be addressed by all creative and productive thinkers. Many books have been written on how to think more productively, most notably a whole series of ideas have been advanced by Edward de Bono. Most of the very sound and useful advice given in such books may be helpful to designers but it is best read in its original form and is thus not reproduced here. There are a relatively small number of principles underlying all this advice which are based on controlling the direction and quality of thought. Even Edward de Bono's famous use of 'lateral thinking' is an exhortation not to rely entirely on what he calls 'vertical think-ing'. He characterises 'vertical thinking' as the tool we use to dig holes deeper and bigger, whilst 'lateral thinking' leads us to dig another hole somewhere else (de Bono 1967). In fact, both kinds of thought are necessary in design, but de Bono and many others repeatedly point out that when thinking, we do not naturally reflect on how we are thinking to see if that could be changed or improved.

Many devices recommended for more productive thinking are based on devices for changing the direction of thought. Looking at a problem from a different direction can often yield quite startling results. In his more recent books, de Bono, has suggested imagin-ing that you are wearing different coloured hats or shoes (de Bono 1991) which he uses to remind us of different characters and per-sonalities. By imagining we are those characters it is often possible to formulate our problem in such a way that new ideas for solving it emerge. Yet another way to challenge the direction of our thought is to interact directly with other people. Techniques such as brainstorming and synectics rely on the assumption that a group of people are not likely all to approach a problem in the same way, and that if the natural variety of the individuals can be harnessed the group may be more productive. We return to these ideas in Chapter 15.

There have been a number of books published more specifically on 'design methods' (Cross and Roy 1975; Jones 1970; Jones and Thornley 1963). However, these are usually not full 'methods' for designing but techniques for controlling the direction of thought at certain stages on the way. So long as the reader does not expect too much from these mental tools and is prepared to adapt them they may well prove useful. It is not the intention behind this book to replicate these 'cognitive recipes' and there is very little evidence that professional designers find such things practically useful. However, underlying many of these mental tricks are a relatively small number of fundamental principles which can also be observed in the design process of successful designers. Some of these princi-ples are explored in this chapter.

Understanding the problem

So often design problems are posed in terms of the solutions expected. As we saw at the beginning of this book, the different design professions are divided not by the kinds of problem they tackle, but by the kinds of objects they create. Even within a single design field such as architecture we tend to think of a project by the building type which it is expected will result, such as office, school, house, hospital and so on. The good design tutor is careful to draw the student's attention to the need to think afresh about the problem without preconceptions about the type of solution. When the Open University began a course entitled 'Man-Made Futures' the course team saw the need to provide this kind of help for students who would not necessarily have the normal levels of contact with their tutors. Perhaps for this reason, Reg Talbot and Robin Jacques invented PIG, or the problem identification game. The game itself is probably rather too elaborate to be a useful design tool in practice, but the ideas behind it are extremely valuable.

The idea of PIG is that the designer distils the problem down to a very short and simple statement from which crucially problematic relationships can be identified. These relationships or 'problem pairs' as the game's authors call them, can then be used to try to develop others and thus expand the understanding of the problem. Five mental tricks are used: asking the designer to think of ways of relating people or issues by 'conflict', 'contradiction', 'complication', 'chance' and 'similarity'. Thus the game might proceed by identifying people involved in the design situation as being in conflict or seeing things from different points of view (contradiction), or seeing that things may not be as simple as originally thought (complication). Like many creative thinking techniques these devices can be used self-consciously to change the direction of thinking which can otherwise become channelled in a single direction.

The model of problems

The model of design problems suggested in this book can be used in very much this kind of way. It is possible to explore a design problem by visiting all the boxes combining constraint generators, domains and functions trying to think of some problems relevant to this project. It is also useful to ask, where in the model do the critical constraints lie? In most design situations there are a limited number of constraints which are absolutely critical and central. In such cases the key to success lies in identifying these factors and paying more attention to them. Again, reference to the model of design problems from time to time during the design process may reveal the rather distorted attention which can otherwise develop. Quite simply, an aspect of the problem can come to interest the designer who becomes determined to find a good solution, however, examination of the whole model may suggest this may not be one of the key factors for success.

Of course, good designers may do this without the need for such tools and such a self-conscious approach. The Malaysian architect Ken Yeang makes this point rather nicely:

> I trust the gut feeling, the intuitive hand, the intuitive feel about the project . . . you can technically solve accommodation problems, you can solve problems of view and so on but which problem to solve first is a gut feeling . . . you can't explain it but you feel that's right and nine times out of ten you are right.
>
> (Lawson 1994b)

Broadbent's method

Perhaps one of the most ambitious programmes of design methods was developed by Geoffrey Broadbent (1973) specifically for use in architecture but which actually has many generic qualities. In reality Broadbent's method probably does not hold together as a total method but relies upon four distinct ways of generating design form which he called, 'pragmatic', 'iconic', 'analogical' and 'canonic' methods. Broadbent arrived at this taxonomy from a study of the history of architecture and shows how each of his four techniques have been used at various times. Broadbent suggests a complete design method could find the designer using all four of his tactics in an ordered and organised way, and then selecting from amongst the solutions produced. There is no evidence of designers actually working like this, but his four tactics are worthy of study and form a very useful addition to the designer's tool kit of tactics for controlling design thought.

Pragmatic design is simply the use of available materials methods of construction, generally without innovation, as if selecting from a catalogue. Provided that the designer has a good grasp of the strengths and weaknesses of traditional and established techniques this method certainly has its uses. It is essentially traditional and conservative and, therefore, a low risk approach unlikely to lead to dramatic failure. This is virtually a pattern-book approach and unlikely to yield great design or move ideas forward. However, it may well prove a valuable tactic in identifying a range of possible forms for all or parts of a design.

Iconic design is even more conservative in that it effectively calls for the designer to copy existing solutions. Speculative house builders seem to work this way by reproducing their standard house types irrespective of the local conditions or external constraints of the site. Whilst this is unlikely to appeal to the creative mind, such an approach does have it's value and supporters. The commercial psychologist, Conrad Jameson (1971), has been critical of architects for beginning their design process with a blank sheet of paper as if each problem were entirely new. By using iconic techniques designers might begin with existing solutions and modify them to meet the new conditions. This might lead to a greater stability and avoid the commonly found errors in which designers miss the clever way in which vernacular designs solved problems, although it is also possible that such a technique could perpetuate errors.

Canonic design relies on the use of rules such as planning grids, proportioning systems and the like. The classical architectural styles and their Renaissance successors offered opportunities for such an approach, and we have already seen how Vitruvius and later Alberti laid down such rules. More recently Le Corbusier's 'modulor' can be seen as an attempt to produce canonical rules that allowed for more iconoclastic designs. Even more recently, system-building relying on modular co-ordination and standard components has typically generated rather dull results using this method.

Analogical design results from the designer using analogies with other fields or contexts to create a new way of structuring the problem. As we shall see later in this chapter this is based on a widely recommended generic technique for creative thinking. Certainly there are clear examples of significant use of analogical thought in design. The use of organic forms in architecture which offer ways of generating beautiful and also efficient structures are characteristic of the architect/engineer Santiago Calatrava whose work we shall hear more of later in this chapter. His design sketchbooks include many drawings of parts of the human body from which he frequently draws inspiration in terms of the way it can flex into many alternative structurally stable configurations to take on different loading patterns. Analogies may be used to give integrity to ways of constructing parts of design solutions. A very good example already quoted in this book (see Chapter 11) is that of Richard MacCormac describing the upper floor worship space in his Fitzwilliam chapel as 'floating free' of the structure below. From this the team described the chapel as a vessel and were eventually to detail its construction in a remarkably boat-like way. Indeed analogies from natural and organic form have often been used in design at all scales, even that of urban design (Gosling and Maitland 1984). In a more contemporary vein, the architect John Johansen has described how he uses an analogy with electronic circuitry and he even talks of the 'chassis', 'harness', and 'components' of his buildings:

> I wanted to borrow the underlying ordering principles and their systematic logic and use them as a model for architectural methodology.
> (Suckle 1980)

Telling a story

Broadbent himself seems to suggest that the 'analogical' methods are the most promising of these four tactics for form generation. This leads us on to another very popular device for helping the designer to generate form, that of narrative. In a way this can be seen as an extension of Broadbent's 'analogical' method, but can go much further than the use of a simple analogy. In what we might call 'narrative' design the designer, or more often design team, tell a story which can be used to link together the main features of the design. To the outsider this may seem a little childish or even quite ridiculous but there is considerable evidence that this technique is quite widely used and genuinely seems to help some designers.

In some fields of design, the story is already effectively there. Most obviously theatre design actually requires the designer to interpret a story of some kind. So in many cases does graphic design, particularly when applied to advertising. However, the idea of narrative has also become popular with architects. In some cases the architect may tell a story about the 'characters' who form the users of the building and the 'roles' they play and the 'rituals' in which they are set. At this level architecture almost becomes a kind of real-world theatrical set.

However, architects do not just restrict themselves to stories about their users, they even tell stories about the very practical construction of their buildings. Kit Allsopp has been using an urban metaphor for the design of single buildings. In particular he has used the 'familiar aspects of everyday urban life' to imagine how his buildings might be organised and, even, constructed (Fig. 12.1). An example of this can be seen in his Law Court building at Northampton (Hannay 1991) where the idea of 'streets, trees, and sky' gave direction to the overall form of the building and the detailing of the structural system. As can be seen from his design sketches the

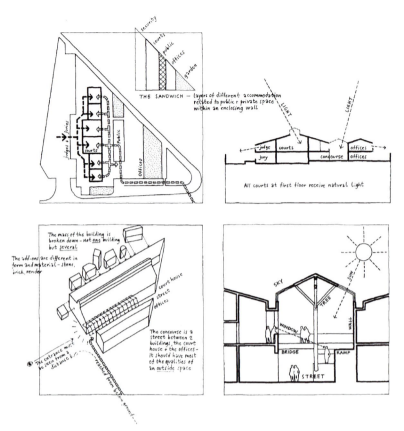

Figure 12.1
Kit Allsopp told a 'story' about 'streets and trees and sky' to help design these law courts at Northampton

site, which was triangular, was divided up into slices or a 'sandwich' as he calls it, the central strip of which is conceived of as a street between two buildings rather than a corridor in the middle of a single building (Fig. 12.2). The 'street' is then detailed as if it were outside space. We can also see that the columns supporting the roof over the 'street' are detailed as if they were an avenue of trees partially blocking out the sky with their canopy. By sticking faithfully to his 'story' about the building, Kit Allsopp has produced a much admired place which is intended not to seem separate from the rest of the urban fabric, thus fulfilling one of the architect's twin

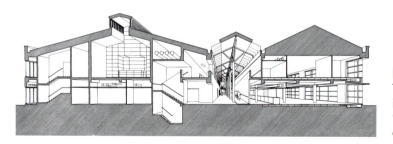

Figure 12.2
The Northampton court building is constructed about its own 'street' complete with an avenue of 'trees'

objectives of 'gravity and accessibility'. Of course, the inside of such a building is quite different from a conventional street in many ways, but that does not really matter here. What matters is that the architect found it helpful to use a story about the building in order to design it and, as a consequence, many aspects of the building feel somehow consistent rather than arbitrary.

The architect John Outram has described a complete design process based on very rich and extremely elaborate stories (Lawson 1994b). His method evolved over a number of years but was always based on the telling of stories with a mythological quality. Outram has described and demonstrated a design process in which he passes the site through seven stages or rites. Here he imagines the place undergoing an evolution rather than the sudden revolution of his design. Thus he imagines the site initially to be a 'grove' on which is then built a 'cenotaph', which is eventually buried ('cataclysm') and built over ('entablement') and then old and new are connected by the folding of a 'valley' into the landscape. Being concerned with decoration Outram goes on to his final rites of 'inscription' and 'façade'. Outram went so far as to reveal these extraordinarily elaborate stories in his submission to the Venice Biennale of 1991, but he accepts that most users of his buildings will not 'read' these stories from his architecture and he is sanguine about this:

> I am arguing the reverse, that it is sufficient for most people that they know there is a meaning, this enables them to engage with the architect at whatever level they choose.

For John Outram the whole design process is based around his own narrative. Such extensive use of narrative is probably rather unusual but then John Outram is an unusual architect who produces unusual architecture! Certainly the architecture of John Outram is very different to that of Kit Allsopp, and this indicates the power and flexibility of story-telling as a design technique. The telling of stories within a design practice about the emerging design solution seems a relatively common technique. As we shall see in Chapter 15, the telling of stories within a design practice also seems to help cement the design team together around this shared but slightly private world.

One or many solutions?

Broadbent's suggestion that his four methods could be used to generate different design solutions has not met with widespread formal approval, but again he points out another very useful concept. Should the design process be based on the deliberate development of one solution or, by contrast, a conscious search for alternative solutions followed by selection and possibly combination? Many questions like this to do with the design process cannot be unequivocally answered, and this one is no exception. It seems that both ways are used by designers who are considered successful. Before exploring the idea of generating alternatives and exploring ways of doing this, let us first examine the case for the single solution approach.

Many designers dislike the idea of generating alternatives and in particular the showing of many alternatives to clients. This seems very much a matter of personal design style and client management, but leads to the fear amongst designers that a client may want to pick ideas from several alternatives that are either impossible or extremely difficult to combine, or that will result in an incoherent and rambling solution lacking in integrity.

The architect/engineer Santiago Calatrava feels that to explore too many alternatives is a sign of doubt and that since eventually the designer must develop only one solution and fight to defend the ideas behind it then it must be believed in to the exclusion of all else:

> You have to let an idea run and proceed with it to be convinced . . . of course you criticise it and you may leave it and start again with something new, but it is not a question of options, it is always a linear process.
>
> (Lawson 1994b)

Perhaps this is similar to what Philippe Starck describes as 'capturing the violence of the idea'. Somehow to leave an idea and search for an alternative may be thought to lose the 'mental inertia' which is needed to develop an idea into a workable proposition. There may be some parallel here with choosing a name for something, a child perhaps. You can look through hundreds of alternatives and none seem particularly to stand out, but when you settle on one and use it for a while it soon becomes special and feels 'right'.

However, Santiago Calatrava was certainly not telling us that he invariably goes straight to this one 'right' idea, but that the process, for him, is based on working on only one solution at once. The architect Richard MacCormac also believes in both evolution and revolution during the design process, but is not enthusiastic about deliberately generating alternatives as a conscious process. He feels that the designer can sense something in the nature of a design problem that indicates whether the generation of alternatives is likely to lead to success:

There are certain kinds of design programme that structure the design very much . . . and you have to have a sense that unless you explore options you are going to miss some tricks, whereas in other cases, for example the St. John's College competition which we won, I rushed headlong as it were into an idea for the project which enthralled the client and which was quite different to the other submissions.

(Lawson 1994b)

Unfortunately, Richard MacCormac has not yet been able to express clearly just how this 'sensing' of the problem nature works. Denise Scott Brown whose practice with Robert Venturi ranges from large-scale planning right down in scale through architecture to furniture and even pottery, also seems to have this feeling that the generation of alternatives works for some problems and not others:

The use of options in planning is to achieve democracy in the process. You have to accommodate more complexity and confront more political options in planning than in architecture.

(Lawson 1994b)

There may well be something in what Denise Scott Brown says here, purely in terms of political expediency, but the idea that there is a hierarchy of design problems with town planning at the top, architecture in the middle and product design at the bottom has limited value. In particular the idea that therefore town planning is more complex than architecture was questioned much earlier in this book and found wanting. As we shall see very soon, Eva Jiricna working at the scale of interior design works very much by generating alternatives. It seems, therefore, more likely that while Richard MacCormac and Denise Scott Brown may feel some problems are more amenable to the generation of alternatives than others, in reality this may be at least as much a matter of the personal style and preference of the designer than an inherent characteristic of the problem.

Generation of alternatives

Let us then explore the use of alternatives and how designers generate them. In such a process, the designer generates many ideas each of which have at least some possible advantages, rather than focusing on one idea too soon. The process then becomes a matter of eliminating unworkable or unsatisfactory ideas and choosing between the remainder, possibly combining some features or several.

Two very different advocates of this approach are Michael Wilford, working at the urban scale and Eva Jiricna working on interiors (Lawson 1994b). Michael Wilford describes it as 'a very systematic process of investigation of options and selection' (Fig. 12.3).

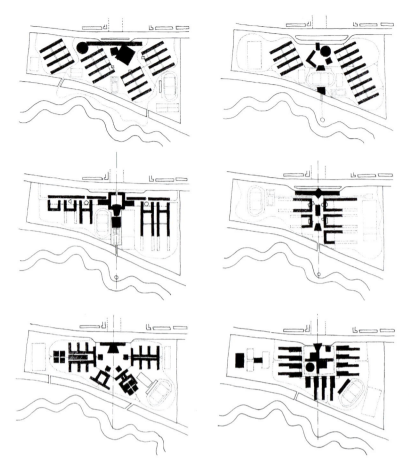

Figure 12.3a
Michael Wilford describes a process involving the generation of many alternatives. These are just some of the alternative layouts considered for Temasek Polytechnic in Singapore. See also 12.3b

Eva Jiricna uses the deliberately calculated stimulus of trying different combinations of materials which, in an echo of an earlier section in this chapter, she calls the 'starting point of the story':

> On the first morning when you start working on the scheme you have got let's say ten and they are all equally possible and then you go through a process of analysing it and develop each of them slightly further on, and then you are left with say five. That process goes on and eventually you are left with one alternative.

It is interesting that these and other designers studied who use the generation of alternatives, often show them to their clients. This seems to become part of the briefing process; a way of drawing more information out of the client about what is really wanted. However, a more detailed discussion of these issues must wait until Chapter 15.

For those who wish to practise the generation of alternatives, it seems necessary to have some basis upon which they are generated.

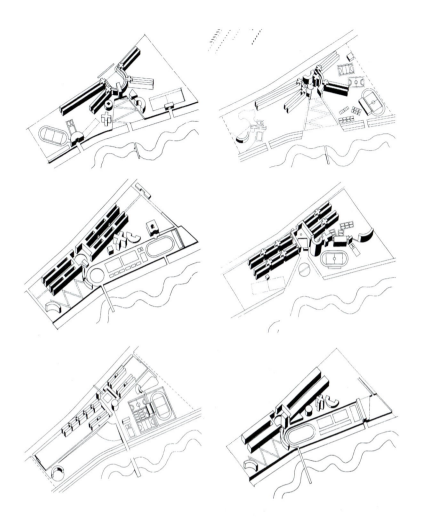

Figure 12.3b
Continued

For Eva Jiricna, it is different materials, for Michael Wilford it is much more about the disposition of major elements on the site. Wilford warns, however, that this process is not easily performed. He has taught in schools of architecture and finds that students often have difficulty producing a range of ideas:

> They can't detach themselves from a particular solution or design to look at others . . . they are locked into a solution without having a full spectrum available to judge whether that is an appropriate solution. Without this the process tends to become ephemeral.

So Wilford is pointing out another benefit to the designer of the alternative generation approach. He is implying in some way that the territory is mapped out, that the range of possible solutions is identified. Of course, designers can never actually know that they have identified all the major alternative solutions to a problem. Often, however, there may be a limited number of basic strategies and an experienced designer such as Michael Wilford may be pretty confident that all the major ones have been found. Identifying all these major alternatives may well be extremely valuable both for discussions with the client and for establishing some firm foundations for the rest of the design process. The tutor in a design school is usually only too well aware of this. When setting a class of students the same problem, it often seems that there are only half a dozen or so valid and sensible basic solutions with many variants and combinations.

Parallel lines of thought

The development of alternative ideas by experienced designers may often be rather more sophisticated than the simple generation of a range of options. When we examine the drawings done during the design process it is often possible to detect, what we might call 'parallel lines of thought' (Lawson 1993a). These parallel investigations represent examinations into different aspects of the design. Thus Eva Jiricna, who likes to work from materials, also has to plan her interiors in organisational terms (Fig. 12.4). The design process cannot simply proceed either from detail to spatial concept or the other way round; both are developed in parallel:

> It is a spatial concept but it goes really parallel to the selection of materials that do exist and the details and they are all joined together and it changes.
>
> (Lawson 1994b)

Robert Venturi echoes this with his characteristically ironic aphorism (quoted more fully in Chapter 3) that 'sometimes the detail wags the dog'. What Jiricna and Venturi are both emphasising here is that, for them at least, design proceeds by investigating both detail and larger-scale issues in parallel. The central issue here is the designer's ability and willingness to allow two or more of these parallel investigations to take place without necessarily trying to resolve them too early.

However, it is not simply a matter of detail or general. Designers can be seen to develop and sustain many incomplete and nebulous ideas about various aspects of their solutions. Sketches done by Robert Venturi for the famous Sainsbury Wing of the National Gallery in Trafalgar Square in London show this quite clearly (Fig. 12.5). There are plans which deal with the problems of circulation, of getting large numbers of people into the new building and connecting it satisfactorily with the axial arrangement of the original Wilkins building.

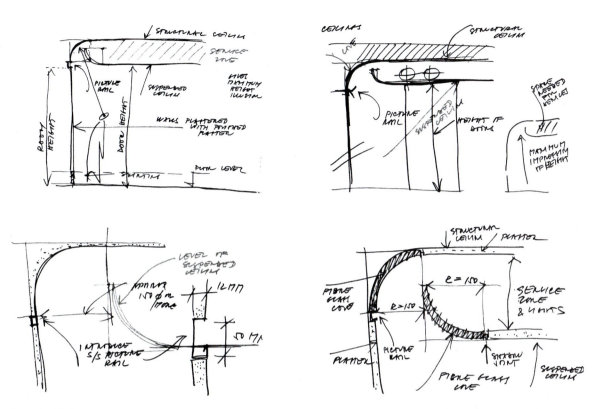

Figure 12.4
Early sketches from Eva Jiricna's design process showing a line of thought about the junction between wall and ceiling

There are also sketches of the elevations, particularly those seen from Trafalgar Square where the new and old buildings come together (Fig. 12.6). The development of this second line of thought about façade makes a particularly interesting case study for us here:

> The main idea for the National Gallery façade, for instance, came on the second day I was thinking about it in London. I was standing there in Trafalgar Square and it came like that, and it has lasted, although it took many months to refine it.
>
> (Lawson 1994)

This comment reminds us of the way an idea can appear suddenly but then need extensive refinement as we saw in Chapter 9. However, it is quite clear from Venturi's description of the whole design process that much of the refinement is carried out in parallel with that of other ideas without attempting to resolve them too soon. The sequence of images shows how Robert Venturi and Denise Scott Brown use a wide variety of techniques for this refinement process. In this case they put the columns from the existing building on to their computer which enabled them to reproduce

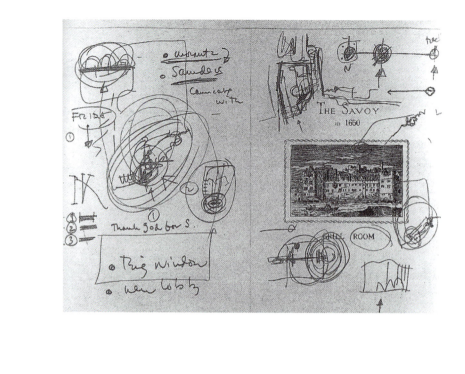

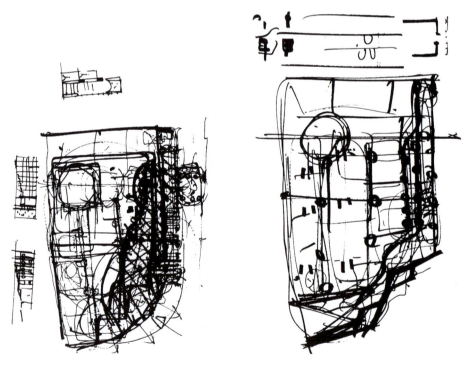

Figure 12.5
Robert Venturi developing a line of thought about the National Gallery
extension as plan

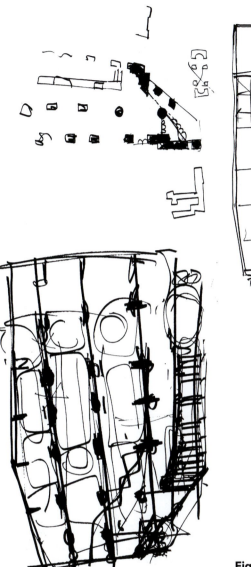

Figure 12.5
Continued

and transform, them at will, sometimes plotting them for use in models or collages combined with more conventional sketching.

In a study of design protocols already referred to in Chapters 3 and 6, Rowe's analysis led him to describe the design emerging through the use of several parallel primary generators:

> In this case study, several distinct lines of reasoning can be identified, often involving the a priori use of an organising principle or model to direct the decision-making process.

(Rowe 1987)

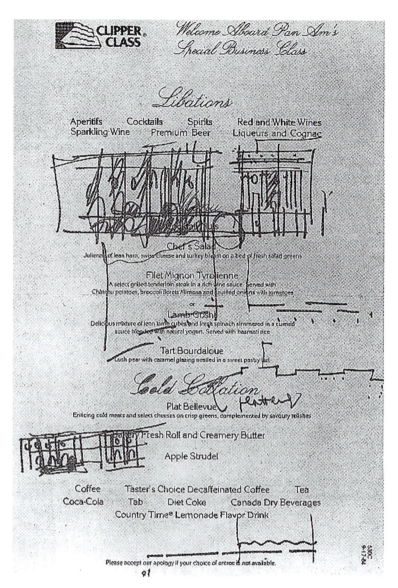

Figure 12.6
A parallel line of thought about the building as elevation

In one protocol where the designers were working on a waterfront site in Chicago, Rowe shows how two primary generators remained in the designers' minds for most of the process with one eventually dominating and partly subsuming the other:

> Perhaps the most distinctive feature of the protocol is the attention paid by the designers to the two large themes of creating a focal point, or landmark, and extending the grid pattern of Chicago, in a linear fashion, out into the lake. Throughout, these two themes seem almost to compete with one another. First one dominates, only to

Figure 12.6
Continued

recede again as the process unfolds. In the end, design effort was focused on the proposal of a single landmark building, although even then its immediate environs were clearly controlled by the idea of the grid pattern.

If we look further into these parallel lines of thought it seems that they often reflect quite conventional ways of thinking about the kind of design under investigation. In Venturi's case he was thinking about a building as plan and elevation. In Eva Jiricna's case she thinks about it as a collection of components and as a spatial organisation. Parallel lines of thought are particularly evident from the sketchbooks of Santiago Calatrava. It is worth remembering that we have already seen that he does not use a process of deliberately generating alternatives. However, his sketches provide clear evidence that he is thinking about the design in many ways simultaneously. Calatrava works by keeping several sketchbooks open at once. As we shall see in Chapter 14, Calatrava prefers small rather than large sheets of paper and these sketchbooks range in size from a small pocket book up to A3. In some he draws with a pen, in others he works freehand but approximately to scale in watercolours, and in some he even performs calculations. Shown here are sketches from two books for his design for the completion of the Cathedral of St John the Divine in New York which was presented for an invited competition. The sketches are in their original sequence but with many gaps since Calatrava is a prolific drawer in addition to relying heavily on models. In the first sketchbook we can clearly see Calatrava drawing mainly cross-sections of the building to develop a structural system. A drawing of the human form shows one of his guiding principles at work as he gains inspiration from this before returning to refine the section of the building (Fig 14.3 p. 253). In the second set of sketches, however, we see more of an emphasis on the building as envelope including concerns about the penetration of sunlight and the relationship of internal spaces to the external ground level (Fig 12.7).

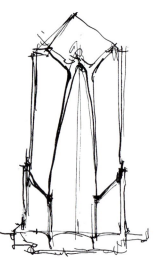

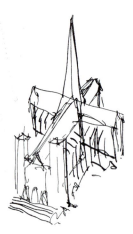

Figure 12.7
A sequence of design sketches by Santiago Calatrava for the cathedral of St John the Divine in New York

In all these drawings and protocols there are areas of vagueness as well as penetrating exploration. This indicates that good designers are able to sustain several 'conversations' with their drawings, each with slightly different terms of reference, without worrying that the whole does not yet make sense. This important ability shows a willingness to live with uncertainty, consider alternative and perhaps even conflicting notions, defer judgement, and yet eventually almost ruthlessly resolve and hang on to the central idea. This suggests that perhaps a particular personality is helpful here and that design education needs to inculcate these vital skills. Amongst other things it also raises some difficult questions about whether computer-aided design systems help or hinder such a process, and we shall return to these, but only after we have explored the role of drawing in more detail. It seems that a common and important characteristic of such design processes is the sustaining of parallel lines of thought.

References

Broadbent, G. (1973). *Design in Architecture*. New York, John Wiley.

Cross, N. and Roy, R. (1975). *Design Methods Manual*. Milton Keynes, Open University Press.

de Bono, E. (1967). *The Use of Lateral Thinking*. London, Jonathan Cape.

de Bono, E. (1991). *Six Action Shoes*. London, Fontana.

Gosling, D. and B. Maitland (1984). *Concepts of Urban Design*. London, Academy Editions.

Hannay, P. (1991). 'Court appeal.' *The Architects' Journal* **4 September**: 30–43.

Jameson, C. (1971). 'The human specification in architecture: a manifesto for a new research approach.' *The Architects Journal* (27 October): 919–941.

Jones, J. C. (1970). *Design Methods: seeds of human futures*. New York, John Wiley.

Jones, J. C. and Thornley, D. G. (1963). *Conference on Design methods*. Oxford, Pergamon.

Lawson, B. R. (1993). 'Parallel Lines of Thought.' *Languages of Design* 1(4): 357–366.

Lawson, B. R. (1994). *Design in Mind*. Oxford, Butterworth Architecture.

Rowe, P. G. (1987). *Design Thinking*. Cambridge Mass, MIT Press.

Suckle, A., Ed. (1980). *By Their Own Design*. New York, Whitney.

13

Design traps

There is a great deal of wishful thinking in such cases; it is the easiest thing of all to deceive one's self.

Demosthenes

The physician can bury his mistakes, but the architect can only advise his client to plant vines.

Frank Lloyd Wright, *New York Times*

Traps for the unwary

No area of human thought is as full of pitfalls as design. Perhaps because design problems are so complex and 'wicked' or tricky it is comparatively easy to make decisions which, with the benefit of hindsight, may seem quite ridiculous. The life of the design critic is in truth far easier than that of the designer! Since designers create things for other people to use they find themselves surrounded by critics all of whom seem to know how to design but just choose not to earn their living that way! No field of design is more prone to exposing its creator's weaknesses than architecture. The great architect Frank Lloyd Wright, responsible for the famous advice quoted at the head of this chapter, was clearly speaking from first-hand experience of this! As a teacher of design students I have seen more design mistakes than most and in many cases they result from the designer falling into a mental trap which it is relatively easy to learn to avoid. This chapter identifies some of the more common traps and discusses ways of avoiding their clutches!

The category trap

The most obvious trap of all for the unwary or inexperienced designer is to identify the problem by the category of solution most commonly found. Thus architects speak of 'housing design' or 'school design'. Whilst schools undoubtedly share much in common, they are also all different. Thus to transfer solutions previously seen at other schools to a new one may be quite inappropriate. What is worse, is that the designer working in this way may not even notice the difference or be aware of the parts of the problem which have not been addressed. Not long ago a group of staff and students in my department became quite understandably fascinated by the urban design qualities of Italian hill towns. This gave rise to a spate of students creating designs based on these ideas without sufficiently examining their relevance to their own sites. While the qualities of these many lovely little Italian towns are indisputable, there are many reasons why they may not work elsewhere. Apart from the topography, the materials, climate and, most importantly but also most easily missed, the variations in culture which cause people to use space differently, all suggest problems with the transfer of these solutions.

This is problematic for designers since they are by their very nature very interested in designs. Architects look at the buildings they visit, industrial designers examine the products they use. Even more alarmingly, these designers study design solutions remotely through magazines and journals which tend to focus attention on purely organisational and visual properties. It is quite understandable and almost inevitable that designers will develop ideas about solutions and bring these to bear on their own problems. The category trap yawns wide open when a designer is looking for an opportunity to use some of these ideas and is tempted to do so too uncritically.

The puzzle trap

As we have already seen in Chapters 6 and 7, design problems are not puzzles. There are no correct or, even, optimal answers to design problems. This means that neither the designer nor others can recognise a 'right' design solution, although designers often experience an emotion similar to the feeling of 'rightness' when a design idea suddenly emerges which seems to satisfy many aspects of the problem. However, we all enjoy puzzles and gain enormous satisfaction from solving them. A visit to any airport bookshop will reveal shelves of crossword puzzles, logic puzzles, brain-teasers and the like for the entertainment of those who find themselves spending more hours than they would choose in and around planes. Add to these the range of rather less portable puzzles such as jigsaws and we can see a whole industry based on our need to solve puzzles.

The fact that we are prepared to put so much effort into solving puzzles which are pointless shows just how much satisfaction we can get from the process. In order to get this satisfaction, however, we seem to need to be able to recognise the right answer. The completed jigsaw or crossword offer just that characteristic. We can become quite obsessed with a particular clue to a crossword puzzle which for a while seems impossible and yet in one moment an obviously correct answer emerges. Such is the satisfaction at this moment that a colleague of mine who was a crossword enthusiast would frequently insist on reading me a particularly difficult clue after he had solved it and then tell me the answer apparently so that I could share the moment of satisfaction with him!

Design problems are not puzzles, but they often have puzzle-like components, and designers rely on this almost obsessional drive to achieve their goals. Planning problems can sometimes be almost like jigsaws. Sometimes predefined components must be arranged, perhaps tables in a restaurant or parking spaces in a car park. More often, however, the components of design problems are not as rigidly predefined as a car parking space and can themselves change size and shape to some extent. This then highlights the first of two aspects of the puzzle trap for a designer.

Designers treating a part of a design problem as a pseudo-puzzle can be trapped into thinking that the elements and rules of this pseudo-puzzle are as inviolate as a normal puzzle. In fact many brain-teasers also rely on our weakness for treating puzzles over-rigidly. The well known nine-dot four-line puzzle is a good example of this (Fig. 13.1). The puzzle is to find a way of connecting all the nine dots by drawing only four lines without lifting the pen from the paper. Most early attempts to solve this puzzle show the thinker implicitly adhering to an extra but not specified rule that no line may go beyond the perimeter of the square defined by the dots. In fact if this rule were to be imposed the puzzle would be impossible hence its brain-teasing quality.

In design, pseudo-puzzles can easily be created by fixing a limited number of constraints and then puzzling out the results. Thus an architect might try fixing the shape of the external envelope of a building in plan and then try to fit the required spaces inside. This is fine so long as the designer remembers later that the building envelope can also be challenged. I had a group of architectural students working on a housing project who were trapped by this for several days (Fig. 13.2). They were trying to decide how many

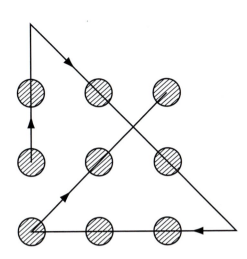

Figure 13.1
Join the dots with only four straight lines without lifting the pen – a simple puzzle that we usually make more difficult than necessary by assuming the lines cannot go beyond the dots

two-person homes would fit on a hillside site. They had decided to use a deck-access system following the contours and were trying to reduce the width of the flat to the minimum in order to fit in the maximum number along the length of the deck which was limited by the site boundary. They had resolved that the bathroom and bedroom would face away from the deck in a northerly direction

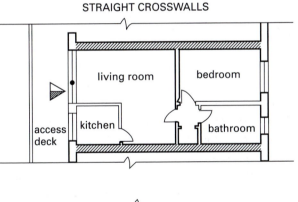

STRAIGHT CROSSWALLS

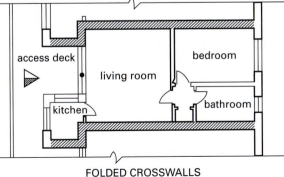

Figure 13.2
Architecture students fall into the puzzle trap

FOLDED CROSSWALLS

leaving the access, kitchen and living-room to face the sun and view across the deck. They had calculated the minimum width of the flat as being the sum of the width of the bedroom and bath-room both of which have to accommodate furniture or fittings of known sizes. So far their thinking was sound. But they were unhappy with the shape of the living space which they felt would be dark and depressing.

During a tutorial we identified that they were indeed pseudo-puzzling and got them to articulate the rules of the puzzle as follows.

1. The structure to be load-bearing cross-walls carrying concrete plank floors.
2. All rooms to be naturally ventilated.
3. Kitchen to be a separate space from the living-room.
4. Internal circulation to be minimised.
5. Living-rooms to overlook the access deck and face south.

However, there was another implicit rule adhered to by all the many designs they had drawn. This rule, never made explicit, was that the cross-walls separating the dwellings had to be parallel and straight. Now it makes sense for these walls to be parallel and thus a constant distance apart but there is no reason why they must be straight. Once we had made their burdensome over-rigid rule explicit and then rejected it, the students quickly found a solution they liked much more. By staggering the kitchen partially in front of the next dwelling the living-room could become a more flexible shape and shallower without increasing the width of the dwelling. This configuration also allowed for the living-room to be recessed from the access deck offering a semi-private external space.

The second aspect of the puzzle trap comes into play only when pseudo-puzzles have been solved. Indeed it is the very satisfaction that we experience when solving puzzles which is likely to ensnare the unwary designer. So pleased are we with the solution that it becomes a focal point of the design and may prevent other much more important ideas from emerging. The pseudo-puzzles which designers might solve are usually only small parts of design problems. More important still, they can often only be defined by making a number of assumptions about other aspects of the design. In the case of our students designing housing, the puzzle was formulated only as a result of assuming a deck-access layout and cross-wall form of construction.

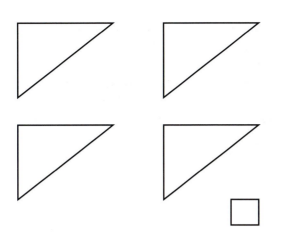

Figure 13.3
The first simple jigsaw puzzle

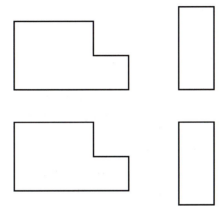

Figure 13.4
The second simple jigsaw puzzle

Consider then the two jigsaw puzzles illustrated here (Figs 13.3 and 13.4). The object in each case is to fit the pieces together in the neatest and simplest way. Undoubtedly the best answers to these puzzles are a square and a rectangle as shown (Figs 13.5 and 13.6). The square in particular has the kind of elegance as a solution which is likely to please the puzzler who discovers it! However, the next and more difficult part of this puzzle is to fit all the pieces from both jigsaws together into a neat and simple form (Fig. 13.7). As can be seen from the suggested solution this entails demolishing the two earlier solutions since they will not fit together neatly (Fig. 13.8).

The unwary designer then can often be found in the second puzzle trap trying to solve the puzzle of how to make use of elegant pseudo-puzzle solutions which are in reality the main obstacle to success, but about which a certain pride and satisfaction is felt. Thus our students designing housing might find it more difficult to return to question the idea of deck access or cross-wall construction. Housing problems often provide ample opportunity for this second puzzle trap. It is all too easy to design rather good house types and then try to fit them on to the site regardless of the problems caused. Regrettably speculative developers frequently go so far as to build such designs so attached are they to their standard house types!

The number trap

In truth we have already rather extensively discussed this trap by devoting the whole of Chapter 5 to 'measurement, criteria and judgement in design'. If a problem or any aspect of a problem can be expressed numerically then all the power of mathematics can be brought to bear on it. Any powerful tool is dangerous, and mathematics is no exception. The incorrect use of mathematical techniques on the wrong sort of numerical systems was thoroughly

Figure 13.5
The nearest solution to the first jigsaw

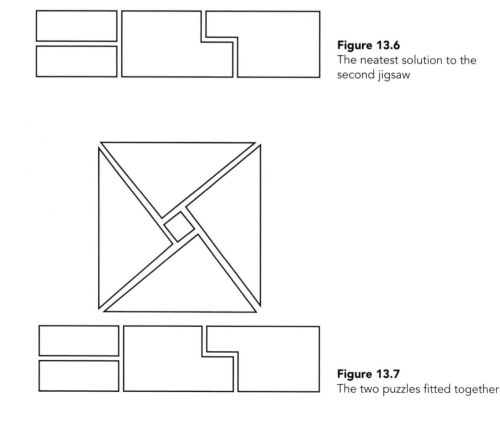

Figure 13.6
The neatest solution to the second jigsaw

Figure 13.7
The two puzzles fitted together

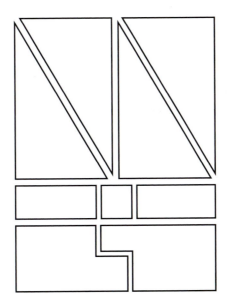

Figure 13.8
A better overall solution may
depend on breaking up the
original solutions

discussed in Chapter 5. However, even if all the rules have been obeyed, one even more tricky aspect of the number trap still remains. The assumption that larger numbers represent things which are bigger, better or more desirable!

I am grateful to Geoff Jones of Building and Urban Design Associates in Birmingham for a very dramatic example of this trap. He was converting some existing houses to flats so the buildings became multi-occupancy (Fig. 13.9). Due to fire regulations this necessitated a partitioning of the staircase to allow for protected escape from the upper floor flat. His drawing shows a small part of this upper floor flat conversion with a block wall surrounding the staircase on the line of the old landing balustrade with the main bedroom occupying space which had been the rear bedroom in the old house. The living space of the new flat was to be at the front of the house. Geoff Jones had cleverly used existing openings and minimised the extent of the alterations. However, the local authority refused planning permission on the grounds that the design did not meet their criterion of a minimum of 12.5 square metre floor area for main double bedrooms. The designers were therefore forced to enlarge the room which could only be done by making rather more extensive structural alterations including new lintels and folded walls.

The planning authority passed the new scheme since the floor area was increased by 0.12 square metres and now just exceeded

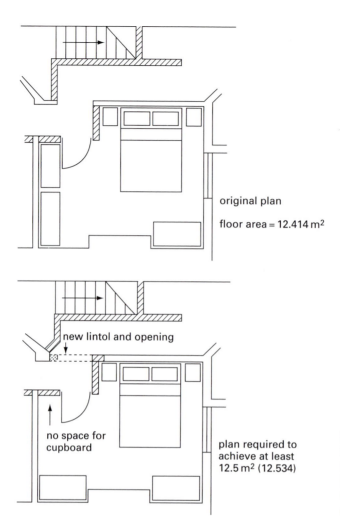

original plan

floor area = 12.414 m²

new lintol and opening

no space for cupboard

plan required to achieve at least 12.5 m² (12.534)

Figure 13.9
Legislators fall into the number trap – the second plan has a larger floor area as required but can accommodate less furniture and is more expensive

the minimum size. This solution was achieved at considerable cost which could hardly be considered value for money. However, even more ridiculously, the actual usable space was now probably lower. As a result of moving the door the space behind it when open was now less than the width of normal furniture preventing the location of a wardrobe or chest of drawers there. In the new design there-fore a dressing-table could no longer be fitted in. However the local authority, taking seriously their responsibility for protecting the public by maintaining minimum standards, insisted on the change! They were truly ensnared by the number trap!

Such faith do we place in numbers that arguments in favour of a design which has some lower number than an alternative will fre-quently fall on deaf ears! Often the gains are difficult to quantify and, therefore, not easily expressed as in the case shown here.

The icon trap

We saw in Chapter 2 how the idea of designing by drawing separated the process of design from that of making or constructing. Today design by drawing is commonplace, to the extent that we shall devote the whole of the next chapter to the subject. Here, however, we shall see how such a powerful tool as the drawing can itself easily become a trap for designers. The design drawing is powerful because, as Jones (1970) pointed out, it gives the designer a 'greater perceptual span'. Thus, designers can see the whole of their proposal and experiment with that image rather than having to try things out in full-scale construction.

However, the drawing itself can easily become a trap for the designer. All designers are, by nature visually sensitive and graphically skilled, so they like to make beautiful drawings and models which, these days, may not just be physical but might be elaborate computer constructions. It is all too easy for the designer gradually to become more interested in what the drawing looks like in its own right, rather than what it represents. Fashions come and go in design drawing styles and media almost as much as they do in design itself.

Some years ago the famous architect James Stirling developed a distinct penchant for axonometrics drawn from below looking up as a kind of 'worm's eye view' rather than the more conventional 'bird's eye view'. A whole generation of architecture students started to imitate this, using these drawings throughout the design process. In many cases decisions were being taken in order that the drawing would compose well rather than the building. Of course we never see buildings from a 'worm's eye view, and rarely from the 'bird's eye view'. But then neither do we ever see buildings in plan or section and rarely do we get near seeing a true elevation. As we shall see in the next chapter, all drawings have their shortcomings as well as their possibilities. There is nothing wrong in producing beautiful presentations, so long as they continue to do their job of revealing and communicating the design so it can be properly understood and thoroughly examined.

The image trap

The designer invariably has an image of the final design held in his or her mind. However, there can often be a mismatch between intention and realisation in design. Over the years I have listened to many hundreds of design students telling me in their crits how their designs will look, feel or what they will be like to live in or use. The natural and perfectly understandable inexperience of the design student means that quite often they are just plain wrong. An architectural student may intend a space to be light and airy or to achieve some particularly dramatic lighting effect, but since he or she has no experience of actually creating such a space their design may be a great disappointment if constructed. All too often these days design students, and some of their tutors who should know better, are content to have the ideas without testing the realisation.

Quite recently an architectural student in my school had drawn an absolutely delightful section through a most imaginative and atmospheric space. Unfortunately the lighting effects shown on the drawing would have been quite impossible from the relatively small aperture he proposed constructing in the roof. This student described his work with considerable verbal skill and no little advocacy but had deceived himself and some of his critics through both his drawn and word pictures of the design.

Such students can be taken to the laboratory or made to do some calculations and be confronted with the results. However, what becomes rather more problematic is when the image in the designer's mind is about some form of social reality. Another architecture student had presented a housing scheme at a crit which I did some years ago. He described how he had separated pedestrians from vehicles which he said would drive into what he called a 'mews court' surrounded by dwellings. His drawings confirmed this showing a leafy sunlit view with a lady carrying a parasol being escorted across some cobbles to a vintage car by a man wearing plus fours, a cap and gauntlet driving gloves. The image then was of genteel behaviour, traditional values and a leisurely lifestyle. The jury became suspicious and asked if furniture lorries could get in and turn round. He had not checked this. We asked if he had thought how to protect the trees from damage by children playing football. He thought the children would play elsewhere. We asked if he thought the residents of his scheme were really likely to own vintage Bentleys or perhaps old Ford Cortinas propped up on bricks while undergoing major repair. He thought that would not matter, so we asked why he had drawn the Bentley. Gradually the whole image conjured up by his 'mews court' began to unravel, but he was very reluctant to see this. He was after all firmly caught in the image trap. He could no longer look critically at his work to test the realisation of his image.

Unfortunately such images are not the exclusive preserve of students. In Sheffield we had three major housing schemes constructed on the same principle in the 1960s. Park Hill was, we were told, based on a 'street' form of access, it was just that these were 'streets in the air' (Fig. 13.10). So famous were these schemes that a considerable amount has been written about them not least by their original architects. They were highly influential and many architects visited and studied them, while English Heritage now believes the only remaining scheme to be worthy of protection through 'listing'.

Jack Lynn in describing the 'streets in the air', argued that Le Corbusier's ideas of Unité d'Habitation with their internal circulation were inappropriate in England:

> Centuries of peace and a hundred years of housing reform in this country had given us the open street approachable from either end and off which every house was entered directly through its own front door . . . Does gregariousness depend on the open air? Why is there so little conversation in the tube trains and lifts? Are there sociable and anti-social forms of access to housing?
>
> (Lynn 1962)

These architects had apparently convinced themselves and their clients that they were indeed constructing 'streets in the air'. So convinced were they that they extended the image to describe the communal refuse chutes as 'the modern equivalent of the village pump'. Again the imagery is one of a quiet bucolic lifestyle in which there is a community spirit. Sadly the reality was rather different. The front doors may have opened off the decks, but the living spaces all looked the other way. The 'streets' were one sided with

Figure 13.10
'Streets in the air' or an example of the image trap?

no 'neighbours across the way to look at. Many of the 'streets' did indeed connect with the ground as the architects claimed but only at the out of town end of the scheme, leaving most residents still needing to use the lifts to get to work or go shopping. So isolated visually were these 'streets' that residents did not feel inhibited in throwing broken household goods such as television sets off them to the considerable concern of those who walked below!

Such images, of course, are vital parts of the designer's process. In the last chapter we saw how many designers like to tell stories and build quite sophisticated images. Without this the ideas cannot be explored and developed. The image trap, however, is never very far away when the design begins to assume the physical and social reality of the images which are being used. They must be regarded as possible hypotheses rather than accepted as developed theses.

References

Jones, J. C. (1970). *Design Methods: seeds of human futures*. New York, John Wiley.
Lynn, J. (1962). 'Park Hill redevelopment.' *RIBA Journal* **69**(12).

14

Designing with others

For better or for worse, the individual is always and forever a member of groups. It would appear that no matter how 'autonomous' and how 'strong' his personality, the commonly shared norms, beliefs, and practices of his group bend and shape and mould the individual.
Krech, Crutchfield and Ballachey, *The Individual in Society*

Everyone is doomed to be the one he wants to be seen by the others: that is the price the individual pays to society in order to remain an insider, by which he is simultaneously possessor of and possessed by a collective pattern of behaviour. Even if people built their houses themselves, they could not escape from this, but instead of having to accept the fact that there is only one place to put the dining table, everyone would at least be enabled to interpret the collective pattern in his own personal way.
Herman Hertzberger, *Looking for the Beach under the Pavement*

Individuality and teams

Throughout this book we have seen that design involves a tremendously wide range of human endeavour. It requires problem finding, and problem solving, deduction and the drawing of inferences, induction and the creating of new ideas, analysis and synthesis. Above all design requires the making of judgements and the taking of balanced decisions often in an ethical and moral context. Designers usually possess highly developed graphical communication skills, and acquire the language of art criticism. Thus it is easy for us to imagine that graphical expression lies at the very heart of design. We have seen how designers' drawings can be viewed as art objects, intended to be exhibited and admired in their own right as objects of beauty. In the next chapter we shall see that designers converse with their drawings. All of this tends to distance designers from the rest of us in a way that can be misleading.

Design can be seen as a very special kind of activity practised by a curious breed of highly creative individuals. In the cinema and theatre, designers are often portrayed in a similar way to artists. These dramatic characters are temperamental and difficult to get on with, and seem consumed and driven by some inner passion which separates them from the rest of society. Sadly many designers seem to want to widen rather than bridge the gap between themselves and others. Their dress, demeanour and behaviour may be unusual and eccentric. In a way this is understandable since it offers a way of claiming authority. What else is a designer selling if it is not his or her creativity? We have come, rather falsely, to associate creativity with originality, so it follows that designers selling their skills want to seem original in as many ways as possible. Design magazines, newspaper reviews and television programmes all tend to reinforce this cult of the individual. As much as anything this probably demonstrates a journalistic response to our need for heroes. The media have recently used the term 'designer' to imply exclusiveness and out of the ordinary, as in 'designer-jeans'. Probably so far, this book has implicitly suggested that design is an entirely personal and individual process. However this need not be so and actually rarely is!

The reality that lies behind the dramatist's simple image and the advertiser's hype is much more prosaic. Designers are not actually special people at all, since we are all designers to a greater or lesser extent. We all design our appearance every morning as we dress. We all design the insides of our own homes, and personalise our places of work. Even planning and organising our time can be seen as a kind of design activity. Professional designers who actually earn their living by designing for others, often work in teams, hammering out, rather than easily conceiving their ideas. It is the team activity which is so often characteristic of the design process which we will study in this chapter. A very important member of that team is the client, and the relationship between client and designer will also come under scrutiny here.

Design as a natural activity

We all develop design skills, but for most of us this is a relatively unconscious process in which are heavily influenced by those around us. We select, buy and then combine clothes and furniture and in this sense cannot avoid being fashion designers and interior designers. We work in our gardens and become amateur landscape architects. In all these activities we are not only satisfying ourselves but also communicating with others and sending out signals about ourselves. Over the years I have acquired a substantial collection of photographs of the way people modify and decorate their houses to express not only individual but also group identities (Lawson 2001). Often this 'customising' has clearly been expensive and may have involved many hours of work. The non-functioning, decorative shutters which can sometimes spread through a housing estate like some kind of infectious disease are an obvious example. Here both time and money have been spent without gaining any strictly functional benefit, but purely to identify and individualise. This action can be seen as part of the process of taking possession of the house, and in many ways distinguishes the 'house' from 'home', by creating a sense of belonging. Too often our creative, professional designers feel such humble efforts to be an insult to their designs.

Of all the designers we have considered in this book, perhaps none understands and accommodates this so well as Herman Hertzberger. The involvement of users in the design process is a dominating feature of Hertzberger's whole attitude towards design. One might therefore expect him to consider this very deeply in the design of houses. Certainly this is true, but Hertzberger reminds us that this process of involvement in place extends from individuals to families and then out into larger communities. Hertzberger (1971) does not, however, see the designer's role as purely passive but as an active facilitator of the process:

> Just as a carcass house can be finished by its occupants and made their personal familiar environment, so also the street can be taken over by its residents. The opportunity to complete one's own house is of importance for self realisation as an introvert process: outside it, the other component manifests itself in the individual's belonging to others. For this reason, a prime concern in the street is to offer provocation and at the same time the tools to stimulate communal decisions. The street becomes the possession of its residents, who, through their concern and the marks they make on it, turn it into their own communal territory – after the privacy of the house, the second prerequisite for self realisation.

Cedric Green has suggested that it is important to recognise the natural way in which we pick up an ability to design (Green 1971).

This fact is often forgotten in schools of design. For Green, the development of design skills is more like the acquisition of language, in that it is a continual process beginning in early childhood. Certainly young children love arranging and rearranging their possessions. This activity is itself part of the process through which we learn not only to classify and categorise, but also to express ourselves. Just as we acquire larger vocabularies and become more fluent in our use of language, so Green argues, do we develop in design.

Although in the UK we have research councils for engineering, physical and social science, the natural environment, medicine, and even an Arts Council, we have no organisation for funding work which might benefit design. Whilst the learning and use of language has long been a field of study, relatively little has been done to understand our development as designers. Indeed design is generally taken for granted in our society and design skills are perhaps rather undervalued. As we grow up, language is taught in a formal and structured way and the study of language is legitimised by its place in our school curricula. Until recently, design was hardly taught at all in schools in the UK. Bits of activity in art, craft, music, drama and other subjects could be said to encourage design abilities, but there was no integrated approach to the teaching of design. At last, the syllabus for the fourteen-year-old child has begun at least optionally, to include design subjects, but there are still blank years from the start of schooling at about aged five when design is hardly taught at all. Perhaps this is another reason why ordinary people sometimes feel a little intimidated by professional designers.

Design games

So it is important to recognise that design is a natural activity and that design students come to their courses prepared through childhood to design. Many have therefore argued that design education should in some way continue this process as well as professionalising it. For some, this implies the use of games. It is through play that children acquire so many of the skills vital to adult life, but the formal use of games as educational tools is a relatively recent phenomenon. This sort of educational game is usually intended not only to develop an appreciation of a problem, but also to explore it in a social context in which the roles of the players are seen as a legitimate field of study (Taylor and Walford 1972):

> The behaviour and the interaction of players in a game can possibly involve competition co-operation, conflict or even collusion, but it is usually limited or partially prescribed. An initial situation is identified and some direction given about the way the simulation is expected to work. Some games nevertheless are still primarily concerned with the desire to 'understand the decision making process', as in role-play; others, however, may be moving towards a prime desire to 'understand the model' or examine the process which the game itself represents.

As we have seen throughout this book, design cannot be practised in a social vacuum. Indeed it is the very existence of the other players such as clients, users and legislators which makes design so challenging. Merely working for yourself can be seen more as an act of creating art in a self-expressionist manner. So design itself must be seen to include the whole gamut of social skills that enable us either to negotiate a consensus, or to give a lead. This in turn implies the existence of tension and even conflict. There is no point denying the effect of such interpersonal role-based conflicts on design.

Designers seek to impose their own order and express their own feelings through design. This is not just pure wilfulness, as some would have it, but a necessary process of self-development through each project, and in many cases a need to maintain an identifiable image to prospective clients. The client, however, is often ambivalent here. Certainly the client is in control in the sense that the commission originates from, and the payment is made by, the client, but in every other respect the designer takes the initiative. The more famous and celebrated the designer, the greater the client's risk, for such designers live in the glare of publicity and are unlikely to wish to compromise their stance. Client/designer tension then is inevitable and an integral part of the problem. In those forms of design where clients are not users, an added element of tension is likely not only between the client body and the users, but also between user groups. Indeed in this case it is actually the designer's job to uncover this tension; a process which can make for an uncomfortable life. I remember only too well working hard to resolve the deep underlying tensions between doctors, nurses and administrators when designing hospitals. Probably one of the most recorded and romantic design processes of the twentieth century was that of the Sydney Opera House. The fact that the architect walked out of the project, that the client had to raise huge additional funds, that a major contractor went financially

237

unstable, that the whole thing took many times longer to build than was envisaged, all contribute to the scene of continuous and substantial conflict. And yet the final outcome is one of the most recognisable and celebrated pieces of modern design anywhere in the world.

The legislator role introduces yet more potential conflict, which can take surprising forms. Conventionally we have the image of the designer and legislator locked in battle, with the designer often representing the unstoppable force and the legislator the immovable obstacle. Richard Rogers' description of his problems with the Parisian fire department, which we saw in Chapter 6, is a dramatic example. However, it is not always so. Sometimes, for example, planning authorities can provide a brake to restrict the client's commercial drive, and the architect, taking a wider urban view, may have considerable sympathy with such restrictions.

This then introduces us to a complication which any student of social relationships would already have recognised as inevitable. Where groups are involved in decision making, not only may tensions exist, but also coalitions and thus factions. Designers then, frequently need social skills to carry through their ideas. Users, clients, legislators and builders or manufacturers must all be persuaded and convinced if the design is really to come to fruition. On the whole the larger the scale of design the more central and vital these skills become. It is therefore not surprising that simulation and gaming techniques have been used in the education and development particularly of town planners, urban designers, and to a lesser extent architects. This is noted by Taylor and Walford (1972) in their study of the educational use of gaming and simulation techniques:

> Urban development gaming has also expanded at a remarkable rate as planning has become more of a total science and less exclusively concerned with the technological aspects of bricks and mortar. Hence planners have built upon the games developed by business analysts, economists, political scientists, organisational psychologists and sociologists to present a more balanced synoptic view of selected aspects of human settlement; they describe, simply, the milieu within which the planner works.

Interestingly, Taylor and Walford, who illustrate their thesis with a number of games, give the details of a game which they call the 'Conservation Game'. In fact this game simulates the final deliberations of the Roskill Commission Inquiry into the third London Airport which was discussed in Chapter 5 of this book. Here, however, the participants of the game are allocated roles in order to bring out the conflicts between the potential gainers and losers at each site. In order to give the game a fresh impetus, sites may be selected for examination other than the four dealt with by the real inquiry. Such a game can simulate and bring to life the social elements of the design process, which this book can only describe. The relationships which exist between people, the ideas for which they stand, and their perception of each other, all contribute to decisions along with the logic and passion of the arguments.

So far we have been concerned with the effect on the design process of the various roles played by the participants in relation to the designer, and the designer has been implicitly seen in the singular. However, this is by no means the only way to design. Large projects such as buildings usually involve a whole design team, and those teams are normally comprised of smaller teams of specialists. A building of any size will need not only architects, but also quantity surveyors, structural and service engineers, and more complex buildings may involve many other even more specialised consultants. Both the individual specialist teams and the overall project team can be seen to exhibit group dynamics, and to behave not just as a collection of individuals. Whilst some architects prefer to be independent, others have deliberately chosen an integrated form of practice in which the various skills are combined into project teams. An examination of professional diaries is likely to show that most architects spend more time interacting with other specialist consultants and with fellow architects, than working in isolation, and yet this is hardly reflected in the curricula of most schools of architecture.

Cedric Green explored the problems of co-operation between architects with a clever adaptation of a children's competitive game called Connect created by the graphic designer Ken Garland for Galt Toys. Garland co-operated with psychologists in the design of symbols in the workplace and this clearly lead him to develop a minimalist approach to graphics which seems ideally suited to the naturally inventive and imaginative world in which children live. He has since used this expertise to develop many other much loved graphical games for children, but would probably have been both surprised and interested to see his game in a school of architecture! Connect consists of a series of tiles with coloured tracks running across them in either straight lines or curves, and sometimes these tracks split or simply stop. In the original game the tiles are dealt out to players who must lay them down in turn following the logic of the tracks, so as to be the first to use up their allocation.

Essentially then this is a kind of graphical dominoes, where the end product can be as visually fascinating as the playing. Green, however, bent the rules in order to produce a game in which a team had to co-operate to produce a design which had to meet various physical and cost requirements.

This idea was extended into a more realistic game, Gambit, by using special magnetic tiles which represented building elements which could be arranged on a grid to create diagrammatic architecture (Green 1977). These designs could be 'costed' according to simple formulae to evaluate capital cost, heating cost, structural efficiency and so on. The members of the teams played out the various specialist roles to be found in the real world building design team. While this technique is unlikely to produce great architecture it does provide a superb vehicle to explore the group dynamics of these teams. The follow-up discussions show how tensions develop and how teams able to deal with these tensions could outplay teams with those seen as 'highly talented designers'.

This illustrates the message of this chapter, that design is often a collective process in which the rapport between group members can be as significant as their ideas. These ideas had already been demonstrated by Rae who had used highly formalised games with design students at the Hornsey College of Art, not intended to model the design process, but specifically to emphasise the significance of group dynamics and the adoption of either competitive or co-operative roles in group performance (Rae 1969). Of course, students also learned about the building design problems themselves, and were forced by the format of the game to confront their own implicit prejudices about what was important in architecture.

Green also developed games for use at the urban scale. In this case students first studied a complete local area in which they were later to design buildings. Arising from this study the students were able to identify key players in the area such as residents, landowners and employers as well as architects, planners and developers. The game began with a Lego model of the area as it stood and the students, playing the roles already identified, began a process of negotiation to explore the future of the area. The enthusiasm with which architecture students adopted roles of which they were normally highly critical, for example highway engineers, was remarkable, and the result was often a rather heated and protracted argument. It seems highly unlikely that such an in-depth analysis could be achieved by individuals, who inevitably find it difficult to represent conflicting points of view in their own mind. Green has also suggested that such a game might profitably be played by players from the real world as a way of 'anticipating and neutralising conflicts which in reality are extremely damaging and usually caused by difficulties of communication and understanding of values' (Green 1971). It would be a brave planning authority indeed which took up Green's suggestion!

Peter Ahrends, Richard Burton and Paul Koralek have not only built a reputation as creative architects but seem to have built some deliberate methods of carrying Green's message into practice. Richard Burton tells us how the three partners adopt roles during a design project in order to represent views to the others (Burton et al. 1971):

> At this stage, and in the conventional way, one or two of us begin a relationship with a client and the same participants continue for the scheme's life. We have observed that the member of the group who deals with the client unconsciously represents the client in the group and acts as a sounding board for the others. He also tends to balance the freer movements of the other two. The difficulties for our group stem, at this stage, from a tendency to have premature ideas based on one aspect of an undigested brief. The advantages stem from the lack of total involvement of two members of the group, one of whom is likely to be detached enough to see some twist in the changes of the direction of the inquiry.

Burton goes on enunciate the value of group dynamics in holding creative ideas in perspective.

> At this point, the group has a distinct advantage over the individual, because ideas can become personal property or one's own intellectual territory. The strength of that territory is considerable, and the difficulty of working alone is often in the breaking of the bonds caused by it. With a group the bonds are broken more easily, because the critical faculty is depersonalised.

Some years later Richard Burton was to demonstrate the power of the group in a remarkable process used for the design of his acclaimed St Mary's Hospital on the Isle of Wight. He assembled a group from the three client bodies representing the various health authorities, members of his ABK team and their consultants. During a three-day period of intensive design activity this group agreed the main headings of the brief, identified three basic design strategies and selected one for further development including rough costings (Fig. 14.1). In fact the final scheme as built was essentially a working up of this final idea (Fig. 14.2).

DESIGNING WITH OTHERS

241

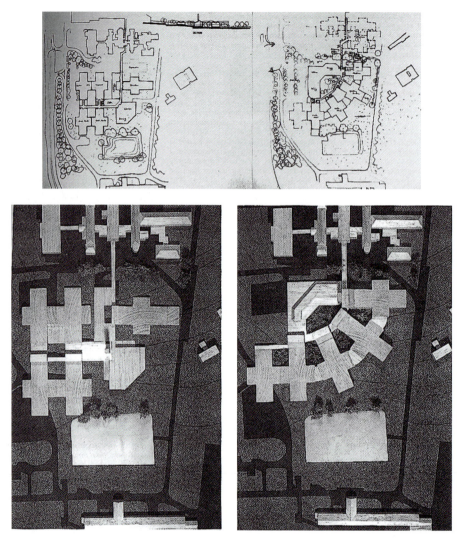

Figure 14.1
Two of three alternative schemes developed by a team of clients and designers over a three-day period for St Mary's Hospital in the Isle of Wight

Group dynamics

All these ideas in some way depend on the concept of a group, which acts not just as a collection of individuals, but also in a manner somehow beyond the abilities of the collective individual talents. This concept resembles the Gestalt psychologists' view as 'the whole being different from the sum of the parts', although in this case it is clearly the relationships between the parts which

Figure 14.2
The selected scheme worked up
later in the design process

contribute most to that difference. Groups as social and psycho-logical phenomena have been studied and written about perhaps as much as any aspect of human behaviour, and there are too many perspectives on the group for us to deal with such an idea more than very briefly here. However, from what has already been discussed in this chapter, it seems at least sensible that designers should be aware of the way their thinking might be affected by group behaviour, and of the way in which they can influence the thinking of other members of groups within which they work.

Much effort has been expended, in the literature on groups, on attempts to define the word itself. As a consequence we are prob-ably more confused now than ever before, but Hare's (1962) description of why a group is not just a collection of individuals will probably serve our purpose here.

> There are then in sum, five characteristics which distinguish the group from a collection of individuals. The members of the group are in inter-action with one another. They share a common goal and set of norms, which give direction and limits to their activity. They also develop a set of roles and a network of interpersonal attraction, which serve to differ-entiate themselves from other groups.

This introduces us to a number of notions which are central to the understanding of group behaviour, the perception of goals, the development of norms, and the characteristics of interpersonal relationships. These ideas are in reality all so interwoven as to be impossible to separate sensibly other than for the purposes of initial analysis. Such analysis is however fairly common now in areas in which groups must perform, although regrettably little has yet been written explicitly about design groups.

It is now not uncommon for competitive teams to employ sports psychologists, not just to develop personal skills but to weld the team together into a more effective unit. It is well known that teams playing away from home are generally less likely to win than those playing at home. By studying football results in the UK and abroad both past and present, Desmond Morris has calculated that in general away teams find it roughly twice as difficult to win as home teams (Morris 1981). There are some obvious disadvantages suffered by the away team which include the journey, unfamiliarity with surroundings and conditions, a hostile crowd and so on. However, all these afflictions are also suffered by touring international teams, and in particularly large measure. In general, however, these teams seem to be able to offset these disadvantages by the social cohesion which develops from the extended contact which is enforced by the tour. It is no accident that touring teams usually play minor opponents they would be expected to beat before the international series begins. Clearly then the performance of a group can be significantly influenced by such factors as group morale, whatever that might be.

Group norms

One of the most significant factors in the formation of effective groups seems to be the development of group norms. Such norms may include conventions of dress, speech and general behaviour and serve to suppress the individuality of members in favour of an expression of attachment to the group. That such a movement towards conformity should be a force for good in a group devoted to creative work seems at first rather strange, and indeed here we find one of the fundamental problems in the life of such groups. However, we shall return to this a little later. It is beyond dispute that in general groups develop norms. Certainly this can be seen very clearly in sporting groups or teams, where uniforms, running jokes, and habitual gestures and terminology abound. Of course, in such cases the supporters also develop such norms, but the behaviour of large crowds is hardly relevant here.

One of the characteristics of group norms is that they often involve some form of regressive behaviour. Standards of behaviour which would, in other social contexts, be seen as rather questionable can become quite normal in small groups. This can be true even though the individual members would also find their own behaviour odd outside the group. I was once concerned with the development of a large open plan headquarters office for a very large nation-wide company. This company had previously been housed in a variety of separate smaller buildings of differing ages and types scattered around the town. The architects department, however, had been familiar with open plan accommodation through their large drawing offices and they had developed such group norms over an extended period. Once relocated in the new office they quickly became regarded as a nuisance by members of other departments due to the rather regressive nature of their group behaviour which involved such things as community singing, rehearsing scenes from the previous night's television comedy programmes, flying paper aeroplanes, and very casual dress.

Tracy Kidder's account of the design of a new Data General computer is rich in material illustrating the importance of group dynamics and interpersonal relationships in the performance of a design team. Kidder (1982) describes how groups sprang up within the team and gained identities through their behavioural norms. In particular the young graduates who joined the team and were regarded as 'kids' by the older hands, were to split into those who designed hardware and were known as 'Hardy Boys' and those who designed microcode and were known as 'Microkids':

> Some of the recruits said they liked the atmosphere. Microkid Dave Keating, for instance, had looked at other companies, where de facto dress codes were in force. He liked the 'casual' look of the basement of Westborough. The jeans and so on. Several talked of their 'flexible hours' . . . There was an intensity in the air. 'I kinda liked the fervour and wanted to be part of it'.

Kidder describes how members of these groups were seduced into them by the atmosphere created by the norms, even though an extremely important norm seemed to be one of very long hours and hard work.

> He was essentially offered the chance for some gruelling work, and he accepted with alacrity . . . There was, it appeared, a mysterious rite of initiation through which, in one way or another, almost every member of the team passed. The term that the old hands used for this rite . . . was 'signing up'. By signing up for the project you agreed to do whatever was necessary for success . . . From a manager's point of view, the practical virtues of the ritual were manifold. The labour was no longer coerced.

245

The results of this astonishing team were that Data General developed one of the most famous series of computers to be designed, and in the face of powerful opposition from larger and much more established companies such as IBM and DEC. There can be no doubt that this group was indeed greater than the sum of its individuals. The documentation of how such creative groups work is rather poor. Possibly this is partly a result of the cult of the individual designer, which seems to be a more misleading than helpful image, and effective groups are probably therefore far more common than the literature might suggest. We have already made mention of the Ahrends, Burton and Koralek partnership who also seem to have built a remarkably creative group described by Richard Burton.

> Over the years we have developed what might be called 'group territory': that is, a pool of common word associations, experience, ideas, and behaviour. We are agile in such territory.

Norms are often not developed without some pain. It is sometimes said that groups go through phases of 'forming', 'storming' and 'norming' before 'performing'. This is because norms to some extent must grow out of the collection of individuals. As each tries to impose his or her character on the group, conflicts are likely to arise before common perceptions of the group's goals and accepted norms develop. During this phase individuals often begin to acquire roles which appear from the outside as caricatures. It can be a strange experience to talk to a member of a group which also contains a fairly close friend. The group may well collectively see your friend in a very different light to you because of the role that has been established for that person in the group. These roles simultaneously often help to facilitate the business of the group and become part of the folklore which binds the group together. Thus a member may quite unjustifiably acquire a reputation as a heavy drinker, giving the group both a running joke and a ready-made excuse to adjourn, ostensibly on his demand to a place of informality.

'Leaders' are obviously valuable in a group which from time to time needs a direction imposed upon it. The dictatorial leader, who directs without consensus, or a multiplicity of leaders, can equally be quite damaging to the performance of the group. The 'clown', who apparently never takes matters too seriously, can be useful in defusing conflicts which otherwise might escalate into permanent rifts within the group. The 'lawyer' who prefers to study the rule book rather than develop the main creative thrust, can paradoxically be most useful in design groups. In such groups the behavioural norms are unlikely to encourage great respect for conformity, regulation and bureaucracy. In general therefore the members are unlikely to be particularly interested in procedure or rules within which they must work. Group members who are so minded, therefore, can be useful in keeping a group on the road, although they are likely to be considerably undervalued by their colleagues. Some roles serve to flatter other group members: the 'dunce' for example, who is in reality much brighter than it appears but who makes others feel they contribute good ideas, or have outstanding talents.

Of course not all roles are productive all of the time, and the skill of managing such groups often lies in recognising the roles members are playing. I have used games to illustrate this to design students, who are likely eventually to become group leaders. In these games, mock meetings were held at which each participant was given a secret 'hidden agenda', and a suggested role through which this could be expressed. Another member was then charged with chairing the meeting whilst uncovering these hidden issues, to attempt to bring them out into the open, and at the end of the game to articulate the roles being played.

One of the problems with group norms is that they can become too powerful and too habitual, and as a result serve to suppress deviance and originality which, when combined with their tendency to encourage regression, can cause groups to lose their grip on reality. Richard Burton seems aware of this when he tells us that it is 'essential that the group should not become a small closed community' and warns that 'we see closed communities as seed-beds of fantasy'. Burton suggests two remedies for this can be found by either changing the group membership, or returning to the idea of deliberate role playing discussed earlier in this chapter.

> We short-circuit many explanations within the group, and this makes it difficult for us to work with anyone who hasn't some working knowledge of group territory. To rely continually on common assumptions can be dangerous, not least because it can lead to stagnation, and so we welcome intervention, which can be either external or from within the group (in which case one partner acts as 'devil's advocate').

Burton's mature perspective on the way his group works is probably rather unusual, and it is more likely that many creative groups are rather less conscious of their performance and of ways of managing and optimising it. For this reason it seems likely that design teams or groups may have a natural life span. It is not surprising that many creative partnerships eventually break up. A highly individual talent may be nurtured and initially nourished by a group, but, rather like a child growing up, such an individual seems to find a moment when it seems inevitable that he or she must leave. Alternatively such a member may continue in the group, but by departing from its norms, eventually become rejected by the group. This can often puzzle those of us outside the group who admire what it has done. At its most extreme such a phenomenon can be seen in the very public splitting of pop music groups such as the Beatles. For years their admirers may totally fail to understand how they could apparently throw away such a productive relationship, and hope they will team up again. Such groups rarely form again, for the conditions which brought them together can never really be recreated. Design partnerships often seem to split up over the most apparently trivial issue and, rather like marital divorcees, become quite antagonistic and publicly critical of each other. Such is human nature, and whilst we can often describe it and sometimes explain it, we can less often control it. Occasionally we can harness it, possibly only for limited periods, to generate what is perhaps the greatest satisfaction we can achieve: creative and productive group work.

Design practices

Design groups are special in a number of ways. They are usually purposive, committed and have pre-defined leadership. Indeed one of the jobs that the principle of a design practice must undertake is to decide how to construct the social organisation of the practice. In a study of the design practices of a number of leading architects, several quite different patterns of organisational structure were observed (Lawson 1994). Perhaps one of the most important issues here is the relationship between the most senior level in the practice and the individual project teams. Of course some design practices have only one single principal while others have three or even many more and may become very large organisations. Where the practice has more than one principal the basic structure can take a number of quite different forms. The principals can effectively operate as semi-autonomous but federated practices each served by their own set of staff. ABK seem to operate generally this way with Peter Ahrends, Paul Koralek and Richard Burton each working with their own groups and on their own projects. Obviously the partners here will still share the infrastructure and discuss and exchange ideas, but they act in a fairly independent way. At the other extreme can be found the famous architectural practice of Stirling and Wilford. Until the untimely and tragic death of James Stirling, he and Michael Wilford shared a room, which in turn looked onto the general office through a large and normally open doorway. These two partners both worked on the same projects and hardly divided at all, even overhearing each other's telephone conversations and discussions with other staff. The practice of MacCormac, Jamieson and Prichard displays yet another structure, which we might think of as a corporate model. Here each of the partners plays a particular role, with Richard MacCormac 'initiating the design process', Peter Jamieson looking after 'technical and contractual matters', and David Prichard being 'very much a job runner'.

All of these practices are highly successful and produce much admired architecture, so all the organisational structures that they represent appear to work. It seems therefore to be largely a matter of personal management style which determines the overall pattern of the design practice. Virtually all the architects in the study knew how big their ideal practice was. The numbers varied but there remained little doubt in the minds of those asked. It almost seems that most designers have their own feeling for how many people they want to be responsible for and to manage. Ian Ritchie advanced the argument that design teams need to be 'about the number of people who can basically communicate well together'. He favours design teams of about five people, and has an ideal practice size of five of these groups.

The principal and the design team

Clearly design depends upon both individual talents and creativity and the group sharing and supporting common ideals. Controlling the balance between individual thought and group work is likely to be crucial. We can see the design team as having both individual and a group 'work space'. In particular there is also the individual work space of the practice principal most concerned with the project. The relationship between the principal and the design team seems at its most critical in the single principal design practice. Here the practice is quite likely to be named after the principal and it is his or her personal reputation which must be defended. The need that this individual titular principal has to find their own mental space can be seen from the observations made by several well-known architects. During the normal working day, single principals such as Herman Hertzberger, Eva Jiricna, John Outram, Ian Ritchie and Ken Yeang can be seen to move around the office or be sitting in the main drawing office space. This is clearly done to engineer maximum contact with the design team staff. However many make particular mention of their need to retire home to do their own design thinking, perhaps in the evening.

How a practice principal intervenes in the design team activity then becomes a matter of critical importance to the way ideas develop and the process is controlled. Richard MacCormac specifically refers to his role as 'making a series of interventions at different stages of the design process'. To manage this successfully requires not only design skill but a sense of timing and an understanding of the psychology of the group. Richard MacCormac talks of deliberately 'creating a crisis' and of finding 'someone in the design team who understands that crisis'. Other designers describe their relationship with their teams in a less confrontational manner. Michael Wilford likens his role to that of a newspaper editor who receives copy from his journalists and then suggests how it might be altered or the emphasis changed.

How design groups understand their collective goals

Design practices are intensely social compared with, for example, legal or medical practices where the partners and junior members work more in isolation. The design practice is most likely to be able to perform effectively once it has 'formed'. We have seen how this often implies the 'storming' or arguing stage, but also the development of group norms. These norms seem to be further reinforced in design groups by the development of a shared language and common admiration for previous design work. It is not unusual for design practices to hold regular meetings to which they invite speakers who are in turn often designers who talk about their work. Similarly trips to exhibitions and places of interest may be used to reinforce the group and develop the common view of good design precedent. This relies heavily on the sharing of concepts and agreed use of words which act as a shorthand for those concepts. The intensity of the design process is such, as we have seen, that this shorthand is frequently needed during conversations about the emerging design. I have noticed how, when visiting a design practice to interview the members, certain words which might normally be thought rather esoteric may crop up quite frequently. In one afternoon at one practice, for example, the rather unusual word 'belvedere' was used by three different people independently whilst quite different issues were under discussion. Similarly, references to other designers, or well-known pieces of design, are likely to be made by way of explanation of what the designers are trying to do.

In a study of how design groups come to develop and share a common set of design ideas, Peng has identified two main patterns of communication, which he calls 'structuralist' and 'metaphorist' (Peng 1994). Peng's study was limited to a very small number of case studies, however an interesting feature of his two patterns seems to confirm my interviews with significant architects (Lawson 1994).

In Peng's structuralist approach, the design team work under the influence of a major set of rules which are known before the project begins and which serve to generate form while nevertheless allowing for a fair degree of interpretation by the group. His example of this is the development by the famous Spanish architect Antonio Gaudi of his design for the Colonia Guell in Barcelona completed at the turn of the century. It is well known that Gaudi was fascinated by the idea of funicular structural modelling. In simple terms this involves building the structure upside down using cords and weights thus allowing the main structural components to take their own logical configuration. Peng points out that the design team, including not only Gaudi but also his structural engineer and a sculptor engaged to provide the decoration, built a funicular model early in the design process which each could refer to for their own purposes. By contrast in Peng's metaphorist approach, the participants introduce their own ideas and attempt to find ideas which can then be used to embrace these, order them and give them coherence.

Earlier in this book we introduced the ideas of 'guiding principles' and 'primary generators' (see Chapters 10 and 11). In Peng's study, we see for the first time, a suggestion as to how these primary generators appear and are understood, not by an individual, but by a whole group. Some designers such as Ken Yeang have written down their guiding principles to form a set of rules which so dominate the design process as to be seen as 'structuralist' in Peng's terminology. Similarly, John Outram has published what he describes as a set of seven stages or rites through which his design process must pass. Outram himself is quite explicit about the impact this has on the design group when discussing the way his own staff respond.

> The staff who get on best are the ones who regard it like another aspect of the game that they are expected to play, you know. There is the district surveyor, there's the quantity surveyor, there's the structural engineer and there's John Outram.

By contrast, other designers confess to not even being able to remember how their group developed the main idea for a design. Richard Burton records that 'at times we have tried to remember who had a particular idea, and have usually found we can't'. This phenomenon is also described by Bob Maguire (1971) who tells us that in his practice ideas can suddenly appear without being the obvious property of any one member of the group:

> It is no one person's idea. We have no clear memory of it except of an experience analogous to doing a jigsaw puzzle very fast.

The architect Richard MacCormac was also quite explicit about this when describing work on the design for his much acclaimed Headquarters and Training Building for Cable and Wireless (Figs. 14.3 and 14.4) (Lawson 1994).

> I can't quite remember what happened and either Dorian or I said 'it's a wall, it's not just a lot of houses, it's a great wall 200 metres long and three storeys high . . . we'll make a high wall and then we'll punch the residential elements through that wall as a series of glazed bays which come through and stand on legs.

We also saw in Chapter 11 the phenomenon at work in another project for the chapel at Fitzwilliam College in Cambridge. The worship space on the first floor eventually became described by the group as a 'vessel'. This was then to inform the way the upper floor was constructed and 'floated free' from, whilst still supported by, the lower floor walls.

While Peng does not envisage this in his own analysis, it seems highly likely that what he calls structuralist and metaphorist patterns of group communication may well coexist in any one design process. Where strong guiding principles are held by the design practice, these are likely to influence each project and suggest a structuralist approach. However, even here the project specific characteristics of the particular combination of constraints may still provide enough novelty which may well encourage an element of metaphorist group thinking.

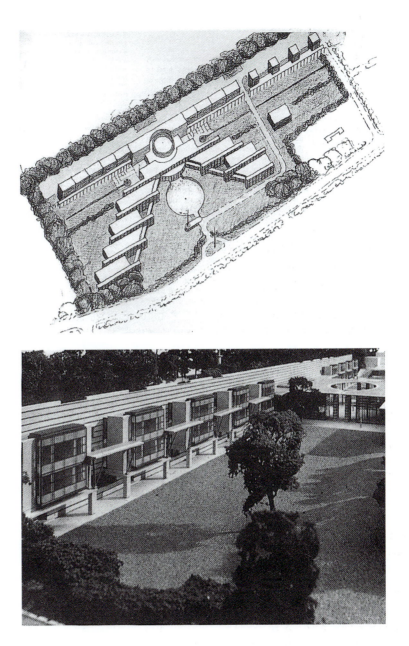

Figure 14.3
A design sketch of Richard MacCormac's design for the Cable and Wireless Training Centre and a later model showing the 'great wall'

The role of the client

Although we cannot help but see the designer at the centre of the design process, we must take care not to neglect the importance of the roles played by others, most notably the client. We have seen how design problems and design solutions tend to emerge together rather than the one necessarily preceding the other.

253

Figure 14.4
The 'great wall' of residential
accommodation as actually built

Michael Wilford describes this as 'gradually embellishing' the brief
with the client as the process develops. Eva Jiricna feels that 'the
worst client is the person who tells you to get on with it and give
me the final product'. Michael Wilford (1991) also sees the client's
role as much more active:

> Behind every distinctive building is an equally distinctive client.

This suggests that the client plays more than just a peripheral role.
Obviously, the client will probably be extensively involved in the
process of drawing up the brief, but many designers seem to prefer
the continuing involvement of the client throughout the process.

In contrast with the image of the designer so often portrayed by the magazines and journals, many designers do indeed enjoy close working relationships with their clients.

We use the word 'client' to refer to those who commission designs rather than the word 'customer'. This suggests that the designer is to be considered a 'professional' and thus to owe a greater duty of care to the employer than might be expected by 'customers'. In essence a client has the right to expect to be protected from his or her own ignorance by such a professional. This is in sharp contrast with the notion of 'caveat emptor', or 'buyer beware' considered the norm in commercial contracts. Such a relationship then must clearly depend upon trust, and good designers can be seen to go about building this trust in a number of ways. Herman Hertzberger tells us that his design process cannot work unless this trust is established and explains this with a catering analogy (Lawson 1994):

> If you have not got a good relationship in the human sense with your client, forget it because they'll never trust you. They trust you as long as they have seen things they have eaten before, but as soon as you offer them a dish they have not eaten before you can forget it.

This important lesson for designers reminds us that if we really want to be creative and innovative, then we must first establish confidence in our clients. Perhaps behaving too outlandishly and effecting too eccentric a position may not work after all. Of course this trust has to be a reciprocal relationship to work and the client must offer their trust in order to get the best from their designer. In today's litigious world when the idea of the professions is under attack from government, this may seem an old-fashioned notion. Clients and designers, however, generally seem to agree that some of the very best design comes from these kinds of relationships. Robert Venturi and Denise Scott Brown talk of their need to have the client 'let the architect be on their side'. In our contemporary world we seem to be encouraged at every turn not to offer trust, so the building client employs a project manager to oversee and protect the client's interests in dealings with the architect. More often than not this serves only to make communication complex and remote, and consequently increases the likelihood of misunderstanding and lack of insight into the real issues by the designer.

Just as the designer works in a team, so often does the client. Few major pieces of design are commissioned by a single individual but more usually by a committee of some kind. When the design and construction processes are lengthy, as can often be the case with architecture, the client committee frequently changes its membership during the commission. Michael Wilford points out that sometimes the changes in personnel in a client body can result in the architect being the only one who has followed a project right through and can remember why decisions were taken. As client personnel change there may also be a temporarily diminished level of commitment to the project which the architect must survive.

> As a result of that you can sense the project languishing on the back burner with nobody agitating it.

Design as a group activity

Critics and commentators will probably continue to present design as the product of highly talented individuals. There is certainly a little truth in this image, for our studies of creativity have suggested that a relatively small number of people are highly creative. However the day-to-day reality of design practice is much more one of team work. Even the enormously talented and creative individual owes much to those who must work to realise the design. Barnes Wallis is quite sure that 'good design is entirely the matter of one single brain' (Whitfield 1975) and this may be true for some people and some projects. It may also be the case that a combination of team and individual work may be more powerful. Moulton, the designer of the famous bicycle, values group working in commercial product design, but only after a technical concept has been originated by an individual. On the other hand Robert Opron, the designer of Citroen and Renault cars, believes in team work from the outset. Opron (1976) however also recognises the inevitable tensions here between the creative individual and the group.

> The real problem is to find executives who are prepared to accept discipline and to subordinate themselves to the interests of the final product.

The great architect and engineer Santiago Calatrava must surely rank as one of the most powerful minds at work in architecture in our time, and yet he finds no frustration in having to work in a team. In fact it seems that it is precisely the need to communicate and co-operate which makes designing so rewarding for him. He explains this by telling a joke about the great painter Raphael. If Raphael had lost both his arms, says Calatrava, he might not have been able to paint but he could still have been a great architect. 'The working instrument of the architect is not the hand, but the order, or transmitting a vision of something' (Lawson 1994). It seems that we take a great deal of satisfaction from successful collaboration whether it is on the sports field, in the musical ensemble or the design practice. Sharing and understanding a set of design ideas and then realising them together can be extremely frustrating, but is also ultimately extra-ordinarily rewarding. This is reflected by the engineer, John Baker, who developed the design and build organisation IDC, who tells us that 'working in this completely integrated team is as thrilling as any experience I have ever had'.

Design process maps revisited

It is time now to return to the maps of the design process that we explored much earlier in the book, but this time in terms of how the process works not inside a single head but when teams and organisations are involved. In Chapter 3 we saw some of the tricky methodological problems that inevitably arise when we try to study the design process. First we looked at prescriptive views of the process in the RIBA and Markus/Maver maps. These apparently quite logical maps suggest we should be able to see clearly defined phases of work at quite different tasks such as briefing, problem analysis and solution synthesis. We have seen empirical evidence that suggests such maps turn out to be unrealistic in practice. We looked at quite abstract laboratory studies of the design process. Then we found that senior design students adopted a strategy that differed from novices and students who studied other subjects. More realistic experiments tended to confirm these results and suggested that designers do not separate out the activities of analysis and synthesis into discrete stages as we would expect from the logical steps that we would predict based on the prescriptive views of the process. Then we found from interviews with designers that even briefing may not be a discrete stage but an activity carried on throughout the whole process.

So which of these pieces of evidence should we find most convincing? In general it seems preferable to have empirical data rather than supposition. However such a view tends to drive us into a more controlled laboratory situation which in turn distorts the process we are trying to observe. Perhaps the interviews are more reliable since such a research method leaves the process untouched and examines it in retrospect. Of course this simply exchanges one distortion for another. How do we know if the memory of the designers we interview is accurate? Perhaps they even have reasons for convincing themselves that they work in particular ways and thus almost deliberately distort their account.

The answer to this conundrum is of course that a good researcher takes all this evidence into account and tries to understand the whole picture. It is also the case that as a research field matures and its participants grow more confident about their subject, the methods they use tend to change. Thus very early design methods research was based on assertion, then on very carefully controlled laboratory work, then on observation of more realistic but still controlled conditions. More recently interviews and longer term investigations of real practice have become more popular. Such investigations also tend to recognise that design is more often than not carried out as a result of actions by many people rather than solely by individuals.

The nature of design organisations

This emphasis on the team has brought with it an entirely understandable wish to return to the idea of clearly defined maps of the design process. One particular set of enthusiasts for this view summarises the argument very succinctly. 'These researchers believe that a shared understanding can be achieved if all of the team members can agree on a shared design strategy' (Macmillan et al. 2001). They argue that in multi-disciplinary design such as construction the benefits of such a shared strategy are that the 'design teams can work in a synchronised and efficient manner'. This argument fails to identify two major problems with such a notion. First the argument assumes that efficiency of process equates with better design and absolutely no evidence is given to support such a position. Everything that we know about the creative process sadly would suggest this is unlikely to be the case. Second the argument assumes that all the participants would actually stick to the process map rather than detour from it should their own design expertise suggest this might be desirable. As we shall see in the next section, what evidence we have again suggests this is unlikely without some form of heavy policing.

So in spite of all the evidence that suggests that design strategies are extremely varied and highly personal, this group of researchers then set out to define yet another version of the process map. Interestingly they conclude that there are probably three levels at which such a map can be drawn which they call 'project specific', 'global' and 'categorical'. The 'project specific' map is rejected effectively on the grounds that it allows too much freedom and variation. The 'global' map is rejected on the grounds that it is practically impossible to achieve. This leaves the 'categorical' process map which is a sort of half-way house in which there is a standard framework imposed which has a series of defined phases but allows for non-generic processes to occur within each phase. Such a position is justified on the basis of some interviews with designers. In these interviews it was found that designers could not clearly remember iterations of their process across the boundaries between the phases defined in the standard map, but they could remember clearly moving from one phase to another. The map is not tested but the validation relies upon interviews with designers in which they are asked if they could work with such a map. As the authors themselves admit, such recollection of the detail of a process sequence is unlikely to be reliable.

One way in which such process maps can be introduced is through some powerful controlling agent operating within the situation. We have seen the growth of increasingly powerful clients in the design world. In construction for example there are banks, transport organisations, retail companies, public authorities and many others who depend for their core business on constructing buildings through which to ply their trade. Such organisations are far from naïve clients and many of them employ architects specifically to brief the architects who design their buildings. Not surprisingly such organisations tend to seek to standardise procedures and impose some control on the design process. For this reason we have seen the renaissance in the popularity of design process maps. In the UK alone there are now many of these published. Some of them are developed by academics working with the supply side of the industry such as the Process Protocol developed by Salford University and Alfred MacAlpine Construction Ltd (Kagioglou et al. 1998). Others are designed specifically to describe design activities for a particular organisation such as the British Airports Authority Project Process (BAA 1995).

Three views of the design process

In a recent project we were able to study the design process by taking several different kinds of data into account (Lawson et al. 2003). We studied a number of client and construction organisations over a four-year period to see how these process maps worked and how realistic they were. In general our data suggested that a shared view of the design process is more myth than reality. This work gave rise to a realisation that there are in fact three views of the design process. The first view is that which is represented by documentation of policies and procedures either by individual organisations or by large groupings such as the RIBA map apparently representing a whole profession. We can also look at the web-sites and brochures of individual design practices which appear to describe their processes. This view of the design process we might call the 'Intentions' view. It tells us what individuals, practices, large organisations and even whole professions intend should happen when design is done. The 'Intentions' view thus tells us what is supposed to happen (Fig. 14.5).

Next we can study what actually happens in practice. That can be done through real-time observation but this is both a lengthy and potentially interventionist process that many commercial organisations find too intrusive. We worked retrospectively looking at six major design projects that had recently been completed by examining all the documentary evidence, interviewing participants and holding focus groups to talk through and draw out a balanced communal view of the actual practice. This gives rise to a view of the design process which we might call the 'Practices' view. The 'Practices' view thus tells us what actually happens in practice.

Obviously we can now study the relationship between the 'Intentions' and 'Practices' views of the design process and learn a great deal more about designing in the real world. However such research immediately throws up a third and, in its own way, even more intriguing view of the design process. Discussion with the participants of large and complex projects often draws out a set of comments not about what they were supposed to do or even what they actually did,

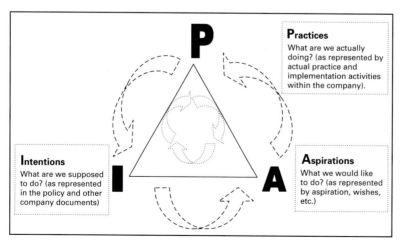

Figure 14.5
Three views of the design process

but rather about what they would really like to do. We might call this the 'Aspirations' view of the design process. Of course those who talk aspirationally can usually also describe, often quite convincingly, what would be preferable about their process. Those who have many years of experience may even reflect on why their aspirational process is not actually realised. The 'Aspirations' view thus tells us what participants in design processes would like to happen.

Such data lead us to the inevitable conclusion that there is no one process map of the design process. This book accepts that pluralist view and we shall not argue here that any one process map is more accurate. It is clear that there is a multitude of ways of linking activities together to make a process map. Some might suit particular individuals or organisations for reasons of personality or management and policy.

The three views related

However before leaving this investigation of design process maps it is worth exploring one other consequence of identifying these three views of the design process. This has to do with the relationship between the three views at any one time and in any one organisation. It must be obvious that these three views or 'Intentions', 'Practices' and 'Aspirations' can be aligned or not (Fig. 14.6). It might at first sight seem that a virtuous design organisation would indeed have them aligned. In such an organisation the participants would actually carry out their process as described in their documentation and indeed would feel happy and content with this way of doing things. What could be better?

Before answering this question let us imagine a different state. This organisation has a clearly described set of intended processes but actually in practice fails to observe these. However many if not all of the participants feel they could improve their performance by working in yet a third way. Such an organisation is what we might call 'totally unsynchronised'. It hardly seems a recipe for success. However there are also three intermediate states in which an organisation can have one of the three views of the design process unsynchronised, with the other two aligned. Each of these organisational states will create different problems for those working inside them and those in other organisations relating to them. Just how all this works is still a matter for investigation but we can already see some of the more obvious implications.

Asynchronous Practices

Synchronous

Asynchronous Aspirations

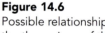

Asynchronous

Asynchronous Intentions

Figure 14.6
Possible relationships between the three views of the design process

For example the unsynchronised practices or aspirations states make an organisation difficult to collaborate with. When practices are unsynchronised other design team members are trying to relate to the published intentions but finding actual practice does not match this. By contrast an unsynchronised aspirations state leaves an organisation in internal difficulty with staff constantly unhappy with practice which may be slavishly following intentions. Such a state suggests a top-down management out of touch with its workforce. Our work suggests such a state to be disturbingly common in large organisations. Again by contrast the unsynchronised intentions state suggests an organisation that is happy with its practice but publishing information likely to mislead those who would collaborate with it. Preliminary studies suggest that the values of the members of organisations in turn influence these states. Designers seem in general themselves not to be too worried about having unsynchronised intentions. Indeed it seems quite common, perhaps almost normal, to find members of architectural offices explicitly recognising that they work in what they would regard as more relaxed and flexible ways than their own published conditions of engagement specify. By contrast, large client organisations more often tolerate unsynchronised aspirations. Again it is common to find staff in such organisations bemoaning the rigid way in which practice is made to follow intention and how this leads to unimaginative or inappropriate solutions.

So what state represents a virtuous design organisation? Again it is unlikely that any one state is always the best for all organisations at all times. Logically it would seem sensible for any organisation to be aiming to be totally synchronised. However is it virtuous to remain totally synchronised? In a changing world, such an organisation might be seen to be complacent, resistant to change and unable to adapt. As conditions change it may well be that those closest to the action tend to see the need for change first. If so then an organisation is likely to move from a totally synchronised state to have unsynchronised aspirations. Probably a good organisation would recognise this and attempt some change.

One course of action here might well be to try to persuade those whose aspirations do not reflect the organisational intentions to change their views or leave. John Outram's comments earlier in this chapter about the need for his staff to understand 'the game they are expected to play' suggests this position. However the management of a more responsive organisation may try to learn from the asynchronous aspirations of the staff and change either the intentions or practices of the organisation. Whether it is important to change the intentions or practices first may depend on the situation. Research is needed into how design and design-related organisations actually behave and change. We know from our work that some are highly adaptable and some are not, some learn much more than others and can transfer knowledge more easily from project to project. The field of design research is now maturing and beginning to be able to deal not just with processes but with the management of those processes in complex organisations.

One other lesson to be drawn from all this is that developing a learning design organisation demands that some effort be put into the sort of reflection we have begun to indulge in here. That is to say a design organisation should try to transfer knowledge gained from the projects it completes in order to develop its processes. Such an effort, it transpires, also offers the opportunity to transfer knowledge about problems and solutions from one project to another. Our research suggests that although this would seem very obvious it often happens far less than seems sensible in actual practice. The ideas discussed earlier in this chapter used by the architects Ahrends, Koralek and Burton represent one possible way of achieving this more effectively. There is a rather delightful paradox here. Many other kinds of organisations have recently been studying the 'project' as an extremely effective management tool. It offers a wonderful focus and intensity of activity that brings people together extremely effectively and nowhere is this more powerfully demonstrated than in the design project. Much recent mid-career management training has been based around the 'away-day' and the project as ways of building teams and collaborative practices. However in the design office the danger seems to be the reverse. The design team has become such an obvious organisational structure that most design offices put nearly all their resource into these teams. This leaves little effort for the conscious reflective thinking that might more easily enable knowledge to be transferred between projects.

Thus the group or team in design can be both a force for enhancing creative thinking within the project and yet also a force for separating out projects and thus an obstacle to learning and developing the organisation as a whole.

References

BAA (1995). *The Project Process Handbook*. London, British Airports Authority (internal publication).

Burton, R., Ahrends, P. and Koralek, P. (1971). Small group design and the idea of quality. *RIBA Journal* **78**(6): 232–239.

Green, C. (1971). Learning to design. *Journal of Architectural Research and Teaching* 2(1).

Green, C. (1977). *Gambit*. University of Sheffield.

Hare, A. P. (1962). *Handbook of Small Group Research*. New York, Free Press.

Hertzberger, H. (1971). Looking for the beach under the pavement. *RIBA Journal* **78**(8).

Kagioglou, M., Cooper, R. et al. (1998). *A Generic Guide to the Design and Construction Process Protocol*. Salford, University of Salford.

Kidder, T. (1982). *The Soul of a New Machine*. Harmondsworth, Penguin.

Lawson, B. R. (1994). *Design in Mind*. Oxford, Architectural Press.

Lawson, B. R. (2001). *The Language of Space*. Oxford, Architectural Press.

Lawson, B. R., Bassanino M. et al. (2003). Intentions, practices and aspirations: Understanding learning in design. *Design Studies* 24(4): 327–339.

Macmillan, S., Steele, J. et al. (2001). Development and verification of a generic framework for conceptual design. *Design Studies* 22(2): 169–191.

Maguire, R. (1971). Nearness to need. *RIBA Journal* **78**(4).

Morris, D. (1981). *The Soccer Tribe*. London, Jonathan Cape.

Opron, R. (1976). The Renault method. *Design* **333**(September).

Peng, C. (1994). Exploring communication in collaborative design: co-operative architectural modelling. *Design Studies* **15**(1): 19–44.

Rae, J. (1969). Games. *The Architects' Journal* **149**(15): 977–983.

Taylor, J. L. and Walford, R. (1972). *Simulation in the Classroom*. Harmondsworth, Penguin.

Whitfield, P. R. (1975). *Creativity in Industry*. Harmondsworth, Penguin.

Wilford, M. (1991). Inspired patronage. *RIBA Journal* **98**(4): 36–42.

15

Design as conversation and perception

Language can become a screen that stands between the thinker and reality. That is the reason why true creativity starts where language ends.

Arthur Koestler

a reflective conversation with the situation

Donald Schön

In this chapter we shall look at design as a process based on conversation and perception. In essence this means how designers come to understand problems and get ideas about solutions through a process that is conversation-like. A process that involves changing the way the situation is perceived by 'talking it through'. As the designer Kenneth Grange put it 'you do have to ferret around . . . to find that which is then suddenly obvious to you' (Cross 2001a).

In a professional context design is very often progressed by teams or groups as we saw in the previous chapter. Sometimes there are teams of designers from the same professional background usually because a job is too large or complex to be handled by one person. Sometimes the nature of the object being created involves many specialist areas and requires a multi-professional design team. In both such cases the design progresses at least partly through the conversations that take place between these team members. Normally such conversations are not recorded and so their importance as part of the process has consequently been rather underestimated in much design research. That these conversations are indeed important only becomes apparent when we study designers in actual practice and talk to them about their process. I held a series of discussions with a number of leading architects that were used as part of my research for *Design in Mind* (Lawson 1994). Those conversations will help us here.

When the architect Ian Ritchie was describing his work he made it very clear that conversations within his team and with other players such as the client were central to his way of working.

> The first move is to talk through the brief, understand what has led to it, understand fundamentally what it is about and that conversation is primarily about building up a level of confidence, of trust. That is the very first move and it's nothing about buildings, it's not about solutions or ideas about buildings.

We shall return to Ian Ritchie's design conversations in due course. What is interesting here is the way in which Ritchie clearly emphasises the importance of his conversations with the client and in this case is quite explicit about using a language that is not about solutions.

First we should introduce a more fundamental way in which design can be seen to be essentially a conversational process. We can even imagine design to be a conversation when performed not by a team but by an individual designer. Donald Schön first suggested this idea when he talked of how a designer 'has a conversation with a drawing' (Schön 1983). In Schön's view, design drawings are part of the mental process of thinking about a design. In this view of design the designer performs the act of drawing not to communicate with others but to pursue a line of thought. As the image of the drawing develops it enables the designer to 'see' new possibilities or problems. More recently we have seen designers using computers and as a result having 'conversational' interactions with their computers about their designs. In the second and third editions of this book I included chapters on designing with drawings and designing with computers. In this edition both those chapters are replaced by this one. Since the third edition of this book I have also written much more extensively on the nature of design drawings and the way knowledge is encoded in them. I have also explored the problems of interacting with drawings or models in computers (Lawson 2004). In this chapter then we shall explore the whole idea of design conversations whether they are between people, between designers and drawings or computers or even carried out reflectively in the minds of individual designers.

Conversations and narrative

One of the most common forms of conversation is that of narrative. As we saw in Chapter 12, narrative can be used as a design tactic. The idea of telling a story in order to develop and give consistency to a design is quite popular. Some researchers from a linguistic background have begun to explore design conversations and concluded that the 'base mode of the conversation is narrative' (Medway and Andrews 1992). Although as designers talk to each other they move through more than one style of conversation, they usually return to a style similar to that of telling a story. We shall therefore begin our investigation by exploring the idea of narrative in order to see how this progresses our understanding conversations in design.

It is not uncommon for narratives to begin with some 'scene setting'. Although of course this may happen at several points in a story, nevertheless it is more common early in the piece. Scene setting most obviously involves describing the situation and the characters or dramatis personae. Major characters must not only be named and introduced but also given some characteristics that will enable us to interpret their utterances and actions. This also happens in design. We shall return to the design conversations of Ian Ritchie to explore this further. The first example is from his project for a new railway station for London Underground.

> We had a conversation yesterday about some smoke vents for the London Underground station which we designed. Obviously these are major features in a project like this.

So the story begins and the designer introduces us to some characters, smoke vents, and tells us that they will be significant in the narrative, or in this case the design. He then describes how the design team conversation explored the nature of these characters and effectively developed 'personalities' for them.

> We came down to air and it wasn't the kind of pragmatic issues and practical issues about how to move air, would air provide us with a central notion of how we could then develop a concept for a building. Is it dirty? Is it clean? What's the hierarchy of the air that's coming up the down pipe? That was finding, if you like, a kind of poetic notion, before we even think about a building or a concept for a building.

This seems rather like an author trying to work out how a character would behave in a dramatic situation given a particular background, personality and motivation. In another example Ian Ritchie was talking about how he arrived at the forms he used for his remarkable glasshouses in the Parc de La Villette development in Paris. He introduced these elements of the building on which he was working, which was to be a kind of science museum (Fig. 15.1).

> We worked on these glasshouses in Paris which were in a way three places where the architect had asked for a view out at the park, he wanted vegetation and landscape, and he wanted to use solar energy. So you had the monumentality of these three glass boxes. Talking with people it became apparent, much more to me than them, that you couldn't do all these things because a greenhouse is about steaming up and not about looking out.

What we see here then is a process of introducing the objects as characters (glasshouses), defining their desired characteristics (views

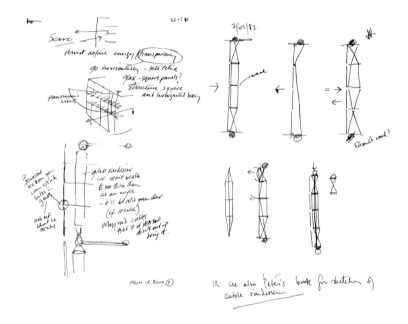

Figure 15.1
Two pages from Ian Ritchie's sketchbook exploring the ideas of transparency and panorama in the design of the glass pavilions at La Villette. The photograph shows the end result

out, vegetation and landscape, solar gain) and then through conversation identifying conflicts between them in terms of the possibilities for physical realisation. This first important step in the design conversation therefore is that of identification. This is very similar to what Schön called 'naming' (Schön 1984). Naming however seems too simple a word to describe properly what is happening here. Even in a normal conversation when you introduce someone, in addition to naming them, you often say something about them, perhaps where they work or who they are married to or some other aspect of their life which is relevant to the current context of the conversation. So it is in design conversations that the significant elements are not just named, but that their very character begins to be explored.

Here, in this design context then, Ritchie leaps in his conversation from the abstract ideas about 'vegetation' and 'solar gain' to his own experience of how these two are normally realised physically in a glasshouse. This experience leads him to see a conflict between the steamed up greenhouse and the 'views out' which are also desired in this case. This central and elaborate process of introducing characters is more than simply 'naming' and we shall therefore call it 'identifying'.

Conversations and negotiations

What we see next in Ian Ritchie's design conversation is a process of reconciliation of the conflict. As we shall see this is done through a very clever trick. It is all a matter of how you look at the problem it seems. Look from the right angle or perspective and the problem vanishes.

> There was a conflict and what we homed in on was in fact a notion of transparency, it wasn't about material. It was about how you define transparency. It took us actually quite a long time, in the end we decided that we had to play something on a clear surface to tell you that it was there. Of course the irony is that you use glass and when you're working perpendicular to it, its magic as it disappears, but as soon as you go oblique to it then it is opaque. So we learned from those conversations about the concept of transparency.

First of all then Ritchie attempts to 'think through' the problem by introducing the idea or concept of transparency. He realises that steamed up glass in conventional greenhouse frames will not achieve the 'views out'. However he also recognises the irony that a perfectly clear glass is invisible and gives no sense of being there. Next he begins to talk about the technicalities of the solution rather than the abstractions of the problem.

> The idea that you have got a transparent plane and it's very big, 40 m high or whatever, you then have to develop an idea of how to hold it up. The notion of transparency; if it's not understood by everybody, very clearly, is very easy to miss, and in fact we missed it – three of us together and though we defined transparency, we ended up with a kind of vertical structure, a square grid. But then we were trying for the bracing of the glass, the wind bracing and everything else, we weren't relating it back to transparencies.

> Certain problems had emerged, things like maintenance, things like cost, and all these are extra. Then we suddenly realised that part of the idea of transparency was panorama, if this transparency had panorama you've got it. To us this implied horizontality which introduced other problems for us like maintaining something with a horizontal structure. Eventually that was how we arrived at the form you see.

Now we can see how this exploration of the materials that could be used in the solution had led to a form with which Ritchie was unhappy. His unhappiness relates to their failure to produce a solution that achieved the 'transparency' he had identified as a key quality of the desired 'views out'. Suddenly comes this moment of insight in which a new concept is introduced, that of 'panorama'. This carries with it an assumption of horizontality in the glazing pattern which changes the form from its previous vertical emphasis.

What is important here is just how much progress is made through this conversation. It matters not at all whether there are one or many designers, the process seems to be the same. A conversational interaction with the situation is taking place in which drawings and ideas each have their place. The ideas are undoubtedly processed through concepts described in words. These words have enormous significance since they represent a complex set of characteristics some of which may help the designer to see a way of proceeding. The drawings appear to reveal problems and enable the designer to see unsatisfactory situations. Together these two powerful forces combine to make the very essence of design thinking. However it is the very introduction first of 'transparency' and then of 'panorama' that enables Ritchie here to view the problem in such a way that all the conflicts are resolved. It looks much more like a form of negotiation than a form of moving from problem to solution based on some theoretical knowledge.

This introduces us to another common form of conversation that is helpful to our enquiry here. We shall now explore the idea of conversation as negotiation. In negotiation two or more parties begin with disparate positions about some common purpose. The parties come into the negotiation taking different views and having different objectives but with a willingness to try to reach some form of agreement that all parties can accept. We can see the design process as one of negotiation too. Famous and public negotiations are often very tricky. For example in any industrial relations dispute or international squabble over territory the parties seem completely irreconcilable for most of the conversations they hold.

The problem and solution views

In fact the negotiation between problem and solution in design turns out to be every bit as tricky to resolve. Earlier on in this book the argument was advanced that problems and solutions have a curious relationship in design. In Chapter 3 we arrived at a diagram showing the design process as a negotiation between problem and solution (see Fig. 3.7). In Chapter 4 we saw how design solutions are often integrated responses to design problems. In fact one of the most beautiful examples of this integration can be seen even earlier in the book in the description by George Sturt of the dished cartwheel (see Figs 2.4 and 2.5). Later in Chapter 6 we saw how the architect Denys Lasdun described features of his National Theatre in London as integrated solutions. In both these examples what we see is that a single idea in the solution, the dish shape of the cartwheel or Lasdun's 'strata', simultaneously solves many problems. As we have also shown in Chapter 5, success in solving those problems cannot necessarily be measured using a single metric. For example we cannot measure the goodness of a view and the energy efficiency of a window with the same kind of scale. Even worse, the relative importance of all the problems a designer is solving is also not easy to establish clearly or objectively. It is no wonder then that negotiating a 'good' solution to a complex design brief is so tricky.

In fact it turns out that this tension between a problem view and a solution view of the situation is at the very heart of the way designers have to think. It is what makes design as an activity not only so challenging and frustrating but also so satisfying and compulsive. We have seen repeatedly in this book that designers tend to be 'solution focussed' rather than 'problem focussed' in their approach. I have written in *What Designers Know* about the way in which designers seem to accumulate knowledge about solutions (Lawson 2004). The role of this knowledge in helping to form the guiding principles we have discussed in Chapter 10 is also explored. In essence designers tend to have relatively little theory that enables them to get from problem to solution. Rather they tend to acquire considerable stores of knowledge about solutions and their possibilities or affordances.

So designers have the task of negotiating reconciliation between these two views of the situation they are dealing with. The problem view is expressed generally in the form of needs, desires, wishes and requirements. The solution view on the other hand is expressed in terms of the physicality of materials, forms, systems and components. Since these two views share no common language this reconciliation requires some very clever mental tricks indeed. In this view of the design process then we do not really see designing as problem solving in the traditional sense of that phrase. We do not see designing as a directional activity that moves from problem through some theoretical procedure to solution. Rather we see it as a dialogue, a conversation, a negotiation between what is desired and what can be realised.

Skilled facilitators of negotiations know that progress is often best made by avoiding some areas of dispute where resolution appears difficult and concentrating on others where things look more promising. Often this results in reaching some agreement on minor areas with a consequent build up of feelings of confidence and trust which then carries over into considerations of the more intractable issues. Some experienced designers have suggested that the drawing may cause problems in this negotiation with a client. The use of words rather than graphical images can offer a less solution-oriented view in this process. The well-known British product designer Richard Seymour has described how he presented ideas to British Rail who wanted to develop a new InterCity train. They had invited a number of leading designers to submit proposals. The Seymour/Powell submission was not based on drawings but on the verbal explanation to British Rail that their design would be 'heroic' in the manner of the British Airways Concorde and that it would once again make children want to become train drivers as in early times (Fig. 15.2). Similarly the Czech architect Eva Jiricna has described how she communicates with her clients in verbal rather than graphical media. She tells how 'I try to express in words what they (the clients) want, and then I try to twist it into a different statement and then draw it' (Lawson 1994). Through this device Eva seems to be able to avoid her clients making prejudgements based on their previous experience of the kinds of rather hi-tech materials she often employs. The verbal

Figure 15.2
Richard Seymour with his design for a train intended to make children want to become engine drivers again

description allows people to interpret shades of meaning not allowed by the drawing. In the same way we can easily be disappointed by the film of a book we have previously read. During the reading we will have built up our own image of the characters and places which the film has no alternative but to contradict.

Nigel Cross has shown the importance of the conjunction between drawing and talking in design groups (Cross 1996). In his study a design group was trying to design a device for carrying a hiker's backpack on a mountain bicycle. Cross showed that well over an hour into the design process one member of the group introduced a design concept with the words 'maybe it's like a little vacuum-formed tray'. Prior to this point the team had been using the word 'bag' as a way of describing to each other what they were trying to create. The word 'tray' was sufficiently evocative without being too prescriptive, and this word then continued to be used by all the members of the team in turn as they drew alternative interpretations of how this might work. In the protocol that Cross was studying this moment of introducing the word 'tray' had enormous impact on the final design. Quite simply it changed the designers' view of the situation.

Eckert and Stacey (2000) showed in an interesting study of fashion designers how conversations about designs are largely based on references to previous solutions. They found that knitwear designers talking among themselves 'describe design almost exclusively in terms of combinations and modifications of design elements that they refer to either by category labels or by their origins'.

An example of this offered by Eckert and Stacey is 'a jumper like the blue one last year, but a bit longer and with a V-neck'. This research also linked the work to a previous study of helicopter designers working for GKN Westland, which suggests that this finding may be fairly generic. Thus a design currently being considered in a process was described as a recombination and modification of elements taken from previously known designs. What this research showed was that enormously complex sets of ideas can be communicated in this simple way. Of course this also showed the extent to which a group of designers needed to share a common understanding and knowledge base in order to collaborate. In the previous example then as the authors point out 'blue' or a 'bit longer' has a different meaning in 1999 than for 1996. This leads to a whole language of design based on an understanding of design concepts and precedent that is extremely powerful and economical but only works if the schemata used are shared. 'Often the referents of the designers' descriptions are nowhere to be seen, but are simply part of the designers' shared cultural experience' (Eckert and Stacey 2000).

Negotiating between the problem and solution view

Maher and Poon (1996) talk of how designers 'play around with ideas to get more understanding about the problem rather than focus on just finding a solution'. They go on to develop what they call a 'co-evolution' model of designing using the paradigm of genetic evolution algorithms. In this model they see a series of solution states each evolving from the previous one in parallel to a series of problem states again each evolving from the previous one. However in the Maher and Poon diagram there are cross-influences in both directions so potentially each evolutionary development is the product of the previous state in both the problem and solution series. They suggest that this highly ingenious notion could be implanted in software to produce design-like thought, although the examples they give do seem to belong to the world of fairly well-defined and highly constrained problems.

In a delightful study Dorst and Cross (2001) showed real evidence of the validity of the Maher and Poon co-evolution model in some design protocols. However even more interestingly they suggest that adherence to this way of thinking may be characteristic of design processes which we consider to be creative. They set nine industrial designers the task of designing a new litter disposal system for new trains on the Dutch railway network. Remarkably all nine designers followed a similar reasoning path which hinged around connecting various separate pieces of information about newspapers. In different parts of the brief these were identified as a significant proportion of the refuse generated on trains, often left behind on luggage racks, and as being a nuisance to the train cleaners. Again elsewhere in the brief, the client expressed a wish to develop a more environmentally friendly image. Each one of Dorst and Cross's designers finally arrived at a solution which involved collecting and keeping newspapers separately from other refuse and designing special containers for them. Thus they effectively took on a new problem; that of designing a container specifically for the cleaners to collect newspapers in. Amusingly Dorst and Cross observe that the designers also all thought they were being original and creative in doing this! As Dorst and Cross point out, this behaviour aligns beautifully with the Maher and Poon co-evolution model. It was possible to see in the protocols a process in which pieces of information in the problem were collected together to form a single idea that led to an evolution in the solution state and a redefinition of the problem.

Framing

So we have discussed the idea of conversation as negotiation. We have seen forms of this negotiation to resolve conflicts and forms of negotiation between the problem and solution view of the design situation. What is common here is the idea that somehow, through a clever mental process, some obstacle or conflict is simply removed by taking a particular view. In all such negotiation the skill lies in finding this view. In the design process the equivalent of this can be seen in an activity that Schön has called 'framing' (Schön 1984). In a way this framing process is similar to the idea of the primary generator which we introduced in Chapter 3 and discussed in Chapter 11. In the sense that it has been used in those discussions a primary generator is most normally a solution-driven idea. Quite simply a suggested form of solution is proposed and the implications of this are then explored. Schön's idea of framing is a rather looser notion and is often seen as more problem driven. In truth it is not entirely clear exactly what Schön meant by a 'frame'. The idea is none the less useful for its vagueness, and we might note in passing that vague language is often helpful in the more sensitive periods of negotiations!

A frame however can be seen to be a sort of window on the world. In our case that world is the design situation. Looked at from some angles the situation looks difficult to resolve whereas from other viewpoints it might seem much less tricky. One way of thinking about this would be the 'video referee' now used in a number of sports such as rugby and cricket. A complex event has just occurred on the field and the referee or umpire was not able to tell in real time from his position what the correct decision should be about this. A so-called 'video referee' then watches video clips from several angles to help make the decision. Some of these angles may be relatively uninformative but sometimes one of them makes the whole situation much clearer and as a result the decision is easily made. In design conversations a frequently employed form of negotiating is to select a particular view of the situation in such a way that what appeared to be difficult becomes clearer or what appeared to involve conflict can be seen to be harmonious. In Ian Ritchie's conversation this was done through the idea of turning 'transparency' into 'panorama'. This slightly different way of seeing what was really required enabled a new design solution to emerge that then allowed the designers to reconcile conflicts.

It is highly likely that experienced designers will have their own ways of framing situations which they have used before and which have proved helpful in the past. We can see that the guiding principles we discussed in Chapter 10 may well offer sources of inspiration about such frames for experienced designers. Nigel Cross studied the British product designer Kenneth Grange who could be described as having a set of guiding principles about the importance of radical constraints or primary functions (Cross 2001a). His varied output is characterised by products that reflect in a very direct and modern way their main purpose, their usability and their construction. So Grange it seems would frame his problems through the eyes of the user. 'I start entirely from the point of view of, can I make the use of the thing better'. One of Grange's most influential and well-known designs was the Kodak Brownie Vecta camera. This was to be seen hanging around the neck of a whole generation of amateur snap-shot takers and at the time became quite iconic. Grange totally reversed the form into a vertical or portrait format rather than the more normal horizontal landscape format. This he did after realising that the vast majority of pictures that were going to be taken with this sort of equipment were of people. According to Cross, it was almost literally the case that he saw the problem through the eyes of his users, and Cross describes this 'as though his ability is primarily perceptual'. Grange also gives us an insight into this process by telling Cross that 'you do have to ferret around . . . to find that which is then suddenly obvious to you'. Grange also refers to 'unlikely analogies' as being the secret of his process. It seems then that this is a process of turning the problem around, describing it in different ways, explaining it to other people, talking to the client, in fact any form of conversation that might reframe the situation until some alignment becomes obvious between what is desired and what can be realised. Such a moment is recognised frequently in the descriptions of creative designers.

Conversations as shared experience

We must also remember however that design is very often a team activity and so the way in which these ideas are shared by the team is likely to be important to us in developing our understanding of the process. The idea of conversation can help us again here too. Another characteristic of normal conversations is the extent to which they reinforce the idea of shared experience. Conversations at work in which colleagues discuss the programmes on television the previous evening or the football or hockey match played by their local teams are obvious examples. The way in which we like to reminisce and recall social occasions from our past offer other popular examples. In a normal everyday conversation one participant may comment on the weather that day. Such a comment only works if the other participants share the ideas about what makes pleasant or unpleasant weather. Imagine how unsustainable such incidental gossip would become if you were talking to an interplanetary visitor unfamiliar with earthly climates. It seems that teams gain social strength through shared experience and that such events and the conversations that surround them offer ways of establishing strong ties and bonds.

Again this seems to have a parallel in design, most particularly in long-lived creative design teams. In the previous chapter we saw some examples of the work of the architect Richard MacCormac. As has been shown elsewhere his practice uses key shared concepts to progress their design ideas (Lawson 2004). Conversations with several members of the practice revealed popular words representing sophisticated sets of architectural ideas. For example the rather unusual word 'belvedere' being used widely in these conversations suggested strongly that the ideas it represented were discussed by the members of the practice. This phenomenon of using simple words or phrases to represent complex sets of ideas that the members of a design practice understand seems particularly significant for creative teams. As we have seen, the design process often involves very fast and intense periods of idea creation. The conversations that go on at these stages must therefore be very high level and rapid too. It simply would not work if every major concept raised in the conversation had to be explained.

The conversation with the drawing

We have already discussed the relative advantages of words and images in designing. However there can be no doubt that the drawing process is generally central to most design processes. In an earlier edition of *How Designers Think* I developed a model of the kinds of drawings that designers use which was based on an earlier taxonomy first suggested by Fraser and Henmi (1994). In fact that model has since been taken rather further and become more elaborate as research has suggested its initial inadequacies. It will not be presented here in its entirety since the reader can find it in *What Designers Know* (Lawson 2004). What is important for our consideration here however is not the whole model but those kinds of drawings with which, as Schön put it, designers have conversations. Technically this is possible with any kind of drawing. Indeed it is possible too with text. When I write this book I do not know in advance every detail of what I am going to say. I have a rough idea, some major themes and an overall structure. As the text begins to emerge on the word processor I may from time to time, and indeed I do, change my mind. In a sense then my own words speak back to me, as if I were talking to myself, and when I hear them I may feel the need to make adjustments. This is what Schön described as 'reflection in action'. I am sure a musical composer must go through a similar process of writing, listening and revising. Perhaps the process is more noticeable in a drawn medium which is not linear and sequential as the text and the score are. The order in which a viewer gets information from a drawing is not determined by the author. Even the order in which we draw is less predictable and structured. When designers are producing drawings entirely for their own benefit as opposed to presenting information to others, this reflective process is almost the whole point of the drawing.

It is these design drawings, sketches, scribbles, diagrams and the like that most offer this conversational potential. This was perhaps most eloquently described to me by the great architect/engineer Santiago Calatrava (Lawson 1994).

> To start with you see the thing in your mind and it doesn't exist on paper and then you start making simple sketches and organising things and then you start doing layer after layer . . . it is very much a dialogue.

A particularly charming example of the designer having such a conversation with a drawing was first shown to me some years ago by Steven Groak who had heard the Italian architect Carlo Scarpa describing how he designed a handrail detail for his wonderful Castelvecchio Museum in Verona. Scarpa worked over several years in the building itself, designing and drawing as construction work proceeded. This process has been lovingly researched by Richard Murphy and is beautifully documented in his excellent book (Murphy 1990). Scarpa's work is notable for the way he has designed around the methods of construction employed by the craftsmen who built the work. So as Scarpa was drawing we may assume that he was also imagining the process of construction and Groak's account of his description of the process confirms this.

In the example shown here Scarpa is designing a balustrade for one of the galleries that leap across the spaces of the Castelvecchio (Fig. 15.3). He is drawing the junction between the handrail and the

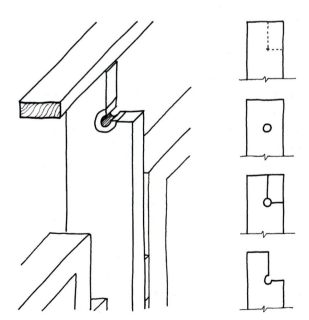

Figure 15.3
A reconstruction after that by Steven Groak of how Carlo Scarpa developed a detail through drawing the construction process

vertical posts which will support it. The width of the handrail is narrower than the posts which are needed to support the balustrade. Almost certainly this is an example of Scarpa resolving the size of a rail which fits comfortably in the hand with the structural depth of the post. However the transition is, typically for Scarpa, very carefully detailed. It is characteristic of Scarpa that such a problem would not be dismissed, or even concealed, and that junctions of these kinds were often clearly articulated. Groak explains how Scarpa achieved this kind of detail by drawing (Groak 1992):

> In drawing the lines to show where the cut edges would be, he encountered the familiar problem of the draughtsman: how do the lines cross? Do they overlap? Or stop at a point? Scarpa realised that the carpenter would face an analogous problem in cutting the piece of timber (although in fact it is not a complicated task for a skilled craftsman). Eventually he decided that the carpenter should drill a small hole at the intersection of the lines, so that the saw would change tone when it then hit the void and produce a clean cut with no overrun. To complete the detail, he then designed it to have a small brass disk inserted in the circular notch left behind . . .

One can see in this sequence of drawings how Scarpa first draws the lines, then sees the problem and finally solves it. Thus the drawing appears to talk back to the designer enabling a problem to be discovered and a solution created.

However there remains the danger which we saw in Chapter 13 of falling into the 'icon trap'. That is to say the drawing begins to dominate the conversation, sets the agenda and ultimately becomes the designed object replacing the original objective. This trap seems at its most dangerous the further designers are away from the process of making. When a design is highly unlikely to be realised then the drawing inevitably becomes more potent. Sadly this is the case for the vast majority of design projects completed by students during their education. No wonder then that students can develop a conversational style with their drawing that is not entirely constructive.

This is then a matter of the balance of power in the conversation. Herman Hertzberger expressed a concern about allowing the balance to go too far in favour of the drawing (Lawson 1994).

> A very crucial question is whether the pencil works after the brain or before. In fact what should be is that you have an idea, you think and then you score by means of words or drawing what you think. But it could also be the other way round that while drawing, your pencil, your hand is finding something, but I think that's a dangerous way. It's good for an artist but it's nonsense for an architect.

One can sympathise with Hertzberger's view here that the design drawing is not in itself an end product in the way a piece of art is. On the other hand research evidence suggests that designers, just like artists, do get inspiration and ideas from their drawings that they did not imagine in advance. Schön and Wiggins (1992) have described this as 'unexpected discovery' and it does appear to be a significant influence in the design process. Suwa and Twersky have studied the way designers work with drawings in a more controlled setting. Their work clearly suggests that designers respond to the geometric properties of drawings as they develop them and from this may 'see' other ideas than those that were in their mind before they began the drawing (Suwa and Twersky 1997). The Scarpa drawing already described here offers an excellent example of this phenomenon. In particular what this research suggests is that these design drawings tend to be of solution features rather than problem states. However it is the formal and figural properties of their own drawings that designers appear to attend to. The work shows that a high level of activity involving such considerations often follows the act of drawing. The drawings then are primarily images of the materiality of what might be, while the designer may also be considering the more abstract sets of needs and wishes. But since the drawings do not actually have to be constructed or manufactured the material constraints on them can be relaxed or tightened at will. It seems then that the drawing does indeed offer the potential to be a 'perceptual interface', as Schön and Wiggins describe it, between function and form (Schön and Wiggins 1992). Goldschmidt has also described this process in conversational terms by calling it the 'dialectics of sketching' (Goldschmidt 1991). She points out how sketches enable a dialogue between 'seeing that' and 'seeing as'. For her 'seeing that' is a way of summarising the process of reflective criticism and 'seeing as' represents the process of making analogies and reinterpretations. In fact it is one of the most flexible and powerful tools for conducting the conversation of negotiation between what is desired and what can be realised.

Conversations with computers

In the first edition of this book I included a whole chapter on designing with computers. At that time using computers in design was relatively innovatory at least in practice if not in theory. Now there are many books on the subject of computer-aided design and there is hardly a design studio where computers have not replaced at least some of the drawing boards. This is not a book about computer-aided design any more than it is a book about drawing. For these reasons it no longer seems appropriate to continue to devote a special chapter here to what is a major subject in its own right. We are however interested here in how designers interact with computers as part of a design process. There are several questions here. Those questions are not so much about what computers can do as what they cannot do. They are not so much about what happens inside the computer but how we converse with it.

Amongst the most fundamental questions we can ask here are: what knowledge do designers exchange with computers, for what reasons and how? They are also really beyond the scope of this book as I have discussed them more thoroughly in *What Designers Know* (Lawson 2004). However a brief discussion of how we converse with computers is useful in the context of seeing design as conversation. In fact much of what is called computer-aided design is in reality computer-aided drawing. Even this does not interest us here as this kind of drawing is most often for presentational purposes rather than as part of the design process itself.

Computers so far cannot design in anything like the sense that we use the verb in this book. They may be able to solve well-constrained problems, but they cannot design in any of the fields we are discussing here. So if computers appear in the design studio, other than as rather smart drawing boards, their purpose must be to aid design. If this is the case then we must assume that the greatest responsibility and certainly the final say will rest with the human designer. Again logically this tells us that the human designer will necessarily be in a conversational relationship with the computer. In fact the designer is going to have to describe the design state and then interpret some modification of it as suggested by the computer.

In general, designers seem to find this experience of using computers a frustrating one. Many well-known and successful designers have articulated their opposition to using computers in their design process. Santiago Calatrava, although using computers for structural design packages such as finite element modelling, prefers to use real physical models to computer-based ones (Lawson 1994). Others rely on computers but leave specialist staff to interact with them. The amazing work of Frank Gehry relies heavily on a great deal of computer technology for its realisation but Gehry himself prefers not even to see the screens of the computers (Lindsey

2001). Gehry is thus lucky to be able to have conversations with the members of his staff led by Jim Glymph who look after all the technology and effectively hide it from him.

Of course the computer can save designers huge amounts of time in the way my computer did for me when I was writing this book. I well remember that the first book I ever wrote had to be done on an old fashioned typewriter. It was a painfully slow process that invited no reflection or interaction. There was no easy way to make simple changes, you just had to type it all again. So of course the editing and interacting capability of computers helps designers to make images. But even here designers often describe it as rather a remote process. As Nigel Cross rather disappointedly asks (Cross 2001b):

> Why isn't using a CAD system a more enjoyable, and perhaps, also more intellectually demanding experience than it has turned out to be?

So what is the problem here? The answer to this simple question is actually rather complex and much of it beyond the scope of this book and certainly this chapter. I attempt some of the answers in *What Designers Know*. Here we should continue to concentrate on this conversational view of design. A real problem with much computer software in general and much CAD software in particular is the way in which the conversation has to be on the computer's terms rather than the human designer's terms. There are several reasons for this. Often the capabilities of the software to perform a multitude of clever tricks, most of which most users will never even bother with, means that the whole system becomes extremely complex to understand. Again my word processing software offers a good example. I have been writing with this system for many decades now but I have never read the manual or gone on any training courses because I am just too busy. As a result I am aware that there are many menu commands and features that I do not use. I can even see that some of them might be useful but only on rare occasions. I know that the opportunities to exploit these features will be so few and far between that even if I learn them I will have forgotten them by the time the next chance to make use of them arrives. So it is with computer-aided design systems but even more dramatically so.

CAD systems suffer from a much worse problem compared with word processors. Putting the text into a word processor is generally an obvious and straightforward task that does not require attention and therefore does not distract me from thinking about what I am actually trying to say. This is not the case with CAD systems. Even simple graphics systems have their own way in which you must enter information. A relatively simple task such as drawing a closed polygon or constructing an arc requires some knowledge about the system itself. A more sophisticated task involving the description of three-dimensional form is an altogether more demanding affair. If the geometry becomes irregular and in particular if it becomes curved and irregular then the whole process is likely to require highly specialist knowledge. No wonder Frank Gehry exploits his luxurious circumstances and has staff who manipulate this knowledge for him.

But even this is not the whole story of the frustration designers have in their conversation with computers. When we talk to other designers, they understand not just the shapes and forms but also the materials, systems and components that the drawings represent. In the case of architecture in particular, designers understand that actually it is what is not drawn that is really important, for architects are really manipulating space. Computers have little or none of this knowledge and are thus generally rather dumb in the conversation. They can perform some clever tricks such as viewing the objects from an infinite variety of angles and rendering them under natural or artificial lighting conditions but here they are really acting as little more than smart drawing boards. If we want to discuss with a computer how well a design might work in some functional or technical way then the computer needs knowledge not just about geometry but about what the graphical elements actually represent. So far this has turned out to be remarkably difficult to achieve reliably and efficiently.

Of course all sorts of research work has been done, and continues to be done to counter all these conversational problems of computers. Some argue that it is simply a matter of time. Once we have big enough and powerful enough computers and we have worked out all the clever algorithms needed, they will talk to us just like another human being, or so this argument goes. Essentially this is the argument behind the whole Artificial Intelligence movement. So successful has this movement been in a relatively short time that the argument appears quite convincing and of course it is remarkably seductive. It is not long ago that the opponents of this movement were saying that although we could write clever little chess playing programs, computers would never beat the grand masters. Well now they can and they have. We already have handwriting recognition and voice recognition and some limited natural language translators. So surely computers that can converse with us meaningfully about design cannot be so far away?

However there is another school of thought (Dreyfus 1992). Such a view holds that there is something quite different about some kinds of human cognition that simply cannot be reduced to the kinds of simple representation needed to put information into computers. This view claims that although we have crude natural language translators, it will never be possible to instruct a computer to translate sensitively and as accurately as people can. Such a view holds that the act of designing as we have discussed it here is probably even more uncodable. Designing is not just an extension of complex problem solving or of playing chess. It involves some cognition that is fundamentally different from those kinds of activities. It is probably one of the main reasons why designers find it so difficult to explain what they do and to discuss their ideas with their clients and users. It is to do with the fact that there is no text book for design students and there are no overarching theories that designers rely upon to practise. It is to do with the apparent lack of boundaries around the knowledge that may be useful when designing even the simplest of objects. Above all it is to do with the curious and beautiful relation between design problems and their solutions. Quite simply it is what this book is all about.

So in terms of our conversational view of design, certainly at least for now, and probably for the foreseeable future, we need an interpreter before we can talk to the computer. This is hardly the direct creative conversation that we have been discussing in this chapter. Our point here is not to attempt an answer to this or any of the other multitudes of problems of using computers in design. That argument belongs elsewhere. Our interest here is the further evidence that this frustration with computers provides of the very natural, conversational and immediate way in which designers think.

References

Cross, N. (1996). Creativity in design: not leaping but bridging. *Creativity and Cognition 1996: Proceedings of the Second International Symposium*. L. Candy and E. Edmonds (eds). Loughborough, LUTCHI.

Cross, N. (2001a). Achieving pleasure from purpose: the methods of Kenneth Grange, product designer. *The Design Journal* 4(1): 48–58.

Cross, N. (2001b). Can a machine design? *MIT Design Issues* 17(4): 44–50.

Dorst, K. and Cross, N. (2001). Creativity in the design process: co-evolution of the problem-solution. *Design Studies* 22(5): 425–437.

Dreyfus, H. L. (1992). *What Computers Still Can't Do: A Critique of Artificial Reason*. Cambridge, MA, MIT Press.

Eckert, C. and Stacey, M. (2000). Sources of inspiration: a language of design. *Design Studies* 21(5): 523–538.

Fraser, I. and Henmi, R. (1994). *Envisioning Architecture: An Analysis of Drawing*. New York, Van Nostrand Reinhold.

Goldschmidt, G. (1991). The dialectics of sketching. *Creativity Research Journal* 4(2): 123–143.

Groak, S. (1992). *The Idea of Building: Thought and Action in the Design and Production of Buildings*. London, E. & F. N. Spon.

Lawson, B. R. (1994). *Design in Mind*. Oxford, Architectural Press.

Lawson, B. R. (2004). *What Designers Know*. Oxford, Architectural Press.

Lindsey, B. (2001). *Digital Gehry: Material Resistance/Digital Construction*. Basel, Birkhauser.

Maher, M. L. and Poon, J. (1996). Modelling design exploration as co-evolution. *Microcomputers in Civil Engineering* 11(3): 195–210.

Medway, P. and Andrews, R. (1992). Building with words: discourse in an architects' office. *Carleton Papers in Applied Language Studies* 9: 1–32.

Murphy, R. (1990). *Carlo Scarpa and the Castelvecchio*. Oxford, Architectural Press.

Schön, D. A. (1983). *The Reflective Practitioner: How Professionals Think in Action*. London, Temple Smith.

Schön, D. A. (1984). Problems, frames and perspectives on designing. *Design Studies* 5(3): 132–136.

Schön, D. A. and Wiggins, G. (1992). Kinds of seeing and their function in designing. *Design Studies* 13(2): 135–156.

Suwa, M. and Twersky, B. (1997). What do architects and students perceive in their design sketches? A protocol analysis. *Design Studies* 18: 385–403.

16

Towards a model of designing

The kinds of knowledge that may enter into a design solution are practically limitless
Goel and Pirolli, *The Structure of Design Problem Spaces*

You think philosophy is difficult enough, but I tell you it is nothing to the difficulty of being a good architect.
Wittgenstein, *Conversation with M.O'C Drury 1930*

This book has relied upon a great deal of research to develop its arguments. Some of the data behind those arguments are the author's but much were collected by others. A brief look back through the book will show that a tremendously wide range of research methodology has been used in design research. It is possible to classify all these approaches.

Ways of investigating design

When the first edition of this book was written in 1980 there was relatively little empirical research into the design process. Most of what had by then been written about designing was based not on gathered evidence but on introspection. A number of designers had simply sat down and reflected on their own practice and what they thought must be happening. Thus many early writers described not a design process they had observed, but one they believed logically must take place. Perhaps some, whose work was then known as 'design methods', even described a process they thought ought to happen. Examples of this sort of work are found in Chapter 3 and would include attempted definitions of design

(Gregory 1966), maps of the process (Markus 1969), and proposed methods of working (Page 1963). These sorts of investigations are now generally regarded as rather vulnerable to the personal perceptions of the investigator. However, they undoubtedly created a valuable stimulus to the nascent field of design research.

Later we saw research that effectively put the designer in a laboratory so as to observe the process under more objective and rigorous empirical conditions. Examples of this sort of work include very artificial and highly controlled conditions in order to abstract designing sufficiently to compare the way non-designers might tackle the same sorts of problems (Lawson 1979). Other more recent work tends to allow designers to work in a more normal way but nevertheless in a controlled and monitored session (Cross et al. 1996). This may represent a very respectable form of research but it is extremely difficult to conduct with a sufficient degree of realism to be relevant to what those designers actually do in practice. The designer is still effectively in a laboratory rather than the normal studio. Timescales are compressed, collaborators and clients are absent or simulated, there is seldom open access to design precedents, no other activity takes place in parallel so there is little time for reflection and so on.

We have also seen work that simply observes designers at work in the field, or rather in the studio. An example of this is the recording and analysing of their normal conversations (Medway and Andrews 1992). While this technique offers more realism it inevitably misses much of the real action. Unfortunately the really interesting things that happen in the design process may be hidden in designers' heads rather than being audible or visible. If we simply listen to what designers are saying or watch what they are doing we are likely to be missing some significant data.

More recently we have seen an increasing use of the simple technique of asking designers to tell us what they do (Lawson 1994; Cross 1996). This might be by interviewing them or reading what they have written about their process. Although a simple idea, the skills and knowledge needed to carry out such interviews are not easily acquired. It is also difficult to know how to analyse the data since what designers write or say should not be entirely trusted. The writings of designers are notoriously misleading and this may be for several reasons. First, designers are often not natural communicators with the written word. Second, they may be writing in order to impress rather than explain and are unlikely to reveal their doubts and weaknesses. Third, because designers are used to 'selling' their designs to clients they seem to develop a post-hoc rationalisation for the process which conceals all the blind alleys which they went down and shows only a logical inexorable progress to what they now wish to present as the 'right' answer. Interviewing designers not about individual projects but about their process as a whole in a confidential way can eliminate some of these problems, but it requires even more skill, as well as extensive knowledge of the designers and their work, to carry out meaningfully and is therefore also very time consuming. However such techniques do have value in that they can be applied to experienced, expert and even famous designers who are unlikely to be willing to take part in laboratory experiments.

There is one further group of research methods that we can use to investigate design processes. Often they are stumbled upon more or less by accident. We can try either to create tools to help designers, such as CAD, simulate design with computers or imagine how computers could be made to design. There are signs that cognitive science is increasingly interested in design because of the challenges that it poses to such models of mental processes (Goel 1995). So far such techniques have tended to reveal the shortcomings of computers and of the computational theory of mind as much as they have provided insights into human designing.

Is a model of designing possible?

Designing is far too complex a phenomenon to be describable by a simple diagram. The early process map diagrams seemed at one time to be logical but turned out to be misleading once we had some empirical data. We have seen that the word 'design' is applied to an extraordinarily wide range of activity including at one extreme something that could also be called 'engineering' and at another something that could be called 'art'. We have seen that design is a highly personal and multi-dimensional process. We have seen that designers often collaborate in teams and that individuals may play quite specialist roles in such teams. Some may be particularly good at early conceptual ideation whereas others may be more skilled in forms of representation such as model-making drawing or computer modelling. Others still may be more skilled in the technical realisation of ideas or even in the actual making of designed objects themselves.

A model of design thinking then must be able to allow for all this richness and variation. At the end of Chapter 6 we developed a model of design constraints. That model is simply one way of representing the possible combinations of constraints that allow for an apparently infinite variety of design problems. Over the years many readers have kindly told me how it has helped them to design and to understand and improve their own design processes. In fact some, on hearing I was writing yet another edition of this book, have even expressed concern that I may have abandoned this model and sought to persuade me not to. Others have rightly criticised the model. Not only is that their right but it reveals yet another of its purposes which is to create a framework within which debate about design can take place. It is very much in that spirit then that I advance another rather looser model but this time not of problems but one of design activity.

The scope of a model

From all we have learned it is clear that there are several groups of activities that take place when we are designing. At the end of Part 2 of this book in Chapter 7 we listed a number of the features of design problems and solutions and of the design process. Now it is time to try to list some of the features of design thinking and the range of abilities that designers need to have. In a seminal paper Nigel Cross summarised the knowledge in the field at the time of writing (Cross 1990). He listed many of the things that designers typically do and from this drew up a list of the abilities they must have. According to Cross, designers 'produce novel unexpected solutions, tolerate uncertainty, work with incomplete information, apply imagination and constructive forethought to practical problems and use drawings and other modelling media as a means of problem solving'. One way or another we have covered all those aspects in this book. Cross however goes on to list the abilities designers must have. 'They must be able to resolve ill-defined problems, adopt solution-focussing strategies, employ abductive/productive/appositional thinking and use non-verbal, graphic and spatial modelling media.' All this suggests that Wittgenstein may have had a point when he claimed, in the quotation at the head of this chapter, that designing is more difficult than philosophy. Cross has a very useful and demanding list here of skills that we have discussed one way or another in this book. So in general this book supports the conclusions Cross arrives at. However we shall now try to go just a little further.

In an attempt to impose some sort of structure on all this it may be useful to think of these design skills under some headings. The most obvious set of skills employed by all designers are those to do with making design propositions. As we have seen designers are often solution focussed and work by generating ideas about whole or partial solutions. These solutions are sometimes developed and sometimes abandoned. We might see this whole group of skills as to do with making moves and we shall therefore refer to them as 'moving'. These moves are most often made through some form of representation. They may be described in words or put into computers or, most common of all, visualised through drawings of one kind or another. We shall call these skills 'representing'. All through this book however we have seen that there is an intriguingly close and yet complex relationship between design solutions and their problems. Another set of skills are clearly those to do with understanding problems and describing them. We shall refer to these as 'formulating'. The way moves are regulated is most obviously through the use of some kind of evaluation of them against some set of criteria however precisely or vaguely understood. There are then clearly a whole range of skills which we shall refer to as 'evaluating'. In addition to all this there is clearly some group of activities which oversee the whole process and provide support for it. A more or less conscious effort is needed to keep the whole design activity on course towards its target. In addition to this designers seem to be very actively looking at and thinking about design even when not actually designing. Donald Schön has most famously written about a range of professionals who seem to depend upon this continuous monitoring and learning process and he calls them 'reflective practitioners'. We shall refer to these skills as 'reflecting'.

Our model of designing is beginning to appear then. We have groups of activities and skills that are all needed and are commonly found in successful design. They are 'formulating', 'moving', 'representing', 'evaluating' and 'reflecting'. Through all this somehow designers seem to be able to negotiate their way to a comfortable, or at least satisfactory, understanding both of the problem and the solution and to give their clients and users at least workable and occasionally beautiful and imaginative designs.

Formulating

1 Ways of understanding design problems

Right back at the beginning of this book we explored the idea of the design process as a sequence of activities. Logically it seemed getting a brief and analysing the problem came before the synthesis of solutions. In Chapter 3 however we saw that such a simplistic model is neither accurate nor helpful. However there can be no argument that designers must be skilled in finding and stating problems and in understanding and exploring them. This group of activities is perhaps best called 'formulating'.

2 Identifying

In the problem-solving view of design these skills include the ability to reformulate and give structure to ill-structured or wicked problems. In the conversational model of design explored in Chapter 15 we saw how designers have to identify, or as Schön would put it, 'name' elements in the design situation. It is almost as if characters are being introduced in a story and their roles and personalities are being explored in order to understand how they will react to events and behave as the story unfolds. Whether we think of it as the reformulation of problems or the identification of elements, making them explicit and developing their characteristics, it is clearly an important and central design skill.

3 Framing

This book has introduced the notion several times that problems can appear different when looked at from different points of view. Perhaps the most important contribution made by Schön and his followers to the debate about design is the idea of 'framing'. This activity involves selectively viewing the design situation in a particular way for a period or phase of activity. This selective focus enables the design to handle the massive complexity and the inevitable contradictions in design by giving structure and direction to thinking while simultaneously temporarily suspending some issues. The skill to create and manipulate frames is a central one in determining how the process will unfold.

In all the original literature by Schön himself there remains a lack of clarity about exactly what a 'frame' is and what it is not. However if we take his notion of a frame almost literally we can image this to be a selective window through which can be seen only part of a wider world beyond. In the problem-solving view of design we might see this as a window on the problem space or a way of expressing and formulating the problem.

If we return to the literature on creative thinking reviewed in Chapter 9 we can now see that much of this deals with how such frames are established. In particular many of the more popular creativity techniques are designed to maximise the number of frames that become available. This might either be through the use of the different perspectives that naturally occur in different minds (brainstorming) or by using deliberate methods of shifting the individual mind into different positions (for example much of what might be found in the writings of Edward de Bono). All this suggests that we should see the skill of 'framing' as one of the most critical and central in the design process.

Representing

1 Ways of representing design situations
Although it is perfectly possible to imagine design taking place without any externalisation at all, in practice designers almost always externalise their thoughts prolifically. Indeed designers are often characterised by their habitual use of these activities. They draw, write, model, make and compute representations of their inchoate ideas for the design they are working towards. They also shuffle and represent to themselves information about the brief or problem.

2 Conversations with representations
As Schön has so eloquently put it designers interact with these representations in a conversational way (Schön 1983). The representations are thus far from being incidental outputs but are rather central inputs to the thought process. Clearly then the ability to execute these representations and manage them is one of the central skills in designing. A designer who cannot sketch is likely not to be able to 'converse' freely with the situation. Drawings are undoubtedly amongst the most central and important of all these forms of representation and those drawings come in several types including most crucially design drawings, diagrams and visionary drawings.

In Chapter 15 we also saw how important words and texts are in the process of thinking about designs. Although textual information is seldom recorded during designing in the way that sketches inevitably are it clearly plays its role in the design conversation.

We also briefly examined the way computers have started to play a role in design thinking too. However the challenge to really make them assist in the design conversation remains ahead. So far their primary role in design has been at the presentation/production drawing end of the process. Computer models like physical models are labour intensive and slow in production and so far remain rather remote compared with the sketch.

The point here however is that the forms of representation used and the skills in using them are likely to have a huge effect on the design process. It is hard to imagine Santiago Calatrava working without his model-maker or Frank Gehry working without his computer modellers. In both these cases the process is highly dependent on both team-working and specialised and skilled representation methods. One only has to look at the architecture of Calatrava and Gehry to see the effects not only on the process but also on the final product.

3 Working with multiple representations
What distinguishes the modern design process from the vernacular design process that we studied back in Chapter 2 is that designers do not actually make their designs, but rather they make representations of their designs. They make drawings, computer models, textual descriptions, physical models and so on. In a way the whole point of such a process is that it enables change and experimentation at much lower cost than would be incurred by making the designs themselves. Such a process then is based on the reduction of risk to the designer. Unfortunately what we have often seen is that the risk can be transferred to the client who pays for the representations to be made real. The skills of choosing and making representations that minimise this risk and that represent the finished design as accurately as possible to the client and to users may also be ones which are critical in the success of real design processes. These skills and the associated risks are often difficult to replicate in design education which may come in for some justifiable criticism at times for this very reason.

We have also seen that drawings, words, computer models and so on all have their own advantages and disadvantages as means of representing emerging design solutions. Some experienced and expert designers have developed and refined their processes and have become selective in the range of representations they make. For most of us this may be dangerous. It seems likely that a key skill for designers generally is not just the ability to make a variety of representations but to select them appropriately in order best to further understand the problems surrounding the current design solution state. Again because of the conversational nature of the relationship that designers have with these representations, it seems appropriate to see representing as another central and crucial skill in design.

Moving

1 Creating solution ideas
So central to design is the activity of solution generation that the word 'design' is sometimes only used to relate to this group of activities. What we have seen now is that there are several activities under this general heading of making design moves. First and most obviously, a new move may be made which has not been seen before in this process. A feature of the solution is placed, or given some shape or some relation to some other element or given some characteristics. Second, a move may alter or develop the existing state of the solution. Where do such ideas come from? We shall develop answers to that question under the section entitled Reflecting.

2 Primary generators
We have seen that designers often develop early ideas about solutions long before they have really understood the problem. This is often done through what Jane Darke called the primary generator (Darke 1978). In turn that is often influenced by the guiding principles we discussed in Chapter 10 and to which we shall return in a later section here. Just as a frame can be seen as a window on the problem space, then a primary generator can be seen as a window on the solution space.

3 Interpretive and developmental moves
Not all moves in design are entirely original to the process. Margaret Boden's distinction of 'h' and 'p' creativity is partially helpful here (Boden 1990). We have four possibilities in a design process. An idea may be entirely novel in all of history (h). Actually such events are relatively rare in our developed and sophisticated world. It might be entirely novel as far as the designer or design team are concerned (p), it might be entirely novel as far as this particular process is concerned and finally it might derive from another idea that has already appeared in this process. Design moves then are frequently the result of reflections on the represented inchoate design and are interpretations of them. Goel refers to such a move

as 'lateral' (Goel 1995). Here we shall use the word 'interpretative' to describe this activity in the sense that the word appears in Laxton's model of design learning which appeared in Chapter 9 (Laxton 1969). Such an activity involves the transformation of an existing idea into a different one albeit carrying through some of the original characteristics.

Goel's distinction between 'lateral' and 'vertical' moves allows us to introduce our final type of move. Here the idea is developed further and given clarity, more detail or substance, or embellished. In a sense the idea is being moved nearer to a realisable and definite form. Goel calls this a vertical move, but here we shall describe it as 'development'. Edison's famous adage of genius being 'one percent inspiration and ninety-nine percent perspiration' is of relevance here. Throughout a complete design process we are likely to see more episodes of interpretation than of initiation, and more episodes of development than transformation. However it may well be that what we recognise as originality or creativity in design depends more on interpretation than development and more on initiation than on interpretation. It may also be the case that each designer has different relative levels of skill in each of these activities and that design teams depend on complementary combinations of these skills to be really effective.

Bringing problems and solutions together

1 Problem and solution are inseparable
In the conversational view of design we might be less inclined to make the distinction between problem and solution. Indeed we might see frames and primary generators as ways of negotiating between a problem and solution view of the situation in order to bring about some resolution between what is required and what can be made. In some design domains the problem may be very clearly stated and success easily measured and thus the process may be more one of moving from problem to a solution which might be almost thought of as optimal. At the other end of the spectrum of design domains the problem may emerge more from an exploration of solution possibilities. Most design domains that we have explored in this book are between these two extremes and, as a result, problem and solution are better seen as two aspects of a description of the design situation rather than separate entities.

2 No clear order of appearance

One of the most persistent themes that can be found running through this book is the idea that, in design, problems do not necessarily precede solutions in the way normally expected in conventional problem solving. In Chapter 3 it was argued that designers are often solution focussed. We saw in Chapter 7 that design problems cannot be comprehensively stated and the information you need to tackle a design problem rather depends on your way of solving it. In Chapter 11 we have seen the idea of the primary generator as a way of getting on with solution production and through that developing more understanding of the problem. In Chapter 15 we have seen the idea of selectively framing the situation so that it is more amenable to solution. Thus we have seen a whole clutch of ways in which thinking about solutions and thinking about problems seem inextricably interwoven in the design process. Recent research has tended to strengthen and support this notion.

3 Briefing is a continuous process

Contrary to the wishes of many who have tried to establish route maps of the design process, briefing appears to be a continuous process. It is certainly not something that happens exclusively at the beginning but rather represents the problem formulation aspects of designing which are often greatly influenced by the emerging potential solutions. However this may well offer us one useful way to distinguish between different design fields. Some design fields have very clearly defined problems that can be quite well described and understood at the beginning of the process or very early in it. Others may characteristically have more open-ended problems that can only be very loosely described and only vaguely understood at the outset. However is seems far better to assume that briefing can continue to take place throughout the process than to assume it is simply an early stage never to be returned to.

4 Parallel lines of thought

We saw in Chapter 12 that designers appear to be able to develop parallel lines of thought about the problem–solution situation. Each line of thought seems to respond to a frame to restrict the view of the problem and to rely on a primary generator to develop ideas about the solution. It seems probable that highly creative designers may be able to sustain several of these parallel lines of thought and allow them to be incompatible or even apparently irreconcilable for periods. Judging when to drop some of them or try to resolve the conflicts between them seems to be one of the key skills required for creative design. Indeed it may even be the case that a creative reframing of the situation allows for a new view in which the various lines of thought can be incorporated into one single higher level set of ideas. The ability to think along parallel lines, deliberately maintain a sense of ambiguity and uncertainty and not to get too concerned to get to a single answer too quickly seem to be essential design skills.

Evaluating

1 Objective and subjective evaluations
Right back in Chapter 3 we looked at some proposed maps of the design process and found them all wanting in some way. However many of them included a phase of evaluation which surely must be there in design. Not only do designers generate alternatives between which choices must be made but also they must know, rather like an artist, when to stop. Cleary then designers must have evaluative abilities. In some aspects of design this can be considerably aided by technology when numerical criteria can be set, for example the energy consumption of a building. However as we saw in Chapter 5, design characteristically involves making judgements between alternatives along many dimensions that cannot be reduced to a common metric. Designers must then have a very particular evaluative skill enabling them to feel comfortable about arriving at such tricky judgements. I know many excellent design critics who are not all necessarily very good designers themselves. As with all the factors summarised in this chapter, some designers are better than others at some of these skills. One often for example finds in a school of design students who will go on to become highly creative, respected and high achieving original designers, nevertheless being usefully taught by tutors who perhaps themselves have never reached such productively creative heights themselves but who are excellent critics.

Designers must be able to perform both objective and subjective evaluations and be able to make judgements about the relative benefits of them even though they may rely on incompatible methods of measurement. Indeed designers may develop their own particular tools for evaluating designs against the criteria that are often important to them either because of the kinds of objects they frequently design or because of the guiding principles they have developed.

2 Suspending judgement

Undoubtedly one of the skills that a designer must have here is to also be able to suspend judgement to allow creative thought to flow and ideas to mature before they are subjected to the harsh light of penetrating criticism. Extremely talented and creative designers are not always very helpful when teaching students as they sometimes fail to appreciate just when and how to do this for a particular student and instead just impose their own ideas and process. Knowing when and how to evaluate as an individual, in groups, and design teams is a core design skill. It may not be the glamorous part of designing but getting it wrong can be very damaging to the process.

Reflecting

1 Reflection in action

Since Schön introduced the idea of the 'reflective practitioner' there has been much more recognition of the importance of this concept of reflecting upon actions. In design at least this seems to be open to two interpretations which we might call 'reflection in action' and 'reflection on action'. The concept of reflection in action is already covered here by combining our formulation, moving and evaluation activities. With such a model the designer is more or less continually reflecting on the current understanding of the problem and the validity of the emerging solution or solutions.

2 Reflection on action

Reflection on action can be seen as higher level activity in which the process is monitored rather than the state of the design. Such a concept clearly involves a mental 'standing back' and asking if the process is going well or might be steered differently. Again the concepts of recognising situations, knowing that certain approaches may be useful in those situations and having a set of skills to carry these approaches out all come into play here. The design constraint model introduced in Chapter 6 may offer some assistance here, as may the model introduced in this chapter. Thus reflection on action can be seen as a combination of asking which problems have been examined and which have been neglected, and then of asking if the processes involved in representing, formulating and moving have all been brought to bear on the case. Again this is a skill and an attitude that is not necessarily easily acquired or remembered.

299

Knowing when to reflect on actions, and how, may be one of the most important skills a designer may possess. A very early design idea can be very easily knocked down by a tough critic and so a delicate process can be brought to a grinding halt by too much early reflection. Failing to reflect on the process can lead a designer to fail to explore important avenues. It may be that normal design education does not necessarily develop this skill as well as it might, being so often rather more focussed on the quality of the end-product of design.

3 Guiding principles

Designers seem to develop their own programme of intellectual endeavour. This results in what we have called 'guiding principles'. These can be seen as a design philosophy or a set of values about what designers hold as important in their own domain. We saw how varied these could be but also how important in guiding the designer in Chapter 10. However the interaction between these guiding principles and each individual design project is clearly a two-way process. Designers effectively use each project as a way of researching their chosen area, progressing their understanding of it and developing their guiding principles. This can then be seen as a third form of reflection, not so much on the individual design but more on the implications the current work has for the wider domain.

4 Collecting precedent or references

Designers rely heavily on reference material and tend to collect this avidly throughout their careers. I have argued elsewhere that designers use more episodic knowledge than many other professions who may use more procedural knowledge (Lawson 2004). This is to say designers of the kind we have been studying here have few rules that tell them how to get from problem to solution, but rather they have a great deal of knowledge about existing solutions and their potential affordances. The ability to execute referential drawings outside the actual process of design seems likely to be central to the development of this episodic knowledge of precedent. In short, designers tend to keep sketchbooks. The skills of observation and recording are thus also central to the ability to store knowledge that may later be used in formulation. Clearly a designer's guiding principles will tend in turn to influence the kinds of experiences and references sought out, gathered, reflected upon and stored.

The search for such reference material is not just an internal cognitive one. It has always been supported by styles, pattern books, libraries and personal sketchbooks and other records. Today however it is increasingly supported by computer-based searches especially across that enormous panorama of possibilities that is now the Internet. Making good use of such material and developing better tools to assist in these searches again provide interesting challenges for those working in the field of information science.

How designers in turn make use of all this precedent when designing perhaps remains one of the biggest challenges still facing the design research field. Why can some designers sometimes draw on references from apparently remote situations and use them in quite novel ways that not only surprise us but also seem entirely relevant to us? Perhaps this is at the very heart of what we mean by creative production.

It certainly seems that experienced practitioners appear to recognise parallels with precedent rather than analyse situations. This process has the double advantage of massively speeding up thinking by side-stepping much lengthy analytical thought, and by making links between problems and solutions. Clearly a very important ability then for designers is to be able to recognise features of situations that make connections with apparently remote sets of ideas.

Skills and values

It seems important and useful to draw a distinction between skills and values. When we ran a major project at my university to develop the idea of working with clients and users in design education we quickly discovered the importance of both these two in engineering change. Put simply we could devise ways of giving students skills for working with clients. However if their tutors did not appear to value the idea of involving clients in the design process this might have little effect on what the students actually did. On the other hand we could lecture the students intensively about the importance of involving clients but unless we developed skills of consultation, listening, and explaining, again we would have little effect on the eventual outcome. To make something work in a design process, the skills and values must both be there together.

The guiding principles that we explored in Chapter 10 are often in reality driven by sets of values. That is to say the designers believe that it is important to design collaboratively (Hertzberger) or with sculpturally expressive structures (Calatrava) or in a sustainable way (Yeang) and so on. In turn this causes those designers to lay relative emphasis on certain slices of the design constraint model we developed in Chapter 6. However this cannot be done unless they also develop skills in relation to these ideas. So for example Yeang has developed a set of procedures to calculate energy consumption and forms of solutions that minimise it. Le Corbusier developed his proportion tool; Calatrava has extraordinarily well-developed sketching and modelling techniques to enable him to produce complex three-dimensional forms and so on. As we see above, this in turns leads these designers to collect precedent that helps them to produce solutions that embody the values they espouse. Thus the process can be seen as a virtuous self-reinforcing cycle across many design projects. Occasionally we also see designers making significant shifts in their value systems, guiding principles and precedent collecting and thus going through phases of producing significantly and recognisably different design solutions.

Epilogue

Many years of research and thinking have gone into this book. The first edition was published almost exactly a quarter of a century ago. When it was first published, design research was a mere babe in arms. It is now a rich and quite sophisticated field but full of contradictions and argument. Perhaps we might feel it has reached those perilous argumentative adolescent years. It is certainly not yet a mature adult. Hopefully this book has shown that just as there are many ways of designing so there are many ways of describing design. Some of those ways have been given more attention in this book than others and inevitably that to some extent reflects the personal position of the author. However research continues to emerge that brings yet new paradigms to bear on the problem.

Only recently Stumpf and McDonnell (2002) suggested we should understand the way designers work in teams by applying ideas from the fields of dialectics and rhetoric. By contrast John Gero and his colleagues offer a model of more or less the same phenomenon explained using the ideas of computer software agents (Gero and Kannengiesser 2004). A trawl through the literature can thus often reveal several alternative interpretations of many of the features of the design process that have been discussed in this book. Some authors will advance their ideas in the forms of 'models' often accompanied by diagrams, others may be in the form of lists, and others simply in prose. The extent to which these ideas actually help you to understand design better is probably more to do with your personal cognitive style, interests and preferences rather than due to some absolute correctness in the model. Some researchers argue persuasively and elegantly that different paradigms are fundamentally at odds with each other (Dorst 1997). On the other hand the more you analyse all these views of design the more you can see parallels in what they have to say about actual practice.

Even after all this effort I remain tormented by a continuing concern. It is that when I read another book or article or listen to a conference paper about the design process I can usually tell whether the author is actually a designer or not. It remains the case that the design process can be learned chiefly through practice and is very difficult to teach well. It is extremely difficult to understand design without actually doing it. For all our empirical science and lofty philosophy we still seem remarkably dependent on our own experience to interpret and make sense of more systematically acquired data. Nigel Cross' wonderful phrase 'designerly ways of knowing' both beautifully encapsulates this problem and stands as a symbol for the tantalising nature of our knowledge about the subject (Cross 1982). Frank Lloyd Wright was greatly influenced by the upbringing he received from his mother who, he was later to explain, believed that he would become a great architect even before he was born. She developed her own system of education for him based on the ideas of Friedrich Froebel. It seems however she believed that his great talent would disappear should he be foolish enough to enquire into its nature. Obviously this book shows that I do not take such a position. To return to the theme of the very first chapter, design is a form of thinking, and thinking is a skill. Skills can be acquired and developed. Those who have a high degree of expertise in such skills often appear willing to learn even more and yet seem capable of performing with little conscious effort. Just how one should approach the nurturing of design skills throughout a design career is something that remains hotly disputed and highly personal. Understanding more about *How Designers Think* is one important step on that journey.

References

Boden, M. (1990). *The Creative Mind: Myths and Mechanisms*. London, Weidenfeld and Nicolson.

Cross, N. (1982). Designerly ways of knowing. *Design Studies* 3(4): 221–227.

Cross, N. (1990). The nature and nurture of the design ability. *Design Studies* **11**(3): 127–140.

Cross, N. (1996). Winning by design: the methods of Gordon Murray, racing car designer. *Design Studies* **17**(1): 91–107.

Cross, N., Christiaans, H. et al. (eds) (1996). *Analysing Design Activity*. Chichester, Wiley.

Darke, J. (1978). The primary generator and the design process. In W. E. Rogers and W. H. Ittleson (eds) *New Directions in Environmental Design Research: proceedings of EDRA 9*, pp. 325–337, Washington, EDRA.

Dorst, K. (1997). *Describing Design: A Comparison of Paradigms*. Delft, Technical University of Delft.

Gero, J. S. and Kannengiesser, U. (2004). The situated function–behaviour–structure framework. *Design Studies* **25**(4): 373–391.

Goel, V. (1995). *Sketches of Thought*. Cambridge, Mass, MIT Press.

Gregory, S. A. (1966). *The Design Method*. London, Butterworths.

Lawson, B. R. (1979). Cognitive strategies in architectural design. *Ergonomics* **22**(1): 59–68.

Lawson, B. R. (1994). *Design in Mind*. Oxford, Architectural Press.

Lawson, B. R. (2004). *What Designers Know*. Oxford, Architectural Press.

Laxton, M. (1969). Design education in practice. In K. Baynes (ed.) *Attitudes in Design Education*. London, Lund Humphries.

Markus, T. A. (1969). Design and research. *Conrad* **1**(2).

Medway, P. and Andrews, R. (1992). Building with words: discourse in an architects' office. *Carleton Papers in Applied Language Studies* **9**: 1–32.

Page, J. K. (1963). Review of the papers presented at the conference. In J. C. Jones and D. Thornley (eds) *Conference on Design Methods*. Oxford, Pergamon.

Schön, D. A. (1983). *The Reflective Practitioner: How Professionals Think in Action*. London, Temple Smith.

Stumpf, S. C. and McDonnell, J. T. (2002). Talking about team framing: using argumentation to analyse and support experiential learning in early design. *Design Studies* **23**(1): 5–23.

Bibliography

Agabani, F. A. (1980). Cognitive Aspects in Architectural Design Problem Solving. PhD thesis, University of Sheffield.

Aish, R. (1977). Prospects for design participation. *Design Methods and Theories* **11**(1).

Akin, O. (1986). *Psychology of Architectural Design*. London, Pion.

Alexander, C. (1964). *Notes on the Synthesis of Form*. New York, McGraw Hill.

Alexander, C. (1966). A city is not a tree. *Design* **206**: 44–55.

Anthony, K. H. (1991). *Design Juries on Trial: The Renaissance of the Design Studio*. New York, Van Nostrand Reinhold.

Archer, L. B. (1969). The structure of the design process. In *Design Methods in Architecture*. London, Lund Humphries.

Asimow, M. (1962). *Introduction to Design*. Englewood Cliffs, Prentice Hall.

Auger, B. (1972). *The Architect and the Computer*. London, Pall Mall.

BAA (1995). *The Project Process Handbook*. London, British Airports Authority (internal publication).

Bartlett, F. C. (1932). *Remembering*. Cambridge, Cambridge University Press.

Bartlett, F. C. (1958). *Thinking*. London, George Allen and Unwin.

Bellini, M. (1977). The typewriter as 'just another limb'. *Design* **348**(December).

Benfield, E. (1940). *Purbeck Shop: A Stoneworker's Story of Stone*. Cambridge, Cambridge University Press.

Berlyne, D. E. (1965). *Structure and Direction in Thinking*. New York, John Wiley.

Bill, P. (ed.) (1990). *Building towards 2001*. London, National Contractors Group.

Boden, M. (1990). *The Creative Mind: Myths and Mechanisms*. London, Weidenfeld and Nicolson.

Boje, A. (1971). *Open-plan Offices*. London, Business Books.

Broadbent, G. (1973). *Design in Architecture*. New York, John Wiley.

Buckle, R. (1955). *Modern Ballet Design*. London, A & C Black.

Burton, R. (1979). Energy in buildings. *Architects' Journal* **170**(44): 922.

Burton, R., Ahrends, P. and Koralek, P. (1971). Small group design and the idea of quality. *RIBA Journal* **78**(6): 232–239.

Cairns, G. M. (1996). User input to design: confirming the 'User-Needs Gap' model. *Environments by Design* **1**(2): 125–140.

Candy, L. and Edmonds, E. (1996). Creative design of the Lotus bicycle: implications for knowledge support systems research. *Design Studies* **17**(1): 71–89.

Chermayeff, S. and Alexander, C. (1963). *Community and Privacy*. Harmondsworth, Penguin.

Clegg, G. L. (1969). *The Design of Design*. Cambridge, Cambridge University Press.

Crawshaw, D. T. (1976). Co-ordinating working drawings. Building Research Establishment.

Crinson, M. and Lubbock, J. (1994). *Architecture: Art or Profession?* Manchester, Manchester University Press.

Cross, N. (1975). *Design and Technology*. Milton Keynes, Open University Press.

Cross, N. (1977). *The Automated Architect*. London, Pion.

Cross, N. (1982). Designerly ways of knowing. *Design Studies* 3(4): 221–227.

Cross, N. (1990). The nature and nurture of the design ability. *Design Studies* 11(3): 127–140.

Cross, N. (1996). Creativity in design: not leaping but bridging. *Creativity and Congition 1996: Proceedings of the Second International Symposium*. Loughborough, LUTCHI.

Cross, N. (1996). Winning by design: the methods of Gordon Murray, racing car designer. *Design Studies* 17(1): 91–107.

Cross, N. (2001). Achieving pleasure from purpose: the methods of Kenneth Grange, product designer. *The Design Journal* 4(1): 48–58.

Cross, N. (2001). Can a machine design? *MIT Design Issues* 17(4): 44–50.

Cross, N. and Roy, R. (1975). *Design Methods Manual*. Milton Keynes, Open University Press.

Cross, N., Christiaans, H. et al. (ed.) (1996). *Analysing Design Activity*. Chichester, Wiley.

Daley, J. (1969). A philosophical critique of behaviourism in architectural design. *Design Method in Architecture*. London, Lund Humphries.

Darke, J. (1978). The primary generator and the design process. In *New Directions in Environmental Design Research: Procedings of EDRA 9*. pp. 325–337. Washington, EDRA.

de Bono, E. (1967). *The Use of Lateral Thinking*. London, Jonathan Cape.

de Bono, E. (1968). *The Five Day Course in Thinking*. Harmondsworth, Allen Lane.

de Bono, E. (1991). *Six Action Shoes*. London, Fontana.

De Groot, A. D. (1965). *Thought and Choice in Chess*. The Hague, Mouton.

Dickson, D. (1974). *Alternative Technology and the Politics of Technical Change*. London, Fontana.

Dorst, K. (1997). *Describing Design: A Comparison of Paradigms*. Delft, Technical University of Delft.

Dorst, K. and Cross, N. (2001). Creativity in the design process: co-evolution of the problem-solution. *Design Studies* 22(5): 425–437.

Dreyfus, H. L. (1992). *What Computers Still Can't Do: A Critique of Artificial Reason*. Cambridge, MA, MIT Press.

Duffy, F. (1993). *The Responsible Workplace*. London, Butterworth Heineman.

Eastman, C. M. (1970). On the analysis of the intuitive design process. In *Emerging Methods in Environmental Design and Planning*. Cambridge, Mass, MIT Press.

Eberhard, J. P. (1970). We ought to know the difference. In *Emerging Methods in Environmental Design and Planning*. Cambridge, Mass, MIT Press.

Eckert, C. and Stacey, M. (2000). Sources of inspiration: a language of design. *Design Studies* 21(5): 523–538.

Edmonds, E. A. and Candy, L. (1996). Supporting the creative user: a criteria based approach to interaction design. In *Creativity and Cognition*. pp. 57–66 Loughborough, LUTCHI.

Elliot, P. (1972). *The Sociology of the Professions*. London, Macmillan.

Fodor, J. A. (1975). *The Language of Thought*. Cambridge, Mass, Harvard University Press.

Forty, A. (1986). *Objects of Desire: Design and Society since 1750*. London, Thames and Hudson.

Fraser, I. and Henmi, R. (1994). *Envisioning Architecture: An Analysis of Drawing*. New York, Van Nostrand Reinhold.

Frazer, J. (1995). *An Evolutionary Architecture*. London, The Architectural Association.

Gardner, C. (1989). Seymour/Powell: a young British design team with international flair. *Car Styling* **70**: 110–132.

Garner, W. R. (1962). *Uncertainty and Structure as Psychological Concepts*. New York, John Wiley.

Gero, J. S. and Kannengiesser, U. (2004). The situated function–behaviour–structure framework. *Design Studies* **25**(4): 373–391.

Getzels, J. W. and Jackson, P. W. (1962). *Creativity and Intelligence: Explorations with Gifted Children*. New York, John Wiley.

Goel, V. (1995). *Sketches of Thought*. Cambridge, Mass, MIT Press.

Goldschmidt, G. (1991). The dialectics of sketching. *Creativity Research Journal* **4**(2): 123–143.

Gosling, D. and Maitland, B. (1984). *Concepts of Urban Design*. London, Academy Editions.

Green, C. (1971). Learning to design. *Journal of Architectural Research and Teaching* **2**(1).

Green, C. (1977). *Gambit*. University of Sheffield.

Gregory, S. A. (1966). *The Design Method*. London, Butterworths.

Groak, S. (1992). *The Idea of Building: Thought and Action in the Design and Production of Buildings*. London, E. & F.N. Spon.

Gropius, W. (1935). *The New Architecture and the Bauhaus*. London, Faber and Faber.

Gross, M. (1996). The electronic cocktail napkin – a computational environment for working with design diagrams. *Design Studies* **17**(1): 53–69.

Guilford, J. P. (1956). The structure of intellect. *Psychological Bulletin* **53**: 267–293.

Guilford, J. P. (1967). *The Nature of Human Intelligence*. New York, McGraw Hill.

Habraken, N. J. (1972). *Supports: An Alternative to Mass Housing*. London, Architectural Press.

Hannay, P. (1991). Court appeal. *The Architects' Journal* **4 September**: 30–43.

Hanson, K. (1969). Design from linked requirements in a housing problem. In *Design Methods in Architecture*. London, Lund Humphries.

Hare, A. P. (1962). *Handbook of Small Group Research*. New York, Free Press.

Heath, T. (1984). *Method in Architecture*. Chichester, Wiley.

Hertzberger, H. (1971). Looking for the beach under the pavement. *RIBA Journal* **78**(8).

Hertzberger, H. (1991). *Lessons for Students in Architecture*. Rotterdam, Uitgeverij 010.

Hillier, B. and Leaman, A. (1972). A new approach to architectural research. *RIBA Journal* **79**(12).

Hillier, B., Musgrove, J. and O'Sullivan, P. (1972). Knowledge and design. In *Environmental Design: Research and Practice EDRA 3*. University of California.

Howell, W. G. (1970). Vertebrate buildings. *RIBA Journal* **77**(3).

Hubbard, P. (1996). Conflicting interpretations of architecture: an empirical investigation. *Journal of Environmental Psychology* **16**: 75–92.

Hudson, L. (1966). *Contrary Imaginations: A Psychological Study of the English Schoolboy*. London, Methuen.

Hudson, L. (1968). *Frames of Mind: Ability, Perception and Self-perception in the Arts and Sciences*. London, Methuen.

Jameson, C. (1971). The human specification in architecture: a manifesto for a new research approach. *The Architects Journal* (27 October): 919–941.

Jenkins, J. G. (1972). *The English Farm Wagon*. Newton Abbot, David and Charles.

Jones, J. C. (1966). Design methods reviewed. *The Design Method*. London, Butterworths.

Jones, J. C. (1970). *Design Methods: Seeds of Human Futures*. New York, John Wiley.

Jones, J. C. and Thornley, D. G. (1963). *Conference on Design Methods*. Oxford, Pergamon.

Jones, P. B. (1995). *Hans Scharoun*. London, Phaidon.

Kagioglou, M., Cooper, R. et al. (1998). *A Generic Guide to the Design and Construction Process Protocol*. Salford, University of Salford.

Kaye, B. (1960). *The Development of the Architectural Profession in Britain: A Sociological Study*. London, Allen and Unwin.

Kidder, T. (1982). *The Soul of a New Machine*. Harmondsworth, Penguin.

Kneller, G. F. (1965). *The Art and Science of Creativity*. New York, Holt, Rinehart and Winston.

Koestler, A. (1967). *The Ghost in the Machine*. London, Hutchinson.

Lasdun, D. (1965). An architect's approach to architecture. *RIBA Journal* **72**(4).

Lawson, B. R. (1972). *Problem Solving in Architectural Design*. University of Aston in Birmingham.

Lawson, B. R. (1975). *Heuristic Science for Students of Architecture*. University of Sheffield Department of Architecture.

Lawson, B. R. (1975). Upside down and back to front: architects and the building laws. *RIBA Journal* **82**(4).

Lawson, B. R. and Spencer, C. P. (1978). Architectural intentions and user responses: the psychology building at Sheffield. *The Architects' Journal* **167**(18).

Lawson, B. R. (1979). The act of designing. *Design Methods and Theories* **13**(1).

Lawson, B. R. (1979). Cognitive strategies in architectural design. *Ergonomics* **22**(1): 59–68.

Lawson, B. R. (1982). Science, legislation and architecture. In *Changing Design*. New York, John Wiley.

Lawson, B. R. (1993). Parallel lines of thought. *Languages of Design* **1**(4): 357–366.

Lawson, B. R. (1993). The quest for the parrot on the shoulder: knowledge about emerging design solutions and its representation in a CAD system. In *Vizualization and Intelligent Design in Engineering and Architecture*. London, Elsevier. 421–430.

Lawson, B. R. (1994). Architects are losing out in the professional divide. *The Architects' Journal* **199**(16): 13–14.

Lawson, B. R. (1994). *Design in Mind*. Oxford, Architectural Press.

Lawson, B. R. (1994). The heart of a new university: building study appraisal. *The Architects' Journal* **199**(8): 43–50.

Lawson, B. R. (2001). *The Language of Space*. Oxford, Architectural Press.

Lawson, B. R. and Riley, J. P. (1982). ISAAC: a technique for the automatic interpretation of spaces from drawn floor plans. *CAD82 Conference Proceedings*, Brighton, IPC Press.

Lawson, B. R. and Roberts, S. (1991). Modes and features: the organization of data in CAD supporting the early phases of design. *Design Studies* **12**(2): 102–108.

Lawson, B. R. (2004). *What Designers Know*. Oxford, Architectural Press.

Lawson, B. R. and Pilling, S. (1996). The cost and value of design. *Architectural Research Quarterly* **4**(1): 82–89.

Lawson, B. R., Bassanino, M. et al. (2003). Intentions, practices and aspirations: understanding learning in design. *Design Studies* **24**(4): 327–339.

Laxton, M. (1969). Design education in practice. In *Attitudes in Design Education*. London, Lund Humphries.

Le Corbusier (1946). *Towards a New Architecture*. London, Architectural Press.

Le Corbusier (1951). *The Modulor*. London, Faber and Faber.

Leach, E. (1968). *A Runaway World*. London, BBC Publications.

Levin, P. H. (1966). The design process in planning. *Town Planning Review* **37**(1).

Lindsey, B. (2001). *Digital Gehry: Material Resistance/Digital Construction*. Basel, Birkhauser.

Lloyd, P., Lawson, B. et al. (1995). Can concurrent verbalization reveal design cognition? *Design Studies* **16**(2): 237–259.

Lynn, J. (1962). Park Hill redevelopment. *RIBA Journal* **69**(12).

Lyons, E. (1968). Too often we justify our ineptitudes by moral postures. *RIBA Journal* **75**(5).

MacCormac, R. and Jamieson, P. (1977). MacCormac and Jamieson. *Architectural Design* **47**(9/10): 675–706.

Mackinnon, D. W. (1962). *The Nature and Nurture of Creative Talent*. Yale University.

Mackinnon, D. W. (1976). The assessment and development of managerial creativity. *Creativity Network* **2**(3).

Macmillan, S., Steele, J. et al. (2001). Development and verification of a generic framework for conceptual design. *Design Studies* **22**(2): 169–191.

Maguire, R. (1971). Nearness to need. *RIBA Journal* **78**(4).

Maher, M. L. and Poon, J. (1996). Modelling design exploration as co-evolution. *Microcomputers in Civil Engineering* **11**(3): 195–210.

March, L. and Steadman, P. (1974). *The Geometry of Environment*. London, Methuen.

Markus, T. A. (1969). Design and research. *Conrad* **1**(2).

Markus, T. A. (1969). The role of building performance measurement and appraisal in design method. In *Design Methods in Architecture*. London, Lund Humphries.

Markus, T. A. (1972). A doughnut model of the environment and its design. In *Design Participation*. London, Academy Editions.

Matchett, E. (1968). Control of thought in creative work. *Chartered Mechanical Engineer* **14**(4).

Maver, T. W. (1970). Appraisal in the building design process. In *Emerging Methods in Environmetnal Design and Planning*. Cambridge Mass, MIT Press.

McLuhan, M. (1967). *The Medium is the Massage*. Harmondsworth, Penguin.

Medway, P. and Andrews, R. (1992). Building with words: discourse in an architects' office. *Carleton Papers in Applied Language Studies* 9: 1–32.

Miller, G. A., Galanter, E. et al. (1960). *Plans and the Structure of Behaviour*. New York, Holt, Rinehart and Winston.

Mitchell, W. J. (1995). *City of Bits*. Cambridge, Mass, MIT Press.

Morris, D. (1981). *The Soccer Tribe*. London, Jonathan Cape.

Mueller, R. E. (1967). *The Science of Art (The Cybernetics of Creative Communication)*. London, Rapp and Whiting.

Murphy, G. (1947). *Personality: A Biosocial Approach to Origins and Structure*. New York, Harper and Row.

Murphy, R. (1990). *Carlo Scarpa and the Castelvecchio*. Oxford, Butterworth Architecture.

Negroponte, N. (1975). *Soft Architecture Machines*. Cambridge, Mass, MIT Press.

Negroponte, N. (1995). *Being Digital*. London, Hodder and Stoughton.

Neisser, U. (1967). *Cognitive Psychology*. New York, Appleton Century Crofts.

Newell, A., Simon, H. A. and Shaw, J. C. (1958). Elements of a theory of human problem solving. *Psychological Review* 65(3).

Norberg-Schulz, C. (1966). *Intentions in Architecture*. Cambridge, Mass, MIT Press.

Norburg-Schultz, C. (1975). *Meaning in Western Architecture*. London, Studio Vista.

Opron, R. (1976). The Renault method. *Design* 333(September).

Page, J. K. (1963). Review of the papers presented at the conference. *Conference on Design Methods*. Oxford, Pergamon.

Peng, C. (1994). Exploring communication in collaborative design: co-operative architectural modelling. *Design Studies* 15(1): 19–44.

Poincaré, H. (1924). Mathematical creation. In *Creativity*. London, Penguin.

Porter, T. (1988). *Designer Primer for Architects, Graphic Designers and Artists*. London, Butterworth Architecture.

Portillo, M. and Dohr, J. H. (1994). Bridging process and structure through criteria. *Design Studies* 15(4): 403–416.

Price, C. (1976). Anticipatory design. *RIBA Journal* 84(7).

Pugin, A. W. N. (1841). *The True Principles of Pointed or Christian Architecture*. London.

Rae, J. (1969). Games. *The Architects' Journal* 149(15): 977–983.

Rand, P. (1970). *Thoughts on Design*. London, Studio Vista.

RIBA (1970). The third London airport: choice cannot be on cost alone says RIBA. *RIBA Journal* 77(5): 224–225.

Roe, A. (1952). A psychologist examines sixty-four eminent scientists. *Scientific American* 187: 21–25.

Rosenstein, A. B., Rathbone, R. R. et al. (1964). *Engineering Communications*. Englewood Cliffs, Prentice Hall.

Rowe, P. G. (1987). *Design Thinking*. Cambridge, Mass, MIT Press.

Roy, R. (1993). Case studies of creativity in innovative product development. *Design Studies* 14(4): 423–443.

Ryle, G. (1949). *The Concept of Mind*. London, Hutchinson.

Savidge, R. (1978). Revise the regs: the plan revealed. *The Architects' Journal* **167**(14).

Schön, D. A. (1983). *The Reflective Practitioner: How Professionals Think in Action*. London, Temple Smith.

Schön, D. A. (1984). Problems, frames and perspectives on designing. *Design Studies* **5**(3): 132–136.

Schön, D. A. and Wiggins, G. (1992). Kinds of seeing and their function in designing. *Design Studies* **13**(2): 135–156.

Stevens, S. S. (ed.) (1951). *Handbook of Experimental Psychology*. New York, John Wiley.

Stirling, J. (1965). An architect's approach to architecture. *RIBA Journal* **72**(5).

Stumpf, S. C. and McDonnell, J. T. (2002). Talking about team framing: using argumentation to analyse and support experiential learning in early design. *Design Studies* **23**(1): 5–23.

Sturt, G. (1923). *The Wheelwright's Shop*. Cambridge, Cambridge University Press.

Suckle, A. (ed.) (1980). *By Their Own Design*. New York, Whitney.

Suwa, M. and Twersky, B. (1997). What do architects and students perceive in their design sketches? A protocol analysis. *Design Studies* **18**: 385–403.

Taylor, J. L. and Walford, R. (1972). *Simulation in the Classroom*. Harmondsworth, Penguin.

Thorndike, E. L. (1911). *Animal Intelligence*. London, Macmillan.

Toffler, A. (1970). *Futureshock*. London, Bodley Head.

Vale, B. and Vale, R. (1975). *The Autonomous House: Design and Planning for Self-sufficiency*. London, Thames and Hudson.

van Bakel, A. (1995). *Styles of Architectural Designing: Empirical Research on Working Styles and Personality Dispositions*. Eindhoven, Technical University of Eindhoven.

Van Norman, M. (1986). A digital modelshop: the role of metaphor in a CAAD user interface. *Design Computing* **1**: 95–122.

Watkin, D. (1977). *Morality and Architecture*. Oxford, Clarendon Press.

Watson, J. D. (1968). *The Double Helix: A Personal Account of the Discovery of the Structure of DNA*. London, Wiedenfield and Nicolson.

Weinberg, A. M. (1974). Can technology replace social engineering? In *Man Made Futures*. London, Hutchinson Educational/Open University.

Wertheimer, M. (1959). *Productive Thinking*. New York, Harper and Row.

Whitehead, B. and Eldars, M. Z. (1964). An approach to the optimum layout of single storey buildings. *The Architect's Journal* (17 June): 1373–1380.

Whitfield, P. R. (1975). *Creativity in Industry*. Harmondsworth, Penguin.

Wilford, M. (1991). Inspired patronage. *RIBA Journal* **98**(4): 36–42.

Wilson, C. S. J. (1986). The play of use and use of play. *Architectural Review* **180**(1073): 15–18.

Wilson, M. A. (1996). The socialization of architectural preference. *Journal of Environmental Psychology* **16**: 33–44.

Yeang, K. (1994). *Bioclimatic Skyscrapers*. London, Artemis.

Yeang, K. (1996). *The Skyscraper Bioclimatically Considered*. London, Academy Editions.

Zeisel, J. (1984). *Inquiry by Design*. Cambridge, Cambridge University Press.

Index

Page numbers for illustrations have suffix f